"Scholars have studied human destructiv[eness from] ... Others have recorded the devastating [dynamics at the] ... Dr. Itzkowitz and Dr. Howell bring the[se perspectives together] with insight and eloquence. From an analysis of psychopathic persons as 'outsiders to love,' contributors speak to the historical, cultural, and even genocidal aspects of psychopathic behavior, all the while offering the reader an uncommon glimpse of the internal experience. In this day when psychopathic personality has the potential to pair with ever greater power, this discerning volume offers a critically needed understanding."

—**Bandy X. Lee**, M.D., M.Div., Yale School of Medicine, Law and Psychiatry Division

"This is a cutting-edge work, an eye-opener. Itzkowitz and Howell, themselves significant contributors to the psychoanalytic literature on psychopathy, encourage us not to limit our definition of psychopathic behavior to the kinds of heinous acts that are reported in the newspapers, but to include evil, noncriminal activities of any kind. Virtually every scholar and clinician who has had something original to say about psychopathy is represented here. This book will be necessary for veterans in its field, and because it so straightforwardly addresses a notoriously difficult subject, it will be crucial to the beginner. It will be widely studied by psychoanalysts, but its appeal will extend to clinicians of every theoretical stripe."

—**Donnel B. Stern**, Ph.D., William Alanson White Institute

Psychoanalysts, Psychologists and Psychiatrists Discuss Psychopathy and Human Evil

Evil—along with its incarnation in human form, the psychopath—remains underexamined in the psychological and psychoanalytic literature. Given current societal issues ranging from increasingly violent cultural divides to climate change, it is imperative that the topics of psychopathy and human evil be thoughtfully explored.

The book brings together social scientists, psychologists and psychoanalysts to discuss the psychology of psychopaths, and the personal, societal and cultural destruction they leave as their legacy. Chapters address such questions as: Who are psychopaths? How do they think and operate? What causes someone to commit psychopathic acts? And are psychopaths born or created? Psychopaths leave us shocked and bewildered by behavior that violates the notions of common human trust and bonding, but not all psychopaths commit crimes. Because of their unique proclivities to deceive, seduce and dissemble, they can hide in plain sight; especially when intelligent and highly educated. This latter group comprise the "successful or corporate" psychopaths, frequently found in boardrooms of corporations, and among leaders of national movements or heads of state.

Addressing a wide range of topics including slavery, genocide, the Holocaust, the individual as psychopath, the mind of the terrorist, sexual abuse, the role of attachment and the neurobiology of psychopathy, this book will appeal to researchers of human evil and psychopathy from a range of different disciplines and represents essential reading for psychotherapists and clinical psychologists.

Sheldon Itzkowitz, Ph.D., ABPP, is an adjunct clinical associate professor of psychology and clinical consultant at the New York University (NYU) Postdoctoral Program in Psychotherapy and Psychoanalysis; guest faculty, the EDCAS Program of the William Alanson White Institute; faculty and consultant, the National Institute for the Psychotherapies (NIP) and the Manhattan Institute of Psychoanalysis. A Fellow of the International Society for the Study of Trauma & Dissociation (ISSTD), he co-edited *The Dissociative Mind in Psychoanalysis: Understanding and Working with Trauma*.

Elizabeth F. Howell, Ph.D., is an adjunct clinical associate professor of psychology at the NYU Postdoctoral Program in Psychotherapy and Psychoanalysis; faculty and clinical consultant at Manhattan Institute of Psychoanalysis; and a Fellow of ISSTD. She is the author of *The Dissociative Mind* and *Understanding and Treating Dissociative Identity Disorder: A Relational Approach* and co-editor of *The Dissociative Mind in Psychoanalysis: Understanding and Working with Trauma*.

PSYCHOANALYSIS IN A NEW KEY BOOK SERIES
DONNEL STERN
Series Editor

When music is played in a new key, the melody does not change, but the notes that make up the composition do: change in the context of continuity, continuity that perseveres through change. Psychoanalysis in a New Key publishes books that share the aims psychoanalysts have always had, but that approach them differently. The books in the series are not expected to advance any particular theoretical agenda, although to this date most have been written by analysts from the Interpersonal and Relational orientations.

The most important contribution of a psychoanalytic book is the communication of something that nudges the reader's grasp of clinical theory and practice in an unexpected direction. Psychoanalysis in a New Key creates a deliberate focus on innovative and unsettling clinical thinking. Because that kind of thinking is encouraged by exploration of the sometimes surprising contributions to psychoanalysis of ideas and findings from other fields, Psychoanalysis in a New Key particularly encourages interdisciplinary studies. Books in the series have married psychoanalysis with dissociation, trauma theory, sociology, and criminology. The series is open to the consideration of studies examining the relationship between psychoanalysis and any other field—for instance, biology, literary and art criticism, philosophy, systems theory, anthropology, and political theory.

But innovation also takes place within the boundaries of psychoanalysis, and Psychoanalysis in a New Key therefore also presents work that reformulates thought and practice without leaving the precincts of the field. Books in the series focus, for example, on the significance of personal values in psychoanalytic practice, on the complex interrelationship between the analyst's clinical work and personal life, on the consequences for the clinical situation when patient and analyst are from different cultures, and on the need for psychoanalysts to accept the degree to which they knowingly satisfy their own wishes during treatment hours, often to the patient's detriment.

A full list of all titles in this series is available at: https://www.routledge.com/series/LEAPNKBS

Psychoanalysts, Psychologists and Psychiatrists Discuss Psychopathy and Human Evil

Edited by Sheldon Itzkowitz and Elizabeth F. Howell

Routledge
Taylor & Francis Group

LONDON AND NEW YORK

First published 2020
by Routledge
2 Park Square, Milton Park, Abingdon, Oxon OX14 4RN

and by Routledge
52 Vanderbilt Avenue, New York, NY 10017

Routledge is an imprint of the Taylor & Francis Group, an informa business

British Library Cataloguing-in-Publication Data
A catalogue record for this book is available from the British Library

Library of Congress Cataloging-in-Publication Data
Names: Itzkowitz, Sheldon, editor. | Howell, Elizabeth F., 1946-
editor.
Title: Psychoanalysts, psychologists and psychiatrists discuss
psychopathy and human evil / [edited by] Sheldon Itzkowitz and
Elizabeth F. Howell.
Description: Abingdon, Oxon ; New York, NY : Routledge,
2019. | Includes bibliographical references and index. |
Identifiers: LCCN 2019036875 | ISBN 9780367205829
(hardback) | ISBN 9780367205850 (paperback) | ISBN
9780429262425 (ebook)
Subjects: LCSH: Good and evil–Psychological aspects. |
Psychopaths.
Classification: LCC BF789.E94 P795 2019 | DDC 155.2/32–dc23
LC record available at https://lccn.loc.gov/2019036875

ISBN: 978-0-367-20582-9 (hbk)
ISBN: 978-0-367-20585-0 (pbk)
ISBN: 978-0-429-26242-5 (ebk)

Typeset in Times New Roman
by Swales & Willis, Exeter, Devon, UK

Contents

Acknowledgments

We invited selected authors we believed would provide our readers with a broad overview of human behavior that falls under the overall title of this volume. Readers might find some chapters more difficult to take in than others. Our goal was to bring us all face to face with the dark side of the human condition, to grapple with and try to understand what often seems to be beyond comprehension. It is too easy for us to dissociate or otherwise avoid confronting and addressing the unthinkable. When that happens on a large societal scale, it allows psychopaths, whether serial killers or corporate executives, to get away with unconscionable behavior.

We want to thank our authors for their excellent contributions. In addition to our own chapters (Sheldon Itzkowitz and Elizabeth F. Howell) we thank J. Reid Meloy for his contribution in understanding the mind of terrorists; Michael H. Stone for his chapter discussing characteristics and dynamics of psychopaths among other negative personality types; Valerie Sinason for her consideration that evil actions are part of the human condition and not the sole dominion of psychopaths; Sue Grand for addressing genocidal actions against Indigenous people and the cruelty of American slavery in her chapter; Cleonie White for her chapter addressing the current political, racial and economic rifts within present-day America; Robert Prince for his contribution to understanding psychopathy and evil as both an individual and social process that can sometimes interlock with each other; Emily Kuriloff for her chapter addressing the concept of evil in psychoanalysis during the reign of National Socialism, and challenging contemporary psychoanalysts to confront evil within the analytic dyad and in culture and society in general; the impact of traumatic dissociation emerges in Richard B. Gartner's chapter as a function of childhood sexual abuse and the potential overpowering effect it can have on the analyst; Mary Gail Frawley-O'Dea for her captivating chapter discussing working with survivors of childhood sexual abuse her experience engaging evil in the form of members of the clergy and disciples, both unwilling to believe in the fallibility of ungodly, and all too human, priest-pedophiles; Adriano Schimmenti for reviewing empirical studies exploring the relationship between attachment styles and psychopathy, and discussing how attachment trauma increases the risk of development of maladaptive behavior such as psychopathy; Neville Symington for re-examining the Oedipus myth, suggesting that the real evil was not the killing of Laius, but Oedipus' succumbing to the role imposed upon him by the Oracle of Delphi and failing to create his own independent life; and Nathalie Y. Gauthier, Tabitha Methot-Jones, Angela Book and J. Reid Meloy for our final chapter, a joint effort that reviews the literature addressing neurobiological correlates of behavioral characteristics of psychopaths and also looks at more current research on individuals whose behavior falls in the category of psychopathy, but who manage to avoid incarceration.

The editors would also like to express their thanks to Kate Hawes and Charles Bath, our editors at Taylor & Francis, for their invaluable assistance in shepherding this project throughout the publication process. And a special thanks to Dr. Donnel Stern, series editor of Psychoanalysis in a New Key, for his wisdom, mentorship and his guidance during the editorial process.

Working on a project such as ours required countless hours actively engaging material that discusses the worst in humankind. The actions of psychopaths and people whose behavior includes unconscionable acts of violence, destruction, greed, etc., can leave one feeling sickened, and enraged. But it also brings into relief the importance of loving and trustworthy relationships, family, friends and colleagues. It is these relationships that provide soothing support, encouragement and the ability to believe in the best aspects of humankind.

Sheldon Itzkowitz would like to express his gratitude and love to his wife Laurie Fredrickson for her love, endless support and encouragement, which helped make this book a reality. Her faith in good conquering evil was an essential counterbalance to the unconscionable cruelty that runs through these chapters.

Elizabeth F. Howell is grateful to her husband, Patrick Flanagan, for his unflagging patience, support and love—showing the kind of connectedness that makes goodness apparent and capable of being mutually created.

Brief descriptions of chapters

In the pages that follow, our readers will find thought-provoking essays exploring our theme from a variety of perspectives. We hope to spark your interest in this important topic and hope it generates further exposition.

Sheldon Itzkowitz examines our topic from a broad psychoanalytic perspective in "Psychopathy and human evil: an overview." The article explores the personality characteristics, organization and cognitive style of the psychopath, as well as the role of superego pathology, contributions from the field of attachment, and the manner in which dissociation plays a role in psychopathy and the potential for conflating this with the dissociative structuring of the mind. The article closes with a brief discussion about "corporate" or "successful" psychopaths and how they have a negative impact on culture and society.

In "Outsiders to love: the psychopathic character and dilemma," Elizabeth F. Howell describes key characteristics of psychopaths, including the power of deceit in a world that generally runs on trust, and the psychopath's ability to tap into and intermesh with people's dissociated need, greed, fears and sadism. Psychopathic character is understood in terms of a dissociative structure of interlocking self-states in which ruthless instrumentality is dominant. The evil in psychopathy originates in a feeling of being an outsider to love, outside and envious of the fabric of the social order and emotional world shared by others. It is argued that while it is human to have some characteristics of evil, sadism and psychopathy, psychopaths themselves fit into a taxon, a category of their own.

The relationship between sexual desire, violent death and fundamentalist beliefs that lead to acts of terrorism is explored by J. Reid Meloy in "Sexual desire, violent death and the true believer." He uses information from contemporary jihadist, ethnic nationalist and single-issue terrorist violence to discuss his ideas about psychopathy, using concepts from psychoanalytic structural theory and object relations theory.

In his chapter, "The place of psychopathy along the spectrum of negative personality types," Michael H. Stone considers psychopathy to be one of a number of negative personality organizations, albeit at the extreme end of the continuum. He discusses narcissistic, paranoid, antisocial and psychopathic personality types, and their characteristics, dynamics and amenability to treatment. Examples of these disorders are provided to enable the clinician to better understand how these types differ.

Valerie Sinason takes on the issue of evil by explaining that one need not be a psychopath to behave in an evil manner. In her chapter, "The perpetrators: the receivers and transmitters of evil," she explains that about a quarter of those with a history of abuse or victimization become perpetrators themselves. Citing her many decades of clinical experience, she believes that despite chilling and evil behavior by people she has worked with, she has never felt anyone was intrinsically evil. Falling on the nurture side of the nature–nurture divide, she believes resilience, attachment patterns, socio-political conditions, capacity for empathy, adverse situations during childhood, fear, obedience and hierarchy all contribute to the development or propensity of becoming a victimizer or perpetrator. A moving case example is presented.

In "The Other within: white shame, Native American genocide," Sue Grand explores the manner in which white American psychoanalysis has failed to fully acknowledge and reconcile African American slavery and the extermination of Indigenous peoples. Using these atrocities as a backdrop, she discusses how these victimized groups are likely to encounter the opportunity to engage in repair and recognition in confronting white racial shame and guilt.

Cleonie White addresses the growing racial and economic divide in the United States being fueled by what amounts to a white supremacist political backlash. The backlash attempts to maintain political and economic power and in doing so identifies the non-white and immigrant populations as the alien "Other" to be feared and rejected. In "American hierarchy: white, 'good'; black, 'evil'," Dr. White examines the antecedents to the current political, social and economic situation. She reviews the African American experience, starting in slavery through what she calls the new Jim Crow laws: the prison industrial complex.

Robert Prince examines evil using the incomprehensible war crimes of Adolf Eichmann in his contemplative article, "Sympathy for the Devil: evil, social process and intelligibility." Prince locates Eichmann by drawing a map of evil with crisscrossing routes named *ideology, deception, banality, thoughtlessness* and *malevolence.* He concludes that evil is "reciprocally located in individual and social processes" helping to make the world both understandable and adding meaning to it; evil, he explains, assaults reality while simultaneously forging it as well.

Emily Kuriloff, in *"Die Hitler in uns* (The Hitler in us): evil and the psychoanalytic situation," discusses how early psychoanalysts identified with the ideal of psychoanalysis being separate and apart from the influence of culture and society. She argues that rigid adherence to theory contributed to destructive ideas and treatment and also at times to inadvertent—and in some cases planned—cooperation with the evils of National Socialism. With the view of the self as a construction, contemporary psychoanalysis is challenged to confront evil as it exists in both analysts and analysands, in culture and society and the influences they have on individuals.

In "Dissociation and counterdissociation: nuanced and binary perceptions of good and evil," Richard B. Gartner extends his ideas on the relational field between analyst and patient. Using material from two of his own cases, Gartner demonstrates how when working with severely traumatized individuals, the "emotional flow" can induce dissociative reactions in the analyst, i.e. counterdissociation. These reactions stem from evil acts that were perpetrated on these patients as children. Gartner clarifies the potential positive and negative aspects of counterdissociation and how he works with these experiences.

Mary Gail Frawley-O'Dea's moving personal account, "Dancing with the Devil: a personal essay on my encounters with sexual abuse in the Catholic Church," captivates us with her first-person account of a clinician working with survivors of sexual abuse. Through her other roles as speaker, author, advocate and expert witness she describes her experience when engaging evil face to face in the form of members of the clergy and disciples, who are all too often reluctant or unable to accept the fallibility of ungodly, and all too human, priest-pedophiles.

In his chapter, "The developmental roots of psychopathy: an attachment perspective," Adriano Schimmenti reviews empirical studies exploring the relationship between childhood attachment styles and psychopathy in adulthood. He discusses and explores how attachment trauma increases the risk of development of maladaptive behavior, such as psychopathy. Defenses such as identification with the aggressor and other controlling and punishing emotional survival strategies combined with experiences of loss, neglect and abuse during childhood may contribute to the emergence of psychopathy.

Neville Symington's fascinating essay, "The murder of Laius," re-examines the Oedipus myth, interpreting Laius as representing an inner psychic reality. For Symington, Oedipus' worst crime was not external (patricide and incest), as is the popular understanding of the myth. By acquiescing to the voice of fate and not actively creating his own independent life, the real evil in the myth is both internal and existential. This inner potential of creating one's freedom from fate as decreed is what is murdered.

We address the potential neurobiological underpinnings of evil with an informative chapter by Nathalie Y. Gauthier, Tabitha Methot-Jones, Angela Book and J. Reid Meloy titled "Psychopaths and the neurobiology of evil." This chapter reviews the literature addressing neurobiological correlates of behavioral characteristics of psychopaths. While the majority of research has been done on incarcerated populations, this chapter also looks at the newer research on those individuals whose behavior falls under the category of psychopathy, but who manage to avoid incarceration; the "successful psychopath."

Preface

The idea for this volume emerged several years ago when we were discussing the status of world events, including increased violent shootings in schools, where children are supposed to be educated rather than terrified and traumatized. We were trying to understand what motivates such aggression and extreme destructiveness to human life. What motivates such terrorism? What is it about the human experience, human development in an interpersonal-relational context that motivates and/or allows such violent, sadistic and often unconscionable behavior? Not so long ago, in many circles, "evil" was almost a dirty word, a word similar to how "psychopath" was considered an unfair characterization until recently. Yet, even as we write, the calamity of the situation increases.

How can psychodynamic clinicians understand the mind and the behavior of the psychopath? The serial killer has emerged as emblematic of the psychopath; but, clearly, not all psychopaths are serial killers. Rather, psychopaths come from all walks of life; many of them are successful psychopaths, or corporate psychopaths. These are people who have the ability and the skill to remain out of the criminal justice system but who behave in ways that place them in the broader category of psychopathy. Unfortunately, these psychopaths can be found in positions of power in the corporate world or in elected office.

We are not claiming that psychopathy has just emerged on the world scene. Obviously, human evil has had numerous manifestations throughout history. What is different now, what is visible in our current civilization, at least in the United States, is the serious erosion of the importance of ethics, basic honesty and consensual reality—where personal beliefs and idiosyncratic interpretation of events have supplanted facts and consensual reality. Modern technology seems to have made it easier for the creation and dissemination of false information and beliefs to gain attention and grow in popularity.

In the following pages you will read about several attributes/characteristics commonplace among individuals who fall under the heading of "psychopathy": extreme or pathological narcissism, lack of empathy and concern for the well-being of others, impairment of conscience (often referred to as superego pathology), and lack of guilt in the face of behavior that harms or destroys the lives of others as long as it satisfies or benefits the psychopath.

What happens when such psychopathic individuals hold high positions in society while managing to avoid attention by the criminal justice system? Corporations (and sometimes governments), the executives who run them, the shareholders that own them, or the voters who elect them have a history of focusing on only one issue, "the bottom line"; i.e. financial and/or fiscal success. Concerns for the impact on human and animal life, the air we breathe, the water we drink, have no seat at the boardroom table. Unfortunately, under these circumstances, many characteristics of psychopathy mentioned above are often valorized when applied to mindless and soulless organizations (whether business or government). What happens when people who are not psychopathic become co-opted by groups or social situations in which their personal benefit is tied to the psychopathic success of others?

Our purpose in putting this volume together was to broaden clinicians' awareness of the breadth of human behavior falling under the heading of "psychopathy." We hope this book leaves the reader with an expanded awareness of our topic and the desire to seek change both in clinical practice and as a member of society.

Contributors

Editors

Sheldon Itzkowitz, Ph.D., ABPP, is an adjunct clinical associate professor of psychology and clinical consultant at the NYU Postdoctoral Program in Psychotherapy & Psychoanalysis; guest faculty at the EDCAS Program, the William Alanson White Institute; on the teaching and supervisory faculty of the National Institute for the Psychotherapies program in psychoanalysis and the Trauma Studies Program of the Manhattan Institute for Psychoanalysis; and is an Honorary Member of the William Alanson White Society. He has presented his work with extremely dissociated individuals both nationally and internationally. His most recent publications include *The Dissociative Mind in Psychoanalysis: Understanding and Working with Trauma*, co-edited with Elizabeth F. Howell. The book received the 2016 Media Award-Written from the ISSTD and the Author Recognition Award from NIP, and was nominated for the 2017 Gradiva Award. "A Dream as an Internal Enactment of Trauma: The Impact on the Analyst's Self" appears in J. Petrucelli and S. Schoen (Eds.), *Unknowable, Unspeakable, and Unsprung: Psychoanalytic Perspectives on Truth, Scandal, Secrets, and Lies*, and "The Interpersonal-Relational Field, Countertrauma, and Counterresilience: The Impact of Treating Trauma and Dissociation" appears in R. B. Gartner (Ed.), *Trauma and Countertrauma, Resilience and Counterresilience: Insights from Psychoanalysts and Trauma Experts*, published by Routledge. He is in full-time private practice in New York City.

Elizabeth F. Howell, Ph.D., is a psychoanalyst and traumatologist specializing in the treatment of dissociative disorders. She is on the editorial board of the *Journal of Trauma and Dissociation*, an adjunct clinical associate professor in psychology for the NYU Postdoctoral Program in Psychotherapy and Psychoanalysis, and faculty and supervisor for the Trauma Treatment Center of the Manhattan Institute for Psychoanalysis. She has written over 35 articles on various aspects of trauma and dissociation and has lectured nationally and internationally on various aspects of trauma and dissociation, as well as on gender and trauma/ dissociation. Her books include *The Dissociative Mind in Psychoanalysis: Understanding and Working with Trauma* (co-edited with Sheldon Itzkowitz), *Understanding and Treating Dissociative Identity Disorder: A Relational Approach, The Dissociative Mind* (all of which won the Print Media Award from the International Society for the Study of Trauma and Dissociation), *Women and Mental Health*, and a forthcoming book, *Trauma and Dissociation-Informed Psychotherapy: Forging Relational Healing and the Therapeutic Connection* (in press). Dr. Howell is the recipient, from ISSTD, of the Cornelia Wilber Award for outstanding clinical contributions in the field of dissociative disorders and the Lifetime Achievement Award. She runs study and consultation groups, and is in private practice in New York City.

Contributors

Angela Book, Ph.D., is an associate professor in psychology at Brock University and is currently the Associate Dean for Undergraduate Studies in the Faculty of Social Sciences. Her research has centered on psychopaths as social predators, including studies on victim selection, social mimicry and fear enjoyment.

Mary Gail Frawley-O'Dea, Ph.D., has engaged clinically with adult survivors of sexual abuse and other developmental traumas for over 30 years. In 2002, she was the only psychologist to address the United States Conference of Catholic Bishops at their seminal meeting on sexual abuse and subsequently wrote *Perversion of Power: Sexual Abuse in the Catholic Church*. She also co-authored *Treating the Adult Survivor of Childhood Sexual Abuse: A Psychoanalytic Perspective*. Dr. Frawley-O'Dea appeared as herself in the Oscar-nominated documentary *Deliver Us from Evil*, and she serves as an expert witness in sexual abuse litigation. Currently, she is Executive Director of

Presbyterian Psychological Services, a non-profit, interdisciplinary mental health resource in Charlotte, NC.

Richard B. Gartner, Ph.D., is Training Analyst, Supervising Analyst, faculty and Founding Director of the Sexual Abuse Service at the William Alanson White Institute. A co-founder of MaleSurvivor.org who is frequently quoted in the media about male sexual victimization, he is the author of *Betrayed as Boys: Psychodynamic Treatment of Sexually Abused Men* (1999). His most recent edited books are *Trauma and Countertrauma, Resilience and Counterresilience: Insights from Psychoanalysts and Trauma Experts* (2017); *Understanding the Sexual Betrayal of Boys and Men: The Trauma of Sexual Abuse* (2018); and *Healing Sexually Betrayed Men and Boys: Treatment for Sexual Abuse, Assault, and Trauma* (2018).

Nathalie Y. Gauthier is a Ph.D. candidate in psychology at Brock University, whose main research focuses on topics in forensic psychology, such as moderators of risk in psychopathy and other personality disorders, violence risk assessment and deception detection. Her current research investigates neuropsychological factors in predicting behavioral outcomes in antisocial youth and adults with psychopathic traits, such as the role of executive function.

Sue Grand, Ph.D., is faculty and supervisor at the NYU Postdoctoral Program in Psychotherapy and Psychoanalysis; faculty at the Mitchell Center for Relational Psychoanalysis; faculty at the trauma program at the National Institute for the Psychotherapies; a Fellow at the Institute for Psychology and the Other; and a visiting scholar at the Psychoanalytic Institute of Northern California. She is an associate editor of *Psychoanalytic Dialogues*, and *Psychoanalysis, Culture & Society*. She is the author of *The Reproduction of Evil: A Clinical and Cultural Perspective* and *The Hero in the Mirror: From Fear to Fortitude*. She co-edited *Trans-Generational Trauma and the Other* and *Wounds of History*, and is the co-editor of the forthcoming books *De-Idealizing Relational Theory* and *De-Centering Relational Theory*. She is in private practice in New York City and in Teaneck, NJ.

Emily A. Kuriloff, Psy.D., is Training and Supervising Psychoanalyst at the William Alanson White Institute in New York, where she is on faculty, and is also Director of Clinical Education. Dr. Kuriloff has also taught at the Institute for Psychoanalytic Study of Subjectivity and the Institute for Contemporary Psychotherapy, and is currently at the Institute for Psychoanalytic Education. The former book review editor of the journal *Contemporary Psychoanalysis*, she has written numerous articles and book chapters concerning the history of psychoanalytic theory and praxis, and the nature of therapeutic action. Dr. Kuriloff is most recently the author of the volume *Contemporary Psychoanalysis and the Legacy of The Third Reich: History, Memory, Tradition*, published in 2014 by Routledge.

J. Reid Meloy, Ph.D., is a board-certified forensic psychologist (ABPP) and consults on criminal and civil cases throughout the United States and Europe. He is a clinical professor of psychiatry at the University of California, San Diego, School of Medicine, and a faculty member of the San Diego Psychoanalytic Center. He has been consulting, researching and writing about personality disorder, psychopathy, stalking, narcissism, criminality, mental disorder and targeted violence for the past 30 years.

Tabitha Methot-Jones is a doctoral candidate in social/personality psychology. Her research interests focus on understanding certain mechanisms that may explain some of the antisocial behaviors associated with psychopathic traits. Specifically, she is interested in examining how these mechanisms may be facilitating negative and violent treatment of women. Presently, her research is focused on examining dehumanization, a social psychological construct, as a mechanism that may help to explain why men high in psychopathic traits tend to engage in sexist and violent behavior and attitudes towards women.

Robert Prince, Ph.D., ABPP, holds a Diplomate in Psychoanalysis from the American Board of Professional Psychology and is a Fellow of the Academy of Psychoanalysis. He is Past-President of Psychologist-Psychoanalyst Clinicians, Section V of the Division of Psychoanalysis of the American Psychological Association (APA), and was formerly on the Board of Directors of the Division of Psychoanalysis of APA and of the Academy of Psychoanalysis. He received his Ph.D. in Clinical Psychology from Columbia University and his Certificate in Psychoanalysis and Psychotherapy from the NYU Postdoctoral Program, where he is Past Co-chair of the Interpersonal Track and one of the founding members of the trauma studies specialization. Among his 35-plus publications are *The Legacy of the Holocaust*; *The Death of Psychoanalysis*, *Trauma and Culture* and *What is Effective in Psychoanalytic Psychotherapy: A Historical Reprise*.

Adriano Schimmenti, Ph.D., DClinPsych, is a full professor of psychodynamic psychotherapy and Director of the MSc Clinical Postgraduate Degree at UKE (Kore University of Enna, Italy). He is also deputy director of the SIPDC (Italian Society of Psychological Assessment), and research director of the IIPP (Italian Institute of Psychoanalytic Psychotherapy). He has been trained in the administration and scoring of the Adult Attachment Interview, the Attachment Style Interview, the Childhood Experience of Care and Abuse, and the Psychopathy Checklist-Revised. He has extensively published in leading journals on the topics of childhood trauma, dissociation, attachment, psychopathy and addictive behaviors.

Valerie Sinason, Ph.D., trained as a child psychotherapist at the Tavistock Clinic and is a psychoanalyst for adults at the British Psychoanalytic Society. She is President of the Institute of Psychotherapy and Disability and Honorary Consultant Psychotherapist at the University of Cape Town. Dr. Sinason is the founder and former director of the Clinic for Dissociative Studies, a member of the Board of Directors of the ISSTD, and a prolific writer.

Michael H. Stone, M.D., is a professor of clinical psychiatry at Columbia College of Physicians and Surgeons. His psychiatric training was at the New York State Psychiatric Institute. He is a graduate of the Columbia Psychoanalytic Institute. Afterwards he served as associate director of the long-term psychotherapy unit at the Institute, specializing in patients with Borderline Personality Disorder; then, as clinical director of psychiatry at the University Health Center in Connecticut, and director of research at the Mid-Hudson Forensic Hospital. He is the author of 260 papers and chapters and 12 books, including *Abnormalities of Personality* and *The Anatomy of Evil*.

Neville Symington, currently a psychoanalyst in private practice in Sydney, Australia, is a Fellow of the British Psychoanalytical Society.

As a young man, he took a diploma in Philosophy and then in Theology. He later did a degree in Psychology and took a diploma in Clinical Psychology. He held a senior staff position in the Adult Department of the Tavistock Clinic from 1977 to 1985. He was also chairman of the Psychology Discipline for the Adult and Adolescent Departments at the Tavistock Clinic in London. In Sydney, he was chairman of the Sydney Institute for Psychoanalysis from 1987 to 1993, and president of the Australian Psychoanalytic Society from 1999 to 2002. In 2007 he started a clinical organization called Psychotherapy with Psychotic Patients. He is the author of *The Analytic Experience*; *Emotion and Spirit* of *Narcissism: A New Theory*; *The Making of a Psychotherapist*; *The Spirit of Sanity*; *A Pattern of Madness*; *How to Choose a Psychotherapist*; *The Blind Man Sees*; *A Healing Conversation*; *Becoming a Person through Psychoanalysis*; *The Psychology of the Person*; and *A Different Path*. He is joint author with Joan Symington of *The Clinical Thinking of Wilfred Bion*, published by Routledge. He also wrote a novel called *A Priest's Affair*, and a book of poetry, *In-gratitude and Other Poems*. He has lectured in Britain, Norway, Denmark, Poland, Portugal, Germany, Italy, the United States, Brazil, Israel, India, Japan, New Zealand and Australia. He has a website at www.nevillesymington.com.

Cleonie White, Ph.D., is a Fellow, faculty and the Supervisor of Psychotherapy at the William Alanson White Institute. She is Adjunct Clinical Assistant Professor at the NYU Postdoctoral Program and faculty and the Supervisor at the Stephen Mitchell Center for Relational Studies. She supervises in the doctoral program in clinical psychology at CUNY and at the Institute for Contemporary Psychotherapy. Dr. White sits on the Editorial Board of Contemporary Psychoanalysis and is an associate board member of *Psychoanalytic Dialogues*. A co-founder of the Study Group on Race and Psychoanalysis at the White Institute, Dr. White also participated in the film *Black Psychoanalysts Speak*. She has written multiple psychological evaluations of immigrants at risk of deportation. Her publications are in the areas of trauma and dissociation, race, class, the immigrant/foreigner Other, identity and creativity in psychoanalysis. Dr. White maintains a private practice in New York City.

Introduction

Sheldon Itzkowitz and Elizabeth F. Howell

Not all psychopaths are in prison—some are in the boardroom.
(Babiak, Neumann, & Hare, 2010)

Even more denied than death is evil—along with its incarnation in human form, the psychopath. Yet, it is imperative now that the topics of psychopathy and human evil no longer be denied. Before us are terrifying signs of societal ethical collapse: increasingly violent cultural divides, climate destruction, the rise of global terrorism, and the specter of global nuclear disaster.

Today, both words, "evil" and "psychopathy," are emotionally loaded. It has become almost impolite, or seemingly "moralistic," to speak of evil and psychopathy, or of any person's behavior as evil—Hitler, Stalin, Milosevic, Ted Bundy, Jeffrey Dahmer, Aileen Wuornos, Rosemary West, the genocide of Native Americans, institutionalized slavery, Armenian genocide, the Shoah, Nanking, Darfur, the current crisis with the Islamic State, and other massive atrocities notwithstanding. The topics of evil and psychopathy have long been marginalized and neglected—even dissociated—in psychoanalysis. Given the shockingly brutal and tragic events that have occurred in the United States and throughout the world during the last century, we believe it is crucial to explore and understand why psychoanalysis has been particularly silent on the topic of evil.

With respect to the silence from psychoanalysts on the concepts of psychopathy and human evil, several colleagues have commented that these ideas smack of morality and religious values and should not be a topic of consideration for psychoanalysis. However, both moralism and egregious lapses of morality have been ever present, but often not confronted face to face in the ongoing history of psychoanalysis. For example, in his "pre-analytic" writings on hysteria, Freud (Howell & Itzkowitz, 2016) identified childhood trauma, often sexual trauma, as the causative factor of traumatic dissociation and hysteria. But it must be asked: what was said and done about the perpetrators who had abused these traumatized patients when they were children? As Freud shifted his focus away from externality and defined psychoanalysis as the exploration of internal unconscious fantasy, real perpetrators of childhood abuse were relegated to the shadows, lurking as ghosts in a repressed maze of infantile fantasy and sexuality. Although improving, holding perpetrators accountable in our culture has been too seldom, too few.

Taking the position that "evil" is a moral or sociological issue is misguided. It precludes psychoanalysts from wrestling with the important question: what is it about the mind and its relational development that results in human beings capable of intentional, unthinkable acts of ruthless cruelty and violence? As Gilligan (1997) stated about violence, "as long as we think of it as a moral problem, we will never be able to learn what causes it or what prevents it" (p. 94).

Evil

Until very recently, popular culture has reduced the word "evil" to a rather archaic term, almost an anachronism. In earlier times, "evil" referred to two things: (1) an overwhelmingly horrible event or force, such as a devastating earthquake (see Chapter 8); and (2) a religious sense of sin within us. Most recently, the use of the word "evil" is having a resurgence, almost a profligate one, too often denoting something or someone the speaker dislikes. For this reason, we wish to discuss and define "evil" very carefully.

To differentiate the evil committed by humans from other colloquial usage such as "the evil of disease or disaster," we are referring to (human) evil as involving predatory, unbridled, ruthless, destructive behavior, conducted without guilt, remorse, or concern about the victims.

But even more specifically, to help avoid collapsing our discourse into a simple moral binary of good versus evil and avoid falling into an abyss of moral relativism we refer to Stone (Chapter 4):

> To invoke once again Wittgenstein's clarification that *the meaning of a word is its usage*, the contemporary meaning of "evil" is less freighted with overtones of religious and philosophical thought; instead "evil" has

become an emotional word that people use when confronted with the actions of another person or group that evokes horror, revulsion, shock, and fright. We hear of some monstrous act, something heinous—such as an atrocity that had caused unspeakable pain and suffering. Our face scrunches up, we wince, our jaw may drop—and we say: "That was horrible … that was evil!"

(p. 95)

Likewise, Otto Kernberg defines the nature of evil as "the shocking expression of primitive aggression, destructive behavior towards others that, in its violence, evinces a wildly excessive quality, a radical callousness, and a lack of compassion that seem to defy the basic nature of humanity" (p. 357). And, in Philip Bromberg's (2003) words,

for humans, selfhood (its cohesiveness, coherence, and continuity), life, and the need to sustain it when it is in jeopardy obliterates all else … in the face of potential (or actual) situations that are taken in as unbearable assaults on the felt core of what defines "who I am to myself." One might also wonder whether it is the perpetration of such assaults on the selfhood of another that comes closest to the essence of what we are trying to capture when we speak of "evil."

(p. 560)

We uncouple the concept of human evil from the burden of its religious past by recognizing that its result does not leave us thinking of demonic possession. Rather it leaves us incredulous—in shock, awe, and disbelief over the all-too-human capacity for purposeful, unbridled destructiveness against our fellow human beings without regard for their pain or lives.

Psychopaths, only a portion of whom are serial killers, rapists, or pedophiles, leave a wave of destruction in their wake (Hare, 1993), often leaving us in a state of confusion and shock over the extreme violation of human trust and bonding.

From sin to instinct

For most of the last few thousand years in Western civilization, through the Judeo-Christian lens, sin was within us, to be dealt with and tamed in accordance with a presumption of free will. Understanding psychology in the tradition of natural science that had, since Galileo's time, supplanted theological belief systems, Freud asserted the universality of aggressive and sexual instincts. He viewed these instincts as so powerful in their striving for satiation that they will inevitably be expressed in some way, often unconsciously. Instincts then were neither good nor bad, but just part of human nature. Sin is bad, even evil, but instinct is natural.

Freud and the secularization of evil

Freud's introduction of his tripartite structural model of mind, which relied heavily on the defense of repression, up-ended the centuries-old battle between good and evil and God and the Devil. In contrast to a belief in exogamous evil, as personified by the Devil or Satan, Freud postulated that people were driven by endogenous forces within themselves, the forces of deeply repressed, instinctual, animalistic impulses; sexual and aggressive drives. The reconstruction of evil in Freudian theory as biological imperatives—as id impulses that need to be sublimated, controlled or at best viewed as expressions of superego guilt—redefined it out of existence as something that should be addressed in and of itself. Long understood within the context of religion, evil became secularized. Once the psychobiological rationale of the drives was accepted, the concept of evil was relocated to the realm of science.

In a major way, by secularizing evil, psychoanalysis challenged the hegemony of organized religious belief in Western culture. No longer was it necessary to invoke Satan or possession by evil spirits as motivating forces behind malicious, evil, and criminal behavior. Freud's theory provided an explanation for criminal acts and antisocial behavior.

Yet this secularized, normalized, and reductive redefinition left us in the position of being unable to identify human evil and psychopathy as something extraordinary when they occur—and therefore left us, as clinicians and theorists of the mind, helpless to do anything about it.

In his structural model of mind, Freud hypothesized a psychic agency whose job it was to help tame and control unacceptable instinctual drives and impulses, which, if left untamed, unsocialized and unsublimated, would allow the development of antisocial behavior. The superego then became the moral center for the drive defense model, and deficits in this agency of mind were understood as the underlying dynamic for the emergence of psychopathy. Therefore, although the term "evil" was avoided, omitted or unseen in psychoanalysis, it has always been present in disguised form. One problem with Freud's model of mind is the assumption that it emerges from the struggles between internal drives and instincts and the inhibiting impact of socialization by caretakers. This assumes caretakers and the surrounding society and culture represent reasonable, rational, and democratic ideals and institutions. He, unlike Erich Fromm, ignored the potential warping effect of family and cultural values, particularly the authoritarian character, on the emerging mind of the developing child.

Recent cultural changes

By the 1960s and 1970s the desirability of losing the shackles of social conformity became more popularized, and psychoanalysis—embedded and responsive as it is to the forces of cultural patterns—kept pace. But somehow, over time, the desirability of viewing sadistic, aggressive, and psychopathic aspects of ourselves in the context of a self, grounded in an ethical moral compass, appears to give way too often to the acceptance of these qualities without a moral context. Greed, the striving for success and the survival of the "corporation," driven by malignant narcissism, is often seen as positive quality among corporate managers.

Walloons (2012), addressing psychopathy in the world of business, writes, "Successful psychopaths are found to be more prevalent in the corporate section of society than in the general population" (p. 44). Citing a study by Babiak et al. (2010), who studied over 200 corporate professionals chosen to partake in a management development program by the corporations by whom they were employed found, that "3.9% of the group scored in the psychopathic range on instruments designed to assess psychopathy … much higher than the 1% that is estimated to occur in the general population" (p. 44).

In the film *Wall Street* (Pressman & Stone, 1987), the main character, Gordon Gekko, epitomizes the corporate psychopath, as heard in his speech to the stockholders of "Teldar Paper" when he exclaims, "The point is, ladies and gentlemen, that greed, for lack of a better word, is good. Greed is right, greed works. Greed clarifies, cuts through, and captures the essence of the evolutionary spirit."

"We live in violent times," writes psychologist Stephen A. Diamond (1996). "The currently raging epidemic of so-called 'senseless violence' has become *the* central concern of the American people, dominating news reportage despite the pressing presence of other serious issues" (p. 1, emphasis in original). These words were written five years before the 9/11 attacks on the United States and before Americans became aware of Al Qaeda and ISIS, and many years before what appears to be a growing epidemic of unreasonable use of force by our nation's police agencies against people of color.

Our questions

Inherent, however, in the increasingly relevant and intertwined concepts of psychopathy and human evil, are extremely complex questions and issues. Who and what are evil or good, according to whom, and to what ends? This question is voiced sarcastically in the 1963 Bob Dylan song "With God on Our Side." For example, Mike Eigen (2007) writes how Mohamed Atta, the key World Trade Center terrorist, described himself and his situation:

> To be obliterated for a godly cause is a thing of beauty and glory. Here the United States is the evil one, the hijackers God's helpers. The mentor instructs Atta that soon all his disturbances will be consecrated: Even his fear is holy, peace is near. Guilt is not even mentioned. It is wiped away by righteousness. The sense of being good obliterates guilt.
>
> (pp. 729–730)

As Piven (2007) documents, Hitler described his struggle as "a battle against 'death and the devil'" (p. 11).

There are many distinctions that must be made and many questions that must be answered or at least addressed. Among these are: where does individual responsibility lie? What about the deindividualizing effects of group membership on the individual's sense of responsibility (see Freud, 1921; Peck, 1983; Staub, 1989)? What about the "banality of evil" (Arendt, 1963), by which people are supposedly, simply and mindlessly, following orders when they commit evil acts? What about the effect of compartmentalization of decision making and technological specialization? With reference to this question, Scott Peck (1983) described the abdication of individual responsibility in favor of ceding to the technological compartmentalization in the atrocity of My Lai in the Vietnam War. One might also ask, would the same people commit evil, murderous acts, if not operating under a group aegis or authority? Under what conditions will people execute evil behavior? Stanley Milgram (1963) found that the majority of his subjects were emotionally capable and willing to deliver what they believed to be severe electric shocks to strangers. Likewise, Philip Zimbardo's (2007) Stanford Prison Experiment illustrated how easily students who were assigned to the role of guard could become vicious in enacting their roles. Other questions: are we all capable of seemingly unthinkable acts of destructiveness and/or violence, in accordance with situational demands? What of the role of terrorism in producing bystanders who are afraid to act? Does evil behavior require dissociative processes, or can it simply be an aspect of acculturation, as Staub (1989) maintains? Does psychopathy exist on a continuum, as a potentiality in all of us, or does it more accurately describe a certain kind of individual, or both?

And, further questions: what are the beliefs/institutions/internal objects, especially in psychoanalysis, that motivate the dissociation of human evil? What are the processes of idealization, terror, and dissociation that foster the nonrecognition of evil? What are the internalized interpersonal/relational experiences that lead people to commit, often repeatedly, unthinkable acts of sadistic violence?

Aspects of evil and psychopathy in culture: acceptance and denial

Erich Fromm (1973) contributed significantly to our understanding of psychopathy. Although he seldom used that term, he wrote extensively of malignant narcissism and malignant aggression. The malignant narcissist is someone whose self-worth and identity are nourished and sustained by "his own entirely subjective conviction of his perfection, his superiority over others, his extraordinary qualities, and not through being related to others or through any real work or achievement of his own" (pp. 201–202). For Fromm (1973), malignant aggression is a quality or characteristic that is unique to humankind. He saw it as destructiveness; cruelty and killing that have no adaptive value and not in response to threat. Rather, it is experienced as a source of pleasure and may even be felt as lustful in and of itself. Sadism is a form of malignant aggression and of it he writes, "passion for unrestricted power over another sentient being—and of necrophilia—the passion to destroy life and the attraction to all that is dead, decaying and purely mechanical" (p. 6). Kernberg (2009) also writes of "malignant narcissism," defining it in terms of antisocial behavior in the context of narcissistic personality disorder.

Dissociation of psychopathy

"Psychopathy is a hidden streak in our accepted cultural mores in which 'successful' exploitativeness is often condoned rather than condemned. At the same time, there is a cultural denial of the existence of human predators" (Howell, 2005, p. 248). Whether in movements or in individuals, evil and psychopathy often are hard to see and process soon enough. As Christopher Bollas writes in a chapter, "The Fascist State of Mind," in his book *Cracking Up* (1995), the evil of psychopaths is often dissociatively unrecognized by others, instead of this evil being understood to be dangerous and destructive. He writes that these gifted practitioners of what he calls "intellectual genocide" may have become socially successful by viciously attacking others, with the odd result that others are acceptingly amused by such "cute monsters" rather than horrified by such viciousness. Ironically it is not so uncommon to find such "cute monsters" in positions of great influence and power (see Chapters 1 and 2; also see Howell, 2005, Chapter 12). Bollas notes, "the act of dissociative acceptance" (p. 196) (the vicious cute monster is really a very nice and charming person) colludes with the function of genocide. By denying the evil before us, we support the fascist state of mind.

Echoing a similar theme, Neville Symington states that in the rest of us psychopaths arouse (1) collusion (because we are understandably frightened), (2) disbelief (*No, surely he can't be that bad—he wouldn't have done or won't do that*), and (3) condemnation. The latter two of these occur because we cannot stand our own sadism and the truth of the psychopath's psychic structure.

Psychopathy in the consulting room

As analysts who are part of this time and embedded in our culture, it is essential that we understand psychopathy. It is vital that therapists be able to understand the character and psychodynamics of psychopathy. This will allow us to help our patients better understand some of the people with whom they interact. Additionally, in those rare instances when psychopaths, themselves, appear in the consulting room, we will be better informed and prepared clinicians. When they must deal with psychopaths, patients often blame themselves for their failure. We need to be able to spot highly psychopathic tendencies in the people our patients interact with so as to address and clarify in the consulting room what our patients are unable to formulate in their minds. Partly because of the psychopath's seductive skills (Meloy, 1988), and partly due to their ability to discern our dissociated needs and wishes, we can all easily become sucked into their views or presentations of themselves as victimized. Also, if our patient happens to have psychopathic characteristics, we must be prepared to deal with the situation before us. Finally, psychoanalysis has—and has had—its own "cute monsters." Our field tends to think of sexual predators and psychopaths as "not me" and "not us," often not really noticing when therapists have committed unethical or psychopathic acts.

Ethical boundary violations and psychopathic behavior have been secreted behind the doors of the consulting rooms since the early years of psychoanalysis. And professional credentials have been used to obfuscate the commission of violations while simultaneously attempting to shift blame onto the victims. Freud was aware of the dalliances between some of his followers and their analysands. He was rightfully concerned that their untoward behavior could be the undoing of his reputation and his "new science." Gabbard (2002), citing Kerr (1993), writes, "sexual exploitation of patients was veritably ubiquitous among Freud's intimate circle. In addition to Ernest Jones, Freud also had concerns about Wilhelm Stekel, Otto Gross, and even the clergyman Oscar Pfister" (p. 381). In such boundary violations, there are overlapping dynamics with psychopathy, such as problems with narcissism, omnipotence, grandiosity, superego pathology, and defensive dissociation.

With respect to Ernest Jones, a more serious and nefarious matter comes to light. In an article that could be considered an indictment of Jones as a pedophile, Kuhn (2002) discusses the 1906 arrest, trial, and acquittal of Jones, who was accused of the indecent sexual assault of two girls, along with indecent exposure towards a number of the children he had examined. Kuhn explains that the children's testimony was deemed unreliable due to their mental incapacity. He writes, "The cross examination of the girls showed that no court of justice could rely on their evidence" (p. 365). Additional evidence from the room in which the children were examined consisted of a table cover containing semen stains, most likely from Jones. It was deemed inadmissible with the help of Jones's attorney.

Not so unlike Hollywood, psychoanalysis has had its own share of Harvey Weinstein-type characters. Consider a more contemporary description of an ethical transgression described in a thoughtful article by Muriel Dimen (2011) between herself and her psychoanalyst, Dr. O. During a moment of fear and vulnerability Dimen, at the moment of leaving her session—it was 1973—asked her therapist for a reassuring hug. The hug ends with her kissing him on the check and his replying: "No, how about a real kiss?" Dimen continues,

> So—it wasn't even a question, because, as the quip goes, there's a "trance" in "transference"—I kissed his mouth. He returned the favor with his tongue—at which point, I recall—as I write—a feeling of shock, and then a feeling of ignoring the shock. He chuckled: "Oops, I'm getting a hard-on, I better stop."
>
> (p. 36)

Dimen thoughtfully grounds us in the zeitgeist, explaining the cultural tumult heightened by the women's movement, birth control, and the beginning of the challenge to male, paternal hegemony as a way of balancing her and her analyst's contribution to this experience. Regardless of the cultural milieu, one might ask rhetorically whether it is ever appropriate or ethical for a psychoanalyst to act towards his/her patient in the manner described by above? We believe it is never appropriate. Dimen's shocked and viscerally disgusted response speaks for itself.

Alas, like the rest of humanity, psychoanalysts are not immune to psychopathy. Like the culture at large, psychoanalysis has too often turned a blind eye to, and implicitly exonerated, its own "cute monsters." That is, "it does not work to Other evil: When evil overwhelms us, it may become a part of us—until or unless we learn enough about it and our relationships to it" (Howell, 2005, p. 10). Yet it is up to psychoanalysts, psychotherapists, mental health practitioners and thinkers—if not us, who else?—to help minimize denial and dissociation so that what is wrong and corrupt can finally be brought into awareness, thought about and acted upon.

Acknowledgments

Sheldon Itzkowitz, Ph.D, & Elizabeth F. Howell. Introduction. *Contemporary Psychoanalysis*, copyright © the William Alanson White Institute of Psychiatry, Psychoanalysis & Psychology and the William Alanson White Psychoanalytic Society, www.wawhite.org, reprinted by permission of Taylor & Francis Ltd, http://www.tandfonline.com on behalf of the William Alanson White Institute of Psychiatry, Psychoanalysis & Psychology and the William Alanson White Psychoanalytic Society.

References

Arendt, H. (1963). *Eichmann in Jerusalem: A report on the banality of evil.* New York, NY: Penguin.

Babiak, P, Neumann, C. S., & Hare, R. D. (2010). Corporate psychopathy: Talking the walk. *Behavioral Sciences and the Law, 28*, 174–193.

Bollas, C. (1995). *Cracking up: The work of unconscious experience.* Toronto: HarperCollins Canada.

Bromberg, P. (2003). Something wicked this way comes: Trauma, dissociation, and conflict – The space where psychoanalysis, cognitive science, and neuroscience overlap. *Psychoanalytic Psychology, 20*(3), 558–574.

Diamond, S. A. (1996). *Anger, madness and the diamonic: The psychological genesis of violence, evil and creativity.* Albany, NY: State University of New York Press.

Dimen, M. (2011). Lapsus linguae, or a slip of the tongue? A sexual violation in an analytic treatment and its personal and theoretical aftermath. *Contemporary Psychoanalysis, 47*, 35–79.

Dylan, B. (1963). With God on Our Side [recorded by Bob Dylan]. On *The Times They Are A-changin'* [LP]. New York, NY: Columbia Records. (January 13, 1964).

Eigen, M. (2007). Guilt in an age of psychopathy. *Psychoanalytic Review, 94*(5), 727–749. doi:10.1521/prev.2007.94.5.727.

Freud, S. (1921). Group psychology and the analysis of the ego. *The Standard Edition of the Complete Psychological Works of Sigmund Freud, Volume XVIII (1920–1922): Beyond the Pleasure Principle, Group Psychology and Other Works*, 65–144.

Fromm, E. (1973). *The anatomy of human destructiveness.* New York, NY: Henry Holt & Co.

Gabbard, G. O. (2002). Boundary violations and the abuse of power commentary on paper by Philip Kuhn. *Studies in Gender and Sexuality*, *3*(4), 379–388.

Gilligan, J. (1997). *Violence: Reflections on a national epidemic*. New York, NY: Vintage books.

Hare, R. D. (1993). *Without conscience*. New York, NY: Guilford Press.

Howell, E. F. (2005). *The dissociative mind*. Hillsdale, NJ: Analytic Press.

Howell, E. F., & Itzkowitz, S. (Eds.). (2016). *The dissociative mind in psychoanalysis*. New York, NY: Routledge.

Kernberg, O. (2009). Afterward. In M. Stone (Ed.), *The anatomy of evil* (pp. 357–360). New York, NY: Prometheus Books.

Kuhn, P. (2002). So, if it were not Jones, who else would it be? Reply to commentaries. *Studies in Gender and Sexuality*, *3*(4), 395–405.

Meloy, J. R. (1988). *The psychopathic mind: Origins, dynamics, and treatment*. Northvale, NJ: Jason Aronson.

Milgram, S. (1963). Behavioral study of obedience. *Journal of Abnormal and Social Psychology*, *67*(4), 371–378.

Peck, M. S. (1983). *People of the lie: The hope for healing human evil*. New York, NY: Simon & Schuster.

Piven, J. S. (2007). Terror, sexual arousal, and torture: The question of obedience or ecstasy among perpetrators. *Discourse of Sociological Practice*, *8*(1), 1–21.

Pressman, E. R. (Producer), & Stone, O. (Director). (1987). *Wall Street* [Motion picture]. United States: 20th Century Fox. Retrieved from www.imdb.com /character/ch0012282/quotes.

Staub, E. (1989). *The roots of evil: The origins of genocide and other group violence*. New York, NY: Cambridge University Press.

Walloons, S. (2012). "The devil in the boardroom: Corporate psychopaths and their impact on business," *PURE Insights:1*, Article 9. Retrieved from http:// digitalcommons.wou.edu/pure/vol1/iss1/9.

Zimbardo, P. (2007). *The Lucifer effect: Understanding how good people turn evil*. New York, NY: Random House.

Chapter 1

Psychopathy and human evil

An overview[1,2]

Sheldon Itzkowitz

The term "psychopath" elicits thoughts of serial killers; pedophiles; sadistic, intentionally cruel persons; or acts of genocide at the hands of tyrants such as Stalin or Hitler. However, psychopathy runs along a spectrum; not all psychopaths are serial killers or mass murderers. There are psychopaths, who may be thought of as "sub-clinical" (LeBreton, Binning & Adorno, 2005) or "successful" (Stevens, Deuling & Armenakis, 2012) unless they commit a fatal error. They are adept at avoiding exposure to either the mental health or criminal justice systems. In fact, these psychopaths are often highly successful and often achieve positions of status in the world of governance or corporations, in which case they have been referred to as "corporate" psychopaths (Boddy, 2010; Wellons, 2012). In this chapter I offer an overview, first addressing the more pathological end of the spectrum, followed by a brief discussion of the more "successful" end, those who share many of the same characteristics but have enjoyed a different outcome in life, e.g. successful psychopaths. In this discussion, to better understand the psychology of psychopaths, I link the following foundational psychological processes: failures in healthy attachment (e.g. disorganized attachment), problems in mentalization (including the inhibition of reflective functioning), malignant narcissism and dissociation. I highlight the work of key theoretical figures, notably Erich Fromm.

Serial killers

It is an unfortunate truism that acquaintances and neighbors of the sub-group of psychopaths known as serial killers are often surprised, shocked even, when they discover the heinous crimes committed so close to home. For example, Yamamoto (2016) writes of Lonnie David Franklin Jr., aka the "Grim Sleeper," neighbors who live in the same South Los Angeles neighborhood as the man accused of slaying nine women and one 15-year-old over two decades are shocked, saying they could never imagine he would do anything remotely like this … [There is] disbelief that Franklin could have killed women and dumped their bodies in alleys and trash bins around Southern California. Rosie Hunter lived down the street from Franklin when she was 10 or 11 years old. All she remembers is a neighborhood mechanic always helping people.

Or in the Associated Press (2009) article about Anthony Sowell,

The man who lived in the house of rotting corpses never gave people a reason to wonder what he was really doing behind closed doors … The suspected serial killer seemed so harmless that when he invited neighbors over for a barbecue in his driveway, they came. So benign that when he beckoned women inside his house that smelled of death, they apparently went willingly.

"Genocide," writes Bollas (1995),

is the quintessential crime of the twentieth century, and genocide is exemplified by the serial killer, a genocidal being who swiftly dispatches his victims and converts the human into the inhuman, creating meaningless deaths that sully the concepts of living and dying.

(p. 185)

For Bollas the serial killer is created in childhood by severe relational trauma. Of the men who become serial killers of "anonymous people" he states they "have suffered a kind of emotional death" (p. 187). He believes the impact of early trauma is overwhelming and drastic and he explains, "In place of a once live self, a new being emerges, identified with the killing of what is good, the destruction of trust, love, and reparation" (p. 189).

How then do they walk among us, sit next to us at work, live in our neighborhoods and even befriend us? How do we understand the surprise and shock of neighbors or co-workers upon learning the "nice, quiet man" living or sitting so closely is someone convicted of committing unthinkably violent and sadistic crimes? The emotional death that Bollas describes is similar to the emptiness, isolation and loneliness that some understand as characteristic of dissociation. Can we conceptualize the previously unknown aspect of this person that suddenly appears and kills as a well-hidden aspect of a psychopath—in which attachment has been dissociated (see Chapter 2), or as a deeply dissociated rageful self-state based on an internalized representation of the person's abuser when he was a child, in someone with a dissociative disorder?

Defining evil

Stone's contemporary definition of evil, referring to, "the actions of another person or group that evokes horror, revulsion, shock and fright" (Chapter 4, p. 95) is remarkably similar to Erich Fromm's. Fromm believed that evil was defined as actions performed consciously and intentionally by someone or a group that intentionally inflicts or causes the victim(s) to suffer physical, psychological or bodily harm and where the perpetrator(s) of evil suffers no real felt sense of remorse or regret over their actions, having no concern for the harm they inflict (Fromm, 1964, 1991).

Erich Fromm's position on evil

The term "malignant narcissism" was first coined by Fromm (1964), but many others, including Kernberg, have since used it and similar terms to refer to the actions of people who carry the diagnosis of "psychopath" (Itzkowitz, 2017). Beginning with DSM-IV (*Diagnostic and Statistical Manual of Mental Disorders*, fourth edition), the diagnosis of "psychopath" was replaced by "antisocial personality."

Fromm was a Marxist and a psychoanalyst. His Marxist leanings grounded his theory of psychoanalysis, and his concept of character in human relations, class structure and the significant impact of society and culture. Where Freud believed that aggression and destructiveness were connected with a fixed quantity of instinctual energy, Fromm saw character as part of the personality that is acquired and shaped by interpersonal-relational experience (Funk & Shaw, 1982). Thus, he uncoupled the etiology of pathological hatred from the instincts and relocated it in the harmful and corrupting elements of human experience as embedded in society. For Fromm, hatred of oneself and hating others are intricately connected and not disparate. As such, he saw destructiveness and the need to destroy as an end product of the obstruction of people's freedom to experience and express themselves to their fullest potential.

In 1947, Fromm wrote, "the degree of destructiveness is proportionate to the degree to which the unfolding of the person's capacities is blocked" (p. 218). In this regard he was referring to the powerful negative role that cultures, societies and governments can have by controlling, obstructing or constricting the development and evolution of the minds and actions of individuals. Therefore, the breeding ground of violence and destructiveness lay in cultures and societies that strangulate the individuals' freedom and ability to thrive and evolve beyond their current life situation.

Fromm (1964), years before Kohut, discussed two forms of narcissism: the benign and the malignant. The benign form of narcissism is associated with and emerges from a productive orientation to living. Joy, self-satisfaction, pride and narcissistic gratification are derived from the fruits of one's labor or production. Productivity is in the service of living. Benign narcissism is self-correcting because the object of one's narcissism is the work, the materials, the process, even the outcome, and the narcissism is balanced by the fulfillment and investment in the work itself. "[B]ut the very fact that the work itself makes it necessary to be related to reality, constantly curbs the narcissism and keeps it within bounds" (p. 77).

In contrast is the malignant narcissist, whose pride, joy and gratification derive from her/his possessions, body, looks, wealth, house, job, etc., rather than anything he/she produces. It is a form of what Fromm termed "non-productivity" and it lacks the "corrective element" seen in benign narcissism. For the non-productive malignant narcissist, one's "greatness" or grandiosity lies in what one *has* and not in one's *achievements*. Therefore, the need to be related or connected to others is limited and in the process of maintaining one's "greatness" or grandiosity, one becomes less related to reality (ibid.). One has to continually feed and support such narcissism "in order to be better protected from the danger that my narcissistically inflated ego might be revealed as the product of my empty imagination. Malignant narcissism, thus, is not self-limiting" (ibid.).

In *The Anatomy of Human Destructiveness*, Fromm (1973) developed and elaborated on his concepts of the biophilic and the necrophilic orientations to living. The necrophilic orientation is what concerns us in discussing the psychopath and human evil. In contrast, "The biophilic orientation develops from within the context of a loving supportive family whose members are themselves biophilic; they love life" (Itzkowitz, 2017, p. 85). Such families are not only loving but also infused with warmth, protectiveness and encouraging of curiosity and growth. Cultures and societies can help facilitate a biophilic orientation. Funk and Shaw (1982) write,

> security in the sense that the basic material conditions for a dignified life are not threatened; justice in the sense that nobody can be an end for the purposes of another; and freedom in the sense that each man has the possibility to be an active and responsible member of society.
>
> (p. 136)

Implicit in the development of Fromm's biophilic orientation is family, community and culture that facilitate and enhance the growth of the individual's sense of worth, esteem, pride, goodness and respect. Gilligan proposes that it is this positive sense of self that can serve as an inoculation against the propensity for violence. He theorizes that there are several precursors to violence, which he identifies as forms of shame, a deep personal and chronic sense of shame. In writing about violent men Gillian explains that they are people who feel "vulnerable not just to 'loss of face' but to the total loss of honor, prestige, respect and status—the disintegration of identity" (p. 112).

Gilligan (1997) notes that emotional health and the stability of a robust sense of self emerges through human interaction within community and culture. He writes, "The relationship between culture and character is an unavoidable socio-psychological reality" (p. 96). The elements of selfhood, community and culture are so connected for Gilligan that they become psychically conjoined to the extent that a threat to the survival of one's culture becomes tantamount to the survival of the self. Violent, incarcerated men cling to a sense of self-esteem and respect to avoid overwhelming feelings of shame and humiliation, which must be avoided at all costs. Shame and loss of respect is tantamount to death: "People will sacrifice anything to prevent the death and disintegration of their individual or group identity" (p. 97). Membership in a sub-group, within the prison system, helps bolster one's sense of esteem, self-respect, safety and cohesiveness. When the sub-group is threatened or shamed, members are likely to experience this as a threat to their individual identity and self-esteem.

Similarly, when a member is threatened or assaulted the sub-group defends their shamed comrade to restore the status of both the individual and the group and to maintain honor, respect and group cohesion. Gilligan (2009), quoting an inmate, writes,

> My life ain't worth nothin' if I take somebody disrespectin' me and callin' me punk asshole faggot and goin' "Ha! Ha!" at me. Life ain't worth livin' if there ain't nothin' worth dyin' for. If you ain't got pride you got nothin'.
>
> (p. 106)

The means by which respect, honor and self-esteem is restored is by violence, a causative factor of inmate-on-inmate violence.

Regarding group or social narcissism, Fromm similarly believed that the majority of a group's members, if not the whole, sustains the ideology of the group. Adherence and devotion to group ideology forms the basis of membership, and the feeling of belongingness inflates individual members' narcissistic needs and enhances group cohesiveness. Cheliotis (2010) clarifies that the underlying ideology of the group need not be reasonable, and I would extend this to include rational as well; the ideology may in fact be pathological. It is developed and sustained by consensus and like-mindedness of the group (see Chapter 8).

In "Group Psychology and the Analysis of the Ego" Freud (1921) makes the argument that group membership often results in identification with the authority of the leader, thereby swapping one's conscience for that of the leader. In the process, previous inhibitions are abandoned and a new freedom to act in tandem with group mores provides increased pleasure. He writes, "A group is an obedient herd, which could never live without a master. It has such a thirst for obedience that it submits instinctively to anyone who appoints himself its master" (p. 81). Obviously, the danger lay in submitting to the moral authority of a corrupt, maniacal, psychopathic leader.

Returning to Fromm's ideas on human evil, we discover his syndrome of decay that includes necrophilia, narcissism and incestuous-symbiosis. It combines malignant narcissism with the love of all that is dead and a regressive, symbiotic-incestuous fixation, which "*prompts men to destroy for the sake of destruction*, and to hate for the sake of hate" (p. 19; emphasis added). By "regressive symbiotic-incestuous ties" Fromm is referring to all that interferes with and prevents the person from living a fully independent life.

Fromm (1973) also used the term "malignant aggression" to refer to cruelty and destructiveness that he believed specific to humankind. He wrote, "man is the only primate that kills and tortures members of his own species without any reason … and who feels satisfaction in doing so" (p. 26). Fromm believed that malignant aggression and destructiveness was a form of negative transcendence, well described by Mauricio Cortina in his 2015 paper, "The Greatness and Limitations of Erich Fromm's Humanism":

> Human destructiveness and extreme sadism can be understood as cases of negative transcendence, i.e. if I don't have the power to be a loving and creative person, I have the possibility of turning to the perverse power to kill and inflict untold suffering on my victims. These perversions may come from histories of children who have been sadistically treated and humiliated by one or more attachment figures and live in families or cultures in which violence is rampant.
>
> (p. 396)

Malignant aggression can also serve as a form of sadistic control. Examples can be seen in brutal dictators such as Stalin and Hitler, in genocide, and I would include psychopaths.

Personality characteristics, personality organization and cognitive style of the psychopath

In her 2003 book *Predators, Pedophiles, Rapists and Other Sex Offenders*, Anna Salter explains that psychopaths fool and deceive us not only as a matter of course but, as a form self-rewarding entertainment. Their lack of conscience allows them to hurt others and commit crimes without remorse and show little distress at being caught and incarcerated.

They excel at seduction, beguilement and manipulation. Their lack of conscience allows them to undermine others, especially others who have naively and mistakenly come to believe in the psychopath's apparent sincerity. Psychopaths often leave others bewildered, hurt and confused (Salter, 2003) when the depths of their insincerity, self-centeredness and selfishness are revealed.

Deceit, hypocrisy and charade

Their skills include the ability to manipulate and dupe others while appearing charming and sincere, to con, deceive and defraud others all while engaging with apparent sincerity and honesty. The kind of person who will smile at you, shake your hand, while simultaneously stabbing you in the back or in the front depending on their level of narcissistic grandiosity.

They are uniquely skilled in being able to lie calmly, sincerely and guiltlessly. The psychopath prides himself and thrives on his success at getting away with his scam. Their ability to adapt, with chameleon-like finesse, and adjust to changes and shifts in cultural circumstances or social environs facilitates their ability to "fit in" and be seen as a compatriot. Once accepted as a member of the group, the seduction and treachery begin. Salter quotes Mr. M.:

> I lived a life of a chameleon, changing colors with the wind. I didn't just live a double life. I lived multiple lives. Whatever life the situation called for I lived it … And I adapted to whatever the situation required … I could feedback to people what I thought they wanted to see and what I thought they wanted to hear.
>
> (p. 35)

The psychopath's ability to establish and maintain a double life is an essential method of deception. They count on the fact that people generally believe that one's public persona is assumed to be the same as their private behavior. They beguile and defraud others by creating the appearance of goodness, kindness, helping others less fortunate or disabled, being charitable, charming, sincere, truthful and trustworthy. For example, Salter explains,

> The Boston Strangler reported that he would suggest that women call the superintendent if they doubted that he was really a maintenance worker. The women took that as a sign that he must be who he says he was and routinely let him into their houses without calling.
>
> (p. 45)

The psychopath is described by many writers (Hare, 1993; Meloy, 1996; Fonagy, 2003; Meloy & Shiva, 2007; Stone, 2009) as someone who is narcissistic, remorseless, lacking conscience and empathy, and who pursues self-gratification regardless of the cost or impact on others, or the suffering they inflict. They are emotionally shallow and superficial people who lack the basic personal qualities and emotions necessary to create and maintain deep, loving, intimate relationships. They want and crave excitement and novelty, without which they become bored easily. *Malignant narcissism is core in this pathological disorder.* Psychopaths' dangerousness is disguised by their capacity for presenting themselves as charming, likeable, amusing, entertaining, quick-witted and interesting people.

Kernberg (1971) cautions us that the external presentation of narcissistic patients often hides deeper character pathology. He lists "the absence of deep object relationships in the present, and severe pathology of their internalized object relationships as expressed in pathological ego and superego structures" (p. 629) as qualities we must be aware of.

J. Reid Meloy, a major contributor to the psychoanalytic study of psychopathy and human evil, describes the psychopath as someone who is suffering "a fundamental disidentification with humanity" (1996, p. 5). In describing psychopathic pathology Meloy and Shiva (2007) explain that at the core of the psychopath is significant narcissistic pathology: "The dominant idealization of the self is that of a predator, which diminishes rage and envy towards others; the dominant idealization of the object is one who will perfectly serve the interest of the psychopath, often as prey" (p. 340).

Meloy (1996) and Meloy and Shiva (2008) explain that the psychopathic character is organized at a primitive, narcissistic level. Failures in the use of repression prevent the development and differentiation of the agencies of mind (id, ego and superego) necessary for neurotic personality organization and the use of fantasy as a way of internalizing and coping with external reality. At this primitive level of psychic organization, splitting (dissociation as defense, not as an organization of mind) and projective identification become primary defenses; and part objects, not whole objects, populate the internal world of the psychopath. Concepts of goodness and badness remain unintegrated, and "identifications and internalizations" when present are usually "harsh or unpleasant." As a result, the psychopath is unable to maintain emotional stability solely through the use of internalized fantasy. *The debasement and deprecation of others, and acting out in the form of cruelty, abuse,*

torture or the annihilation of others, serves the crucial role of stabiliz-
ing his grandiose self-structure. Pretense, deceit, deception and vio-
lence are the tools of the psychopath's trade.

Meloy and Shiva (2008) explain that psychopaths are under-socialized and immature with a limited range of affects: "Consciously felt emotions include excitement, frustration, rage, boredom, envy, dysphoria, and shame" (p. 342). They add:

> More mature feelings that require whole-object relatedness and a capacity for secure attachment are missing. These include anger, fear, guilt, depression, sympathy, gratitude, empathy, remorse, sadness, loneliness and reciprocal joy- emotions that are broad, deep, and complex.
>
> (p. 342)

Blair et al. (1996) suggest the presence of a violence inhibition mechanism in normal human development. This mechanism is "activated by distress cues" and is "responsible for the development of moral emotions (e.g. guilt, empathy)" (p. 16) and the ability to differentiate between "moral transgressions," defined by the presence of a victim(s) and "conventional transgressions, defined by the social disorder they cause (e.g. talking in class, public nudity)" (p. 23). They studied groups of autistic and psychopathic individuals with regard to the inhibition of violence and found that autistic individuals were able to "pass tests of violence inhibition mechanism performance showing that they are able to … make the moral/conventional distinction and … show physiological arousal to the distress of others" (p. 17). However, "psychopaths fail tests of violence inhibition mechanism; they do not make the moral/conventional distinction and are hypo-responsive to the distress of others" (ibid.). These researchers conclude, "the psychopath appears to lack the emotional apparatus to feel empathy" (p. 22).

In his classic text "Neurotic Styles" David Shapiro (1965) examines the characteristics and the thinking style of the psychopath. He explains psychopaths lie effortlessly, persuasively and frequently. A psychopath is insincere and

> acts on whim, his aim is the quick, concrete gain, and his interests and talents are in ways and means. From a long-range point of

view, his behavior is usually erratic, but, from the short-range point of view, it is often quite competent.

(p. 157)

Regarding consensual morality, Shapiro believes the psychopath is usually well aware of their societal moral values, but he is generally disinterested in them except when they can be used and manipulated for his own advantage.

Shapiro presents an interesting view of psychopathy as a variant of the impulsive style. He questions whether conscience and moral values such as justice, honesty, personal integrity, good faith and being responsible are possible when a person's character style constitutes impulsive functioning. He explains that moral values, principles and aims are abstract and highly developed concepts requiring a high degree of emotional and cognitive development. Additionally, they require the capacities of self-reflection and delay of gratification and therefore run counter to those who need and seek out more immediate forms of gratification and reward.

Explaining that having a normal conscience implies the successful internalization of an external authority, usually a parental figure, Shapiro adds that this implies the capacity to stand outside of oneself and view oneself and one's actions from the perspective of a socially internalized moral code. This kind of critical, self-reflective ability is not characteristic of impulsive individuals. When it does exist for them, Shapiro believes it exists not in a highly developed form but more perfunctory, limited manner.

The contemporary literature on attachment styles lends support to Shapiro's ideas about the psychopath's impairment in reflective function. Several studies (Fonagy, Moran & Target, 1993; Fonagy, 1999; Dozier, Stovall-McClough & Albus, 2008; Taubner et al., 2012) indicate that attachment pathology, especially disorganized attachment, disrupts and interferes with the child's capacity for mentalization and the development of reflective functioning. Left untreated, this can result in reduced capability or inability to read the mental state of others and recognize others as separate centers of subjectivity. Hence, experience of failures of empathy is a common finding among psychopaths.

Superego pathology

In traditional, structural theory, the etiology of psychopathy is understood to be superego pathology (Greenacre, 1945; Kernberg, 1970a, 1970b; Meloy, 1996). In accounting for antisocial behavior or psychopathy, Shapiro notes that pathology of the superego "is commonly attributed to the absence, inconsistency, or excessive harshness of parental authority" (1965, p. 158). Further, superego pathology is related to "the nature of the existing mode of thinking, and the prevailing forms of emotional experience" (ibid.) that is available to the child during the internalization process.

For Kernberg (1971) pathology and "distortions of ego and superego structures" occur in pathological narcissism, along with pathological internalized object relationships. In describing impulse-ridden character types, Kaufman (1958) explains that superego pathology is in evidence because it is functioning at an underdeveloped, primitive level where its ability to function as a moral guide is impaired. He explains that the capacity to feel guilt is the result of "a state of tension between the ego and the superego" (p. 548), which then indicates the presence of this intrapsychic agency. The psychopath's inability to experience guilt reveals pathology in this agency of mental functioning.

Kernberg (1992) has coined the term "psychopathic transference" in addressing the superego pathology of borderline patients. In a psychopathic transference, patients attempt to deceive the analyst by lying, withholding information, etc., in a conscious effort to prevent the analyst from being able to accurately assess the patient's mental state. Kernberg cautions that this tendency must be addressed directly for the treatment to be effective: "it is for this technical reason—*and not for any 'moralistic' one*—that the therapist has to address the problem of opening the field of communication by resolving psychopathic transferences" (p. 13; emphasis added).

The role of attachment

The centrality of mentalization and subsequent emergence of reflective functioning, i.e. the child's ability to recognize and know the mind of an "other" cannot be overemphasized (Gergely, Fonagy, & Target, 2002; Yakeley & Meloy, 2012). Of particular note in this chapter is that capacities for reflective functioning and emotional empathy that emerge from healthy, early attachment relationships are missing in the psychopath (Taubner et al., 2012). For optimal development of these capacities the child's attachment relationships must be free of unremediated overwhelming and disorganizing early childhood trauma. "Attachment trauma," write Schimmenti and Caretti (2016), "can generate impairments in several psychological domains, including affect regulation, attachment, cognition, dissociation, and self-concept" (p. 339). Indeed, Liotti (2004) has indicated that attachment disorganization results in the collapse of the successful integration of consciousness "and may be the first instance of dissociative reactions during life" (p. 483). Early childhood relational trauma, particularly if it is persistent, sets the stage for early emergence of dissociation, possibly the dissociative structuring of the mind, and the impairment of reflective functioning and empathy.

Additionally, failures in the caretaker's capacity for mentalization, the ability to know and reflect to the child an accurate, even if somewhat exaggerated, representation of her/his self can lead to marked problems in attachment and the child's ability to develop an accurate representation of her/his own experience. If the caretaker is troubled, disturbed and/or aggressive the child is likely to become frightened by the caretaker and thus internalize a distorted image of the caregiver, one that is foreign, bad or aggressive. Yakeley and Meloy (2012) explain that "The person is then forced to develop an identity around an alien persecutory, internal object, or introject, that is unable to think or feel and has to be defended against by violent means" (p. 235). The need for attachment, because it creates feelings of danger and disorganization in the young child, is primarily what is dissociated in psychopathy.

Levy and Orlans (2000) explain that the precursors of the adult psychopath and the antisocial personality can be found in significant problems in early attachment patterns and relatedness. Furthermore, disordered behaviors such as absence of conscience, impulsivity, failures in empathy, "enuresis, animal torture, fire-setting, pathological lying, chronic day- dreaming, and violent fantasies" (p. 12) are early symptoms of those who go on to become serial killers.

Researchers studying the role of attachment in people with personality disorders (PD) (Dozier, Stovall-McClough & Albus, 2008; Lorenzini

& Fonagy, 2013; Taubner et al., 2013) indicate that a higher rate of insecure attachment exists in PD than in the general population. In addition, those with PD have experienced higher rates of significant childhood trauma; early physical abuse is a risk factor in developing antisocial PD in adulthood. Craparo, Schimmenti and Caretti (2013, n. p.) noted there exists a link between early interpersonal-relational trauma, child abuse, disorders of attachment and the development of psychopathy. They studied a group of convicted, violent offenders and found "convicted male offenders with high levels of psychopathic traits were more likely to have experienced abuse and neglect during childhood, and they were even more likely to have experienced relational trauma at an early age." Their findings indicate that those who display severe psychopathic traits in adulthood are most likely to have experienced significant early childhood trauma. (Of course, having been a recipient of early trauma is the larger category. Abuse often results in more benign outcomes).

Taubner et al. (2012) studied the role of mentalization and psychopathic traits and found the ability to mentalize had a moderating effect on levels of aggression, even in individuals who scored higher on traits of psychopathy. Individuals with psychopathic tendencies who showed a higher ability to mentalize displayed less proactive aggression than those with average or low ability to mentalize. The authors concluded that difficulty or failure in mentalization contributes to "a pronounced deficit in understanding self and others in high affective situations" (p. 18). Levinson and Fonagy (2004) studied groups of prisoners, PD patients and controls. They found that "prisoners were more likely to be dismissive in their attachment patterns, and the prisoners' capacity for reflective functioning was more impaired than that of the PD patients" (p. 225). The more violent offenders displayed the largest deficits in reflective functioning. The authors concluded "disavowal of attachment related experiences" and impairment in reflective functioning were in part related to severe childhood trauma. It appears that one outcome of healthy attachment and the capacity for mentalization—i.e. the recognition of the "other" as a separate, subjective, individual— increases the development of empathy and mitigates against non-defensive (primary) aggression and violence; abilities that are either absent or defective in the psychopath.

The role of dissociation

Dissociation played a central role in the origins of psychoanalysis. In their early writings Freud and Breuer identified dissociation as the splitting of consciousness, resulting in abnormal states of consciousness, hypnoid states, and "double consciousness" (Breuer & Freud, 1893–95). Had Freud not shifted his attention from the impact of interpersonal-relational trauma on the mind to the fantasy model, he might have discovered what later researchers and writers (e.g. Schore, 2003, 2004; and Bromberg, 2011) have indicated. In traumatic dissociation, the mind/brain becomes overwhelmed, entering into a state of emotional hyperarousal, causing a shift in the level of consciousness and the inability to process experience symbolically. As a result, multiple centers of consciousness begin to emerge and may remain dissociated from each other as well as the rest of consciousness, thereby creating a mind structured by dissociation.

However, after breaking with Breuer, Freud shifted the etiology of neurosis from trauma to fantasy, rejecting the significance of hypnoid states and multiple centers of consciousness, and replaced dissociation with repression (Howell, 2005; Howell and Itzkowitz, 2016).

Howell (2014) explains when a child is engaged with caretakers who are alternately sources of nurturance and trauma, she is confronted with incompatible affective states of the need for caretaking-attachment and overwhelming, paralyzing fear. This fear intensifies the attachment to the caretaker/abuser. Because this situation is untenable, the young child's mind/brain responds to this fear dissociatively, with a shift in consciousness to a trance-like state where the abuser becomes a focus of attention in a depersonalized and derealized way.

This can involve the automatic unconscious mimicking and internalization and emulation of aspects of the abuser's personality and ways of relating including the focus on the caretaker's desires, during trance-like states (Howell, 2014; Liotti, 2006). In this case, what is imitated is internalized in an altered, dissociative state. In this instance, the mind itself becomes structured by dissociation and multiple centers of consciousness, dissociated self-states, emerge. See Howell (2002, 2014) for more on the etiology of internal aggressive–persecutory dissociated states.

Contemporary writers such as Bromberg (1998, 2006, 2011), Stern (2003) and Howell, (2005, 2011, 2014) have been bringing the impact of trauma and the dissociative structuring of the mind to the foreground of psychoanalysis. This allows us to differentiate between those who commit crimes, even murders, in dissociated states and true psychopaths.

Dissociation in DID v. psychopathy

What I have described above is characteristic of dissociative identity disorder (DID). However, while aggressive or perpetrating states are common in DID, my experience (with a non-criminal population) indicates these states usually direct their criticism and aggression against the self/body and are not homicidal. Dissociated self-states are understood to contain thoughts, feelings and memories that are able to enter into a psychoanalytic relationship with a clinician trained in working with (extreme) dissociative disorders. More importantly, they are not without conscience and the capacity for experiencing guilt, which, by definition, precludes the person from being considered psychopathic. Finally, especially in the early phases of treatment, the aggressive and perpetrating states of extremely dissociated patients are frequently unconscious. In contrast, the true psychopath consciously, carefully and deliberately creates and carries out his aggressive, destructive and hurtful plans.

Moskowitz (2004) describes the case of a California high school student, "Andy," who shot 15 people; two died. He explained, "No one saw it coming. As is often the case in adolescent mass murders, Andy was considered quiet and nice, and those who knew him were mystified that he could commit such an act" (p. 21). When discussing his experience while committing the crime Andy explained, "I don't think crazy is the right word. It's, like, an out-of- body experience—when I was in my body, I was out of my body at the same time … I didn't feel like it was actually me doing it" (ibid).

Moskowitz provides some illuminating statistics regarding violent crime and dissociation:

> Approximately 25% of prison or jail inmates demonstrate "pathological" levels of dissociation … and that a somewhat smaller percentage meet diagnostic criteria for a dissociative disorder … A few studies specifically addressed dissociative identity disorder (DID), with the most conservative finding a prevalence of 6.3% in a hospitalized

(psychiatric and medical) male prison sample, most of whom had been convicted of violent offences.

(p. 9)

Stein (2007, 2016) has linked dissociation caused by childhood trauma and criminal, violent behavior. She believes that most violent crimes are committed by offenders who "operate somewhere between repetition compulsion and dissociated enactment" (2007, p. 114). And she believes that criminal profilers make the mistake of attributing willful control to behavior that is dissociative in nature. Based on her research and clinical experience, she explains that dissociation has often been ignored and seriously under-diagnosed in the criminal justice system. Moreover, she experienced a bias on the part of forensic clinicians against dissociation. She explains,

> If anything, the reluctance to chart dissociative phenomena has hardened, companion to the belief that most inmates are lying about either their abuse history, their symptoms, or the memory of their crimes in order to twist things to their legal advantage.
>
> (2007, p. 235)

This remains a thorny issue since deceit and deception are endemic accoutrements of the psychopath, but not all offenders or inmates are psychopaths. According to Stein, dissociation and dissociative disorders are a more reasoned explanation for amnesia of post-violent and criminal behavior. She explained, "offenders rarely claim not to have committed crimes, only to not remembering committing them" (p. 233).

Stein (2001) offers an example of how dissociation can play a role in criminal violence. She presents "Sonny," a man who while in a dissociated state killed a friend. But "Sonny" also has other named parts, e.g. "Robert," "Lawrence," "The Protector" and "Junior." It seems clear that Sonny's mind is structured by dissociation. She writes,

> Not infrequently, Sonny blames Bobby's murder on the "Protector" or fingers him as an accomplice. Alternately, he claims that the "Protector" only witnessed the murder. "He comes when I'm in physical danger. He came the night when I murdered somebody."
>
> (p. 446)

Sonny acknowledges the murder, but has no memory of the experience.

Should we consider someone like Sonny a psychopath? Might the killer part of Sonny be a dissociated psychopathic part? Unfortunately, Stein does not give us sufficient information to know if the killer part has more qualities characteristic of a true psychopath. Therefore, it is plausible to consider this an example of a dissociated, angry, rageful part who, once triggered, distorted his experience of Bobby's behavior, acted impulsively and killed him. As for Sonny, he admitted to the homicide, even though he does not recall it. Stein explains that he feels sadness and guilt over what he did, ruling him out as a "true" psychopath.

Importantly, Moskowitz (2004), cautions us against precipitously conflating DID with psychopathy, as popular media and culture tends to: "*it is important to note that there is no evidence to suggest that most persons with DID are violent to others; many are violent to themselves, and others manage to avoid engaging in any form of violent behavior whatsoever*" (p. 9; emphasis added).

The "corporate, successful" psychopath

Stein believes law-breaking exists on a continuum "that includes completely legal forms of manipulation, corruption, and risk taking, as well as specifically outlawed acts" (2007, p. 114). For example, the Trump administration, cloaked in business attire, seems to have overtaken aspects of our government in true Machiavellian style. In line with the psychopathic personality and its cognitive style, the administration has intentionally created an atmosphere of deception, manipulation and iniquity that has overtaken our daily lives, and seeks to undermine and sabotage our belief and reliance on consensual realty. In point of fact, "As of Aug. 5, his 928th day in office, he had made 12,019 false or misleading claims, according to the Fact Checker's database that analyzes, categorizes and tracks every suspect statement the president has uttered" (Kessler, Rizzo, and Kelly, 2019).

Clearly then, not all psychopaths are serial killers nor are all psychopaths incarcerated. There are many who enjoy positions of fortune, fame and power while they conduct their personal, business or professional lives in a manner that would place them within the category of psychopathy. In a recent study Stevens, Deuling and Armenakis (2012) explain that successful psychopaths are likely to engage in unethical decision making due to their propensity to morally disengage "in response to ethical dilemmas in the workplace" (p. 146). Yet they remain seen by others as charming and likeable, perhaps due in part to their intellectual gifts and their manipulative and superficial charm, despite their disagreeable and destructive behavior. Some eventually enter either the mental health or the criminal justice systems. Some, however, remain hidden in plain sight. These impostors use their cognitive skills to "size up their prey" and hide behind a façade designed to seduce and manipulate their victims into seeing them as who they wish/need them to be: "the ideal friend, lover, partner" (Babiak & O'Toole, 2012).

Some present themselves as role models and pillars of the community while consciously, not dissociatively, improving their lot in life at the cost to others, frequently embezzling private, public or corporate funds for their own use and enjoyment. Think of Bernard Madoff, the Enron scandal, the Bank of America and JP Morgan Chase, the bank that sold "the shoddy mortgage-backed securities before the financial crisis hit in 2008" (Henning, 2014) and the recent Wells Fargo scandal.

Boddy et al. (2010) state, "modern society is suffering from a plague of poor leadership in both the private and public sectors of the economy" (p. 121). While there is heterogeneity among psychopaths, there are some common attributes they seem to share: failures in empathy and a seeming lack of conscience. In discussing non-criminal psychopaths Wellons (2012) describes two sub-types: primary and secondary psychopathy. Primary psychopaths are likely to show behavior often equated with psychopathic business executives, such as "arrogance, callousness and manipulative behavior." They tend to score high on tests displaying "enhanced cognitive functioning." Secondary psychopathy, on the other hand, is characterized by "impulsive-antisocial lifestyle traits." When compared with primary psychopathy, this group's performance suggests these,

> individuals would be higher in the social deviance aspects of psychopathology and might be more likely to act in impulsive, irresponsible, and law-breaking ways while primary psychopaths were cognitively capable of functioning within society.
>
> (p. 43)

Such "successful" or "corporate" psychopaths are able to function in society and avoid incarceration. In a study of corporate professionals (see Babiak, Neumann & Hare, 2010) the prevalence of psychopathy *"occurred in 3.9% of the sample, much higher than the 1% that is estimated to occur in the general population"* (p. 44; emphasis added). Those who scored high in psychopathy were perceived by their co-workers as strategic thinkers and good communicators. However, they were also seen as poor team players, with poor management skills and poor performance reviews. Of significant interest is the fact that "Most of those with high psychopathic traits were high-ranking executives" (p. 43). In general, these corporate psychopaths are of concern, because they lack a healthy capacity for empathy and they act on their own self-interests, not those of their colleagues, and not in the interests of the corporation or society at large (Boddy, 2010; Wellons, 2012).

Consider the following examples. Gates et al. (2017) reported that Volkswagen admitted to installing software in 11 million cars that enabled the vehicles' computer to "knowingly" deceive the findings of emissions test data, specifically nitrogen oxide (NOx) emissions. During emissions testing, equipment that would lower the cars NOx emissions was enabled so the car appeared to meet the appropriate emissions criteria. However, this same equipment was turned down when the car was being operated normally. The authors explain the possible reason for this was "most likely to save fuel or to improve the car's torque and acceleration." However, NOx is an ingredient causing "ground level ozone or smog" and reparatory diseases such as bronchitis and emphysema (see Tox Town, n.d., for additional information).

As a second example, consider the landmark Paris Climate Accord signed by 196 nations agreeing to correct the devastating impact of climate change. In her *New York Times* article, Friedman (2017) provided a link to the draft of a recent report on climate change by scientists from a number of federal agencies. She explains that the report "contradicts claims by President Trump and members of his cabinet who say that the human contribution to climate change is uncertain, and that the ability to predict the effects is limited." Friedman continues,

The authors note that thousands of studies, conducted by tens of thousands of scientists, have documented climate changes on land and in the air. 'Many lines of evidence demonstrate that human activities, especially emissions of greenhouse (heat-trapping) gases, are primarily responsible for recent observed climate change.'

Yet President Trump has decided to pull the United States out of the agreement. Why? Is our withdrawal really about a disagreement over the science? Or is it perhaps an issue of personal wealth and corporate profits at the expense of the welfare of humanity and wildlife? One must ask: Who stands to gain, or profit from our refusal to adhere to the agreement and continue polluting the environment; the fossil fuel industry, the automotive industry? Then there are the powerful lobbyists, paid handsomely to influence congressional votes to help ensure the enrichment of the industries employing them. With the Paris Climate Accord as a powerful example, we see our leaders, corporations and lobbyists, evidencing psychopathic traits of having no conscience, no strong sense of morality or empathy. Their endgame is their own benefit and the benefit of their shareholders only. Even when it puts all of humanity and wildlife at risk.

Acknowledgments

Sheldon Itzkowitz, Ph.D. Psychopathy and Human Evil: An Overview. *Contemporary Psychoanalysis*, copyright © the William Alanson White Institute of Psychiatry, Psychoanalysis & Psychology and the William Alanson White Psychoanalytic Society, www.wawhite.org, reprinted by permission of Taylor & Francis Ltd, http://www.tandfonline.com on behalf of the William Alanson White Institute of Psychiatry, Psychoanalysis & Psychology and the William Alanson White Psychoanalytic Society.

Notes

1 The author wishes to acknowledge there is body of literature on the neurobiology and genetics on aspects of psychopathy, the discussion of which is beyond the scope of this chapter.
2 I wish to express my gratitude to Dr. Elizabeth F. Howell and Dr. Barbara Nussbaum for their valuable comments on earlier versions of this chapter.

References

Associated Press (2009, November 6). Neighbors: Serial killing suspect seemed OK. Retrieved from www.nbcnews.com/id/33736578/ns/us_news-crime _and_courts/t/neighbors-serial-killing-suspect-seemed-ok/#.WZHU-a2ZOgQ.

Babiak, P., Neumann, C. S., & Hare, R. D. (2010). Corporate psychopathy: Talking the walk. *Behavioral Sciences & the Law, 28*(2), 174–193.

Babiak, P., & O'Toole, M. E. (2012). The corporate psychopath. *FBI Law Enforcement Bulletin.* Retrieved from https://leb.fbi.gov/2012/november/the-corporate-psychopath.

Blair, J., Sellars, C., Strickland, I., Clark, F., Williams, A., Smith, M., & Jones, L. (1996). Theory of mind in the psychopath. *Journal of Forensic Psychiatry, 7*(1), 15–25.

Boddy, C. R. P. (2010). Corporate psychopaths and organizational type. *Journal of Public Affairs, 10*, 300–312.

Bollas, C. (1995). *Cracking up.* New York, NY: Hill & Wang.

Breuer, J., & Freud, S. (1893–1895/1955). On the psychical mechanism of hysterical phenomena: preliminary communication. *Standard Edition*, Vol. 2. London: Hogarth Press.

Bromberg, P. M. (1998). *Standing in the spaces.* New York, NY: Psychology Press.

Bromberg, P. M. (2006). *Awakening the dreamer: Clinical journeys.* New York, NY: Analytic Press.

Bromberg, P. M. (2011). *The shadow of the tsunami.* New York, NY: Routledge.

Cortina, M. (2015). The greatness and limitations of Erich Fromm's humanism. *Contemporary Psychoanalysis, 51*(3), 388–422.

Craparo, G., Schimmenti, A., & Caretti, V. (2013). Traumatic experiences in childhood and psychopathy: A study on a sample of violent offenders from Italy. *European Journal of Psychotraumatology, 4*, n.p.

Dozier, M., Stovall-McClough, K. C., & Albus, K. E. (2008). Attachment and psychopathology in adulthood. In J. Cassidy & P. R. Shaver (Eds.). *Handbook of attachment: Theory, research, and clinical applications*, 2nd edition (pp. 718–744). New York, NY: Guilford Press.

Fonagy, P. (1999). Male perpetrators of violence against women: An attachment theory perspective. *Journal of Applied Psychoanalytic Studies, 1*(1), 7–27.

Fonagy, P. (2003). Towards a developmental understanding of violence. *British Journal of Psychiatry, 183*, 190–192.

Fonagy, P., Moran, G. S., & Target, M. (1993). Aggression and the psychological self. *International Journal of Psycho-Analysis, 74*, 471–485.

Freud, S. (1921). Group psychology and the analysis of the ego. In *The standard edition of the complete psychological works of Sigmund Freud*, Vol. XVIII (pp. 67–144). London: Hogarth Press and Institute of Psychoanalysis.

Friedman, L. (2017, August 7). Scientists fear Trump will dismiss blunt climate report. *New York Times.* Retrieved from www.nytimes.com/2017/08/07/cli mate/climate-change-drastic-warming-trump.html?_r=0.

Fromm, E. (1947). *Man for himself.* New York, NY: Henry Holt & Co.

Fromm, E. (1964). *The heart of man: Its genius for good and evil.* New York, NY: Harper & Row.

Fromm, E. (1973). *The anatomy of human destructiveness.* New York, NY: Henry Holt & Co.

Fromm, E. (1991). *On being human.* New York, NY: Bloomsbury Publishing.

Funk, R., & Shaw, M. (1982). *Erich Fromm: The courage to be human.* New York, NY: Continuum.

Gates, G., Ewing, J., Russell, K., & Watkins, D. (2017, March 16). How Volkswagen's 'defeat devices' worked. *New York Times.* Retrieved from www.nytimes.com/interactive/2015/business/international/vw-diesel-emissions-scandal-explained.html?_r=0.

Gergely, G., Fonagy, P., & Target, M. (2002). Attachment, mentalization, and the etiology of borderline personality disorder. *Self Psychology, 7*(1), 61–72.

Gilligan, J. (1997). *Violence: Reflections on a national epidemic.* New York, NY: Vintage.

Greenacre, P. (1945). Conscience in the psychopath. *American Journal of Orthopsychiatry, 15*(3), 495–509.

Gilligan, J. (April 2009). Sex, gender and violence: Estela Welldon's contribution to our understanding of the psychopathology of violence. *British Journal of Psychotherapy.* Retrieved from https://doi.org/10.1111/j.1752-0118.2009.01118.x.

Hare, R. D. (1993). *Without conscience: The disturbing world of the psychopaths among us.* New York, NY: Guilford Press.

Henning, P. J. (December 29, 2014). The year in white-collar crime. *New York Times.* Retrieved from http://dealbook.nytimes.com/2014/12/29/the-year-in-white-collar-crime/?_r=0.

Howell, E. F. (2002). Back to the "States": Victim and abuser states in Borderline Personality Disorder. *Psychoanalytic Dialogues, 12*(6), 921–957.

Howell, E. F. (2005). *The dissociative mind.* New York, NY: Routledge.

Howell, E. F. (2011). *Understanding and treating dissociative identity disorder: A relational perspective.* New York, NY: Routledge.

Howell, E. F. (2014). Ferenczi's concept of identification with the aggressor: Understanding dissociative structure with interacting victim and abuser self-states. *American Journal of Psychoanalysis, 74,* 48–59.

Howell, E. F., & Itzkowitz, S. (Eds.). (2016). *The dissociative mind in psychoanalysis: Understanding and working with trauma.* New York, NY: Routledge.

Itzkowitz, S. (2017). Erich Fromm: A psychoanalyst for all seasons. *Psychoanalytic Perspectives, 14*(1), 81–92.

Kaufman, I. (1958). Panel reports: Superego development and pathology in childhood. *Journal of the American Psychoanalytic Association, 6,* 540–551.

Kernberg, O. F. (1970a). A psychoanalytic classification of character pathology personalities. *Journal of the American Psychoanalytic Association, 18,* 800–8028008.

Kernberg, O. F. (1970b). Factors in the psychoanalytic treatment of narcissistic personalities. *Journal of the American Psychoanalytic Association, 18*, 51–85.

Kernberg, O. F. (1971). Prognostic considerations regarding borderline personality organization. *Journal of the American Psychoanalytic Association, 19*, 595–635.

Kernberg, O. F. (1992). Psychopathic, paranoid and depressive transferences. *International Journal of Psycho-Analysis, 73*, 13–28.

Kessler, G., Rizzo, S. & Kelly, M. (August 12, 2019). President Trump has made 12,019 false or misleading claims over 928 days. *Washington Post*. Retrieved from www.washingtonpost.com/politics/2019/08/12/president-trump-has-made-false-or-misleading-claims-over-days/.

LeBreton, J. M., Binning, J. F., & Adorno, A. J. (2005). Subclinical psychopaths. In J. C. Thomas & D. L. Segal (Eds.), *Comprehensive handbook of personality and psychopathology, personality and everyday functioning*, Vol. 1 (pp. 388–411). Hoboken, NJ: John Wiley & Sons.

Levinson, A., & Fonagy, P. (2004). Offending and attachment: The relationship between interpersonal awareness and offending in a prison population with psychiatric disorder. *Canadian Journal of Psychoanalysis, 12*(2), 225.

Levy, T. M., & Orlans, M. (2000). Attachment disorder as an antecedent to violence and antisocial patterns in children. In T. M. Levy (Ed.), *Handbook of attachment interventions* (pp. 243–259). San Diego, CA: Academic Press.

Liotti, G. (2004). Trauma, dissociation, and disorganized attachment: Three strands of a single Braid. *Psychotherapy: Theory, Research, Practice, Training, 41*, 472–486.

Liotti, G. (2006). A model of dissociation based on attachment theory and research. *Journal of Trauma & Dissociation, 7*(4), 55–73.

Lorenzini, N., & Fonagy, P. (2013). Attachment and personality disorders: A short review. *FOCUS, 11*(2), 155–166.

Meloy, J. R. (1996). *The psychopathic mind: Origins, dynamics & treatment.* Northvale, NJ: Jason Aronson.

Meloy, J. R., & Shiva, A. (2007). A psychoanalytic view of the psychopath. In A. R. Felthous & H. Sass (Eds.), *The international handbook of psychopathic disorders and the law*, Vol. 1 (pp. 335–346). Chichester, UK: John Wiley & Sons. Retrieved from www.researchgate.net/profile/John_Meloy/publication/228002741_A_Psychoanalytic_View_of_the_Psychopath/links/0912f50a68d9331e49000000.pdf.

Moskowitz, A. (2004). Dissociation and violence: A review of the literature. *Trauma, Violence, & Abuse, 5*(1), 21–46.

Salter, A. C. (2003). *Predators, pedophiles, rapists, and other sex offenders: Who they are, how they operate, and how we can protect ourselves and our children.* Cambridge, MA: Basic Books.

Schimmenti, A., & Caretti, V. (2016). Linking the overwhelming with the unbearable: Developmental trauma, dissociation, and the disconnected self. *Psychoanalytic Psychology, 33*(1), 106–128.

Schore, A. (2003). Early relational trauma, disorganized attachment, and the development of a predisposition to violence. In M. F. Solomon & D. J. Siegel (Eds.), *Healing trauma: Attachment, mind body, and brain* (pp. 107–167). New York, NY: W. W. Norton.

Schore, A. N. (2004). The human unconscious: the development of the right brain and its role in early emotional life. In V. Green (Ed.), *Emotional development in psychoanalysis, attachment theory and neuroscience*. New York, NY: Brunner–Routledge.

Shapiro, D. (1965). *Neurotic styles*. New York, NY: Basic Books.

Stein, A. (2001). Murder and memory. *Contemporary Psychoanalysis*, 37(3), 443–451.

Stein, A. (2007). *Prologue to violence: Child abuse, dissociation, and crime.* Mahwah, NJ: Analytic Press.

Stein, A. (2016). A tale of two offenders: Why dissociation is under-diagnosed in forensic populations. In E. F. Howell & S. Itzkowitz (Eds.), *The dissociative mind in psychoanalysis: Understanding and working with trauma* (pp. 231–240). New York, NY: Routledge.

Stern, D. (2003). *Unformulated experience*. Hillsdale, NJ: Analytic Press.

Stevens, G. W., Deuling, J. K., & Armenakis, A. A. (2012). Successful psychopaths: Are they unethical decision-makers and why? *Journal of Business Ethics*, *105*, 139–149.

Stone, M. (2009). *The anatomy of evil*. New York, NY: Prometheus.

Taubner, S., White, L. O., Zimmermann, J., Fonagy, P., & Nolte, T. (2012). Mentalization moderates and mediates the link between psychopathy and aggressive behavior in male adolescents. *Journal of the American Psychoanalytic Association*, *60*(3), 605–612.

Tox Town. (n.d.). Chemicals and contaminants. Retrieved from https://toxtown. nlm.nih.gov/text_version/chemicals.php?id=19.

Wellons, S. (2012). The devil in the boardroom: Corporate psychopaths and their impact on business. *PURE Insights*, *1*(Article 9), 42–45. Retrieved from http:// digitalcommons.wou.edu/pure/vol1/iss1/9.

Yakeley, J., & Meloy, J. R. (2012). Understanding violence: Does psychoanalytic thinking matter? *Aggression and Violent Behavior*, *17*(3), 229–239.

Yamamoto, J. (2016, February 16). "Happy-go-lucky guy": Residents in disbelief that neighbor accused of "grim sleeper" murders. NBC. Retrieved from www. nbclosangeles.com/news/local/grim-sleeper-franklin-trial-south-los-angeles-serial-killer-neighbors-react-369048401.html.

Chapter 2

Outsiders to love

The psychopathic character and dilemma

Elizabeth F. Howell

In the words of a criminal psychopath, a barrister, residing in one of the Dangerous and Severe Personality Disorder (DSPD) wards of Broadmoor, a high-security psychiatric prison in England:

> I realized from quite early on in my childhood that I saw things differently than other people … But more often than not, it's helped me in my life. Psychopathy (if that's what you want to call it) is like a medicine for modern times. If you take it in moderation, it can prove extremely beneficial. It can alleviate a lot of existential ailments that we would otherwise fall victim to because our fragile psychological immune systems just aren't up to the job of protecting us.
>
> (Dutton, 2013, p. 36)

In "Wisdom from Psychopaths," published in *Scientific American Mind*, a subsidiary publication of *Scientific American*, the barrister's interviewer, Kevin Dutton, rhetorically inquires: "Might this eminent criminal defense lawyer have a point? Is psychopathy a 'medicine for modern times'? The typical traits of a psychopath are ruthlessness, charm, focus, mental toughness, fearlessness, mindfulness and action. Who wouldn't at certain points in their lives benefit from kicking one or two of these up a notch?" (Dutton, 2013, p. 36). Noting the characteristic autonomic hypoarousal of psychopaths, Dutton elaborates: "And such inner neural steel, such inestimable indifference in the face of life's misfortunes, is something that all of us, perhaps, could do with a little bit more of" (p. 41). According to Dutton (2013),

> A psychopath's rapacious proclivity to live in the moment, to "give tomorrow the slip and take today on a joyride" … is well documented— and at times can be stupendously beneficial. In fact, anchoring your

thoughts unswervingly in the present is a discipline that psychopathy and spiritual enlightenment have in common.

(p. 43)

Although clearly not writing from the perspective of society or that of the psychopath's victims, Dutton is not alone in his viewpoint. Psychopathic "values" are increasingly often a given, not to be hidden. It is not surprising that the results of an online survey that Dutton conducted, "The Great Britain Psychopathy Survey," singled out chief executive officer (CEO) as the professional position with the highest proportion of psychopaths.

Unfortunately, there *is* some observable accuracy to the statements by the men Dutton quotes. All other things being equal, a person who is not constrained by guilt, loyalty, or concern about harm to the other will likely "win" against others who *are* constrained by these qualities. Psychopaths leave a swath of destruction behind them. As J. Reid Meloy (2001c), a foremost expert on psychopathy, noted, "If one needs to know where the psychopath has been, one searches for the damage" (p. 192).

Who is the psychopath?

"Their hallmark is a stunning lack of conscience; their game is self-gratification at the other person's expense. Many spend time in prison, but many do not. All take more than they give." So states Robert Hare (1993), author of *Without Conscience* (p. 1). Hare further describes the "sub-criminal" psychopath, who may operate on "the shady side of the law," and/or whose criminal acts may never be detected or prosecuted: "For them antisocial behavior may consist of phony stock promotions, questionable business and professional practices, spouse or child abuse, and so forth. Many others do things that, although not illegal, are unethical, immoral, or harmful to others" (p. 68). Hare emphasizes the consistency in their lack of ethics: "If they lie and cheat on the job—and get away with it or are even admired for it—they will lie and cheat in other areas of their lives" (p. 114). And he further observes: "If we can't spot them, we are doomed to be their victims, both as individuals and as a society" (p. 6).

Today, the term closest in meaning to psychopathy in the fifth edition of the *Diagnostic and Statistical Manual of Mental Disorders* (DSM-5; American Psychiatric Association, 2013) is "antisocial personality disorder" (ASPD). However, ASPD, in the DSM-5 categorization, which rests primarily on behavior criteria, fails to focally address the psycho-dynamics and some of the salient personality characteristics that contribute to the dangerousness of the psychopath. In addition, the criteria for psychopathy are more specific than for ASPD. Stone (2018) notes that, although about 75–80% of incarcerated prisoners meet criteria for ASPD, only about 15–25% meet criteria for psychopathy. Not everyone in prison, especially those serving sentences for minor drug convictions, qualifies as either antisocial or psychopathic. And there are convicts with dissociative disorders, brain damage, and/or mental retardation who are neither (Lewis, 1998; Stein, 2004). Furthermore, many psychopaths who have seriously harmed others have never had any criminal justice encounters.

A collapse of various studies noted by Stone (2018) suggests a lifetime prevalence of psychopathy of about 1% of the population. Although the proportion of female psychopaths is only slightly less than that of males, almost all violently offending psychopaths are male (Verona & Vitale, 2006, cited in Stone, Chapter 4).

Psychopaths are unable to love in the way that requires accepting the other person as separate and agentic. Their relationships are instrumental and exploitative; others are viewed as pathological narcissistic extensions of the self. They are motivated by power, not affection; they strive for control and domination; and, as Meloy (2001c) notes, their inner and outer worlds are populated by predatory–prey relationships. Meloy (2001c) describes three primary characteristics of psychopathy: aggressively narcissistic behavior often expressed in repetitive devaluation of others; chronic emotional detachment from others; and deception (i.e., mendacity). Meloy (2001c) notes a significant positive correlation with sadism. Both Hare (1993) and Meloy (2001a, 2001b) discuss a genetic component, an issue beyond the scope of this article.

Other characteristics

Mimicking

Psychopaths are dangerous, and like Oscar Wilde's Dorian Gray, the danger is generally not visible on the outside. "His mask is that of robust mental health. Yet he has a disorder that often manifests itself in conduct far more seriously abnormal than that of the schizophrenic" (Cleckley, 1941, p. 383). In his classic book *The Mask of Sanity*, Herve

Cleckley describes how the psychopath mimics normality: "His rational power enables him to mimic directly the complex play of the human living" (p. 383). The psychopath appears to be sincere and charming, yet is fundamentally insincere. Cleckley's checklist of behaviors identifying the psychopath includes superficial charm, lack of truthfulness, lack of remorse, unreliability, inability to love or to experience genuine emotions, and extreme ego centricity, among others. Hare (1993) later improved upon and revised Cleckley's checklist, developing the diagnostic checklist most frequently used now: the Psychopathy Checklist Revised (PCL-R). He added factors such as grandiosity, impulsivity, and a history of juvenile conduct disorder. The addition of grandiosity is especially important, for grandiosity is often the psychopath's Achilles heel, exactly what lands them in trouble.

Instrumentality

Aside from his checklist, Cleckley (1941) had a behavioral diagnostic criterion for psychopathy based on his own experience:

> A saying current among psychiatric residents, secretaries, medical associates, and others familiar with what goes on in my office may illustrate … that excellent evidence for the diagnosis of psychopathic personality can be found in my own response to newcomers who seek to borrow money or cash checks. It is rather generally believed that only psychopaths are successful and that in typical cases success is inevitable.
>
> (p. 342)

Psychopaths are known for their stunning ability to manipulate. Cleckley coined the term "semantic dementia" to describe psychopaths, because what he considered their demented aspect was revealed in their use of words. Rather than using words to express complexly symbolized personal meaning, the psychopath uses them manipulatively to achieve instrumental ends, to mimic emotions, to press buttons. In this way, words often "work," functioning as triggers to elicit certain behaviors. They read their victims' needs and desires to know how to manipulate them—with words. "They use their listeners' reactions as 'cue cards' to tell them how they are *supposed* to feel in the situation" (Hare, 1993, p. 130; emphasis in original).

Even when the psychopath uses words that have symbolic meaning, such as religious words, the psychopath is not thinking that way. Symbols evoke a complexly contextual array of meaning that awaken the creative network of the whole person, illuminating both the thinker and the subject of contemplation. In contrast, psychopaths tend to think concretely, in a way that lacks emotional meaning. This is exemplified by a remark that "dumbfounded" Hare. The criminal in question commented that the person he murdered had "learned a hard lesson in life" (Hare, 1993, p. 41).

Psychopaths often use their knowledge of how certain words—including buzzwords, such as *trust, trust me, believe me, growth, sincerely*—"work" to engender a sense of a relationship in others. Even the mental health professional may overestimate the psychopath's capacity to undergo the anxiety of psychological growth (Meloy, 1988). Unfortunately, psychopaths can become *more* dangerous as a result of treatment where they learn the appropriate buzzwords with which to con (Rice, 1997).

Although the psychopath uses words to manipulate, upon closer and frequently retrospective examination, something may be "off." The words and the thoughts often do not link together, and the narrative may be confusing (Hare, 1993). The words are frequently accompanied by a dramatic display of facial and hand expressions, as well as by an appeal to various human vulnerabilities. For example, I once had the remarkable experience of being hood winked in the blink of an eye. In the late 1990s, I was exiting my office building and a well-dressed man, walking with his bicycle, approached me. Speaking very rapidly, gesticulating, and indicating anxiety, he said he was a photographer and that he needed to borrow $6 to pay for a cab because he had left some expensive photography equipment worth thousands of dollars in an insecure location; he said he had to get to it right away. He promised that he would return and repay me the next day. He gave me his name, Jack Smith, and showed me a number on his cell phone that he said was his number. He told me that I could call him if he did not show up, but that of course he would. Somehow, his behavior evoked my sympathy. I opened my wallet, intending to pull out $6, but in the process, I moved a $10. Seeing the $10 in my hand, he grabbed it, and sped off on his bicycle. The next day, I realized that the things he said did not make sense. Yet, somehow, the urgency and sincerity that he projected prompted me to let my guard down, and even to believe the unbelievable. His story was inconsistent. Yet, this memory itself is consistent with Hare's observations, that the psychopath's frequently dramatic style of communication, in this case complete with rapid speech and stated urgency, can effectively cause the other person to momentarily lose track of consistency. It was only when I looked up "Jack Smith" in the New York City phone book and found several pages of Jack Smiths that I finally realized I had been snookered. Way beyond my humiliation at my stupidity, I felt damaged, as if the insides of me had been gouged out, even though it was only $10. For weeks it was hard for me to get the incident out of my mind.

There is another person's language to which I must refer. Describing the problematic language of the president of the United States, Charles Blow in a *New York Times* Op-Ed (July 17, 2017), decried Trump's language because "it has the power to degrade truth itself." Blow explains that Trump's use of language is "a way of reducing language to the point that it is meaningless because the use of it is mindless, and in that compromised state, language becomes nearly worthless. As a consequence, truth becomes relative, if not altogether removed" (p. A19). He suggests that Trump (and his family and surrogates) lie "first by directly and intentionally saying things they know well aren't true, and second, by obfuscating by linguistic obtuseness, by overusing a nebulous relativism and by spouting an excess of superlatives to stand in for meaningful description and disclosure." Blow highlights Trump's excessive and indiscriminate use of the word "beautiful," noting, "*It is a device rather than a descriptor*" (emphasis added). In addition, one may note the hypnotic cadence, the up and down tones, much like a brimstone-spouting preacher drawing others into a spell.

Instrumental verbal maneuvers: lies

Psychopaths also "win" by lying—an advantage of being undeterred by scruples. Psychopaths know they are lying—or perhaps it might be better to say that whether their utterances are truth or lie is personally unimportant. What matters is achieving a certain end. With successful lies, the psychopath can often influence the appearance of reality—even influence interpersonal reality itself—by waving a verbal magic wand.

Such lies, instrumental verbal maneuvers, combined with characteristic lower anxiety, can be stunningly successful. For example, Hare (1993, p. 194) recounts how Jeffrey Dahmer was able to talk the police into leaving a bleeding and naked teenager, who had escaped his apartment, in Dahmer's hands. He told the police that the boy was a consensual adult lover and that they were having a "lover's spat." Soon after the police left, he murdered the boy.

This ability to influence reality by theft, lies, and undermining others reinforces the illusions of omnipotence and absolute entitlement. Devaluation, which targets others' shame, works to make those others feel and behave less adequately, shoring up the psychopath's self-esteem. For example, a devaluing father, mother, husband, or wife may create the very kinds of inadequate children and spouses that they criticize. A devaluing, scary boss creates ineffective, frightened, and dependent employees.

Ultimately, however, such "success" may compromise reality testing. When the psychopathic process works, it may superficially appear to be adaptive and indicative of good reality testing. However, when the psychopath is deprived of the ability to lie, cheat, steal, and control others with charm, promises, threats, or force—activities that shore up omnipotence, entitlement, and devaluation—deficits may then begin to appear and gain expression in massive paranoia and emotional instability.

The synergy of psychopathic acumen with victims' vulnerabilities

Often people are simply vulnerable to—rather than culpable or collusive with—the psychopath's deceptions, exploitations, and betrayals. But psychopaths may also elicit acquiescence and/or "evil" behavior in others. How is it that people fail to recognize and deny evil in front of them, as well as collude with the psychopath?

The social fabric of our world runs on trust. In general, people do not expect to be deceived or betrayed. Psychopaths have a stunning ability to read which people will be vulnerable. Altruistic people are frequently vulnerable. (Contrary to suggesting that we should all be guarded cynics, I think that it is better to be able to trust, but to be aware that the world is not always safe.) Once engaged in helping another in need, people tend to let their guard down. Ted Bundy was known to feign injury, such as a broken arm or injured leg. By appealing to some women's willingness to help an injured person, he would gain the advantage to assault, torture, and murder them (Rule, 1980).

As Christopher Bollas (1995) notes, "Even though we know that the world is in part dangerous, and even though we are aware of our own destructive ideas and feelings, we seem able to delude ourselves that the world and the self are basically benign" (p. 190). Further, the structure of evil exploits our primitive belief in the goodness of the other. However much the child's projective processes may invest the parent with nasty qualities, he ultimately knows the difference between his imagined constitution of the parent as a monster (e.g., in dreams, daydreams, willfully vindictive sulking) and the moment when a parent does something that is truly monstrous (p. 200).

I would add to Bollas's statement that when the parent *has* done something truly monstrous, aspects of such terrifying experiences are likely dissociated by the child, who may then be blinded to later similar dangers (see Gartner, Chapter 10).

Psychopaths are often expert at tapping into, and intermeshing with, the dissociated emotions and needs of potential victims—victims' self-states holding limitless wants, unformulated yearnings, unspeakable terrors that have not been adequately experienced, formulated, and integrated. For example, longing for love becomes believing that promises will be kept, despite the evidence. Or, dissociated greed or need may be tapped with vague or explicit promises of jobs, status, or money. By creating the illusion that the psychopath has the power to bestow higher-level positions, jobs, or money, those with some position in an organization may engender a need-based idealization in others. For example, Bernie Madoff's prearrest reputation was as a singularly trustworthy, solid person, who would provide his clients with unusually high financial growth (Henriques, 2011). Some of his victims may have had dissociated affect states of need and greed, such that they did not consider the likelihood that he must be cheating in some way and that they were colluding. Of course, some consciously collude.

Psychopaths often shift their self-presentation in accordance with changing situations. For purposes of manipulation, they may create a false feeling of resonance in a relationship with another. Meloy (1988, 2001b) describes this "as-if" mimicking as simulations, emphasizing "malignant pseudoidentification" (1988, p. 139) in which the psychopath simulates certain interests or feigns admiration to exploit the other's feeling of connection due to shared interests or narcissistic needs. Neville Symington (1980) notes,

People collude with him because their own infantile longings are aroused. Disbelief in the psychopath's greed and destructiveness is

> a defense against sadism in those who treat [talk] with him ... To adhere to the evidence rather than disbelieve, requires us to accept our own sadism which we deny all the harder when it is being stirred by the psychopath ... If we accept what we see in the psychopath then we have to accept our own sadism. It may be more comfortable to believe that he and ourselves are good.
>
> (p. 297)

Accepting one's own sadism includes accepting that sadism, cruelty, and destructiveness—although unacceptable—sometimes feels good. What the psychopath lacks is a countervailing capacity for love and concern for the other. I was recently struck by an Op-Ed piece by Said Sayrafiezadeh in the *New York Times* (August 27, 2017). The author describes how as a half-Jewish, half-Iranian immigrant young child, he had been painfully ridiculed for his accent and appearance. Then, as a nine year-old, "yearning to align with power" he joined two other boys in ridiculing and exiling another boy.

> I was operating in a realm beyond logic, where matters of right and wrong, of good will, of humanity, no longer held any sway ... I was propelled by something far more fundamental and intoxicating and disturbing, something that could not be argued away with the use of reason: It had felt good.
>
> (p. A9)

Likewise, Piven (2007) writes of the widespread ecstasy and exhilaration of killing enemy soldiers and how—specifically in the Holocaust—"the sheer proliferation of murder, rape, torture, and humiliation attests to the intense joy in these acts, that they are enacted willingly, angrily, hatefully, and often pleasurably" (p. 3). Freud (1920) proposed innate aggression and the death instinct and then, in 1921, described how people may abandon personal principles under the sway of an autocratic leader.

Sheldon Itzkowitz (2018) powerfully describes the influence of groups and cultures in shaping extreme aggression and antisocial behavior.

On an even more disturbing note, psychopaths manipulate, not only overtly, but often covertly, by creating or eliciting profound fear and terror that may be difficult for the other to identify or formulate. For example, experts Hare (1993), Meloy (1988), and Stone (2018) discuss the "predatory" or psychopathic stare, a penetrating look that can be highly unnerving and intimidating in ways that are often hard to process consciously, making people feel like they are prey. Stone (2018) describes a "thousand-yard stare" that so unnerved him and inspired so much fear that he had to excuse himself and briefly use the bathroom. This stare was from a murderer who was shackled in the courtroom and hence of no physical danger. It is interesting that the forensic psychiatrist who had testified the day before had had the same exact experience. (Meloy & Meloy, 2002, have documented physiological responses reported by professionals who interviewed psychopaths, suggestive of a "primitive, autonomic, and fearful response to a predator," p. 21).

Sometimes, an unnamable, unreferenceable kind of fear may bind people to do the will of psychopaths. People may not know why, or even that, they are frightened. Illustrating the power of this kind of fear and intimidation, a patient told me of an incident with her ex-husband, a chronic liar and philanderer. She came outside her house to find three police cars in the driveway and her husband yelling at the chief of police and two other officers. He had been taking one of his unregistered antique cars for a ride and was stopped for an illegal license plate. He insisted that he was simply on the way to get it inspected, even though he had no appointment. Somehow the officer followed him back to their home, where that officer felt he needed to call for backup. The man was able to intimidate three police officers and did not get a ticket.

Developmental pathology

As Meloy (2001a) observes, it is important to remember "when one gazes on the psychopath there is less than meets the eye" (p. 13). One should keep in mind that they (psychopaths) "possess an emotional range and depth and object relatedness similar to, although not identical with those of a young toddler prior to sustained interaction with his peers" (p.16). Those who behold and interact with the psychopath tend to fill in the blanks, swayed by hearing heartening words like "trust," and attributing levels of maturity and emotional complexity that are consistent with their own. Psychopaths do not wear signs on their foreheads announcing their potential dangerousness.

Conversely, psychopaths do not emotionally understand the moral thought of others, but see it in terms of their own. Thus, when they accuse others of lying, psychopaths aren't projecting, in the sense of an unconscious defense mechanism. The defense of projection requires that the act of projection is unconscious—that the projector is unconscious of the personal ownership of the faults seen in others. For example, when Bernie Madoff attempted to exonerate himself on the basis that his victims were venal (they sensed his too-good-to-be-true successes were unethical but continued to invest with him; Henriques, 2011), he was right in many cases, but only because he consciously saw himself in them. Another more recent example is when Donald Trump accuses real news of being fake news: he is not projecting; he is just lying.

Knowing that lying, being "crooked," or exploiting others, are considered "bad," psychopaths attempt to tarnish their adversaries with such accusations. Psychopaths are aware of their own lies, but believe they can hide it, often using another lie to cover the first one.

For the psychopath, it is a dog-eat-dog world, in which one must always overcome others first. At the same time, in a startlingly dissociated way, the psychopath also believes that others are suckers. Along with believing that everyone is as venal and depraved as they themselves are, psychopaths also know that others are capable of trust, and will likely trust another if told the "right things." In this way, the gullible will show their necks to the psychopath's teeth.

Inadequate theories of morality

I began this chapter with a summary of an article recently published in the *Scientific American Mind* that extolled the benefits of psychopathy, an example of a true Orwellian "double-think" of modern morality: What is bad is good! What happened? For many in our culture, Freudian superego theory replaced theology as a more scientific means of assessing the origins and meaning of morality. Psychopathy has often been understood in psychoanalysis as due to "superego lacunae," holes or inadequacies in the superego. But, the equation of superego with morality is problematic. Superego as morality is derived from the premise that the parents' superegos are internalized by the child, via the Oedipal crisis, thus replicating the parents' and the culture's mores. This theory is criticized on the basis that it is relativistic and that, therefore, superego is often corrupt

(Kohlberg, 1971; Sagan, 1988). For example, infanticide, stoning of dissenters, and sadistic murders of those of a different religion or gender orientation are valued, even required, as aspects of certain cultural moral codes. The ISIS version of the Quran is an example.[1]

Superego: shame and guilt

A major problem with Freud's model of superego is that it bypassed the primacy of attachment. Helen Lewis (1971) solved the problem of the corrupt superego by repositioning morality as an outgrowth of attachment and re-grounded superego as an attachment regulator: "Morality is the affective-cognitive outcome of attachment. Threatened attachment, which first evokes protest aimed at the caretaker—'other,' is then trans-formed, mainly by identification into states of shame and guilt that aim at maintaining the attachment" (Lewis, 1983, p. 173). Emphasizing the innate capacity for attachment, she wrote: "Human beings are social by biological nature and … shame and guilt are 'givens' whose function it is to maintain the basic affectional bonds" (p. 227). Following her view that the most viable model of the superego is that of an affect regulator (rather than internalized mores), she understood shame and guilt as superego affects (Lewis, 1981, 1983), especially shame, which emerges earlier in the child's development and has adaptive, psychobiological aspects that regulate attachment. Shame is involved in both the deactivation and reactivation of attachment and in the switches of psychobiological states (Schore, 2003).

Lewis (1981, 1983) posited that shame modulates a child's behavior. For this to be effective, the experience of shame itself should be within tolerable bounds: pro social and empathic behavior depends upon tolerated, experienced shame (Schore, 2003). (Lewis, among others, has distinguished between guilt and shame, noting that guilt is more about the specifics of what one did; but shame is more of a global feeling of deficiency, about who one is.) An earlier writer on shame, Helen Lynd (1959), linked shame to the feeling of being outcast, not acceptable for human company, expelled from human bonds, which is consistent with the concept of shame as a powerful socializing affect. (See Howell, 2005, pp. 233–234, on the Coriolanus complex).

Attachment, shame, and guilt are needed to hold antisocial behavior in check. This is consistent with internalized prohibitions, but it also assumes the capacity for concern, which internalized prohibitions do not.

Developmental precursors

The evidence (Meloy, 2002; Schimmenti et al., 2017) increasingly points to a failure in the attachment system of psychopaths, and this failure is often also associated with severity of childhood abuse and neglect. Noting the problem for attachment to predatory parents, Meloy (1988) states, "The experience of the mother figure as an aggressive predator, or more benignly as a passive stranger, leaves the child no choice but to disavow a primary emotional attachment to an actual object outside the child's skin boundary" (p. 54). Hence, among psychopaths, there is a dearth of deep and positive identifications with care givers and a deactivation of attachment need. Meloy (2001a) notes a problem with early identifications, and in particular, to a "dearth of soothing internalization experiences [in psychopathy]" (p. 10). Drawing on Grotstein's (1982) concept of identification with a stranger self-object, a fantasy that helps the normal infant anticipate the real presence of a predator, Meloy (1988) notes that in the psychopathic process, the "stranger, or predator self-object as a narcissistic identification is the predominant archetypal internalization of the infant" (p. 46).

Bowlby (1980) described three phases in disruption of early attachment: protest, despair, and detachment. Once entrenched, detachment precludes bonding with others, and it is often irreversible. In one of his earliest studies on attachment, Bowlby (1944) focused on how maternal rejection and neglect had left a group of juvenile delinquents indifferent and affectionless. Bowlby (1980) used the word "deactivation" to describe a psychological defense against disorganization in the face of attachment loss. This deactivation involved the exclusion of all affect and thought that "might activate attachment behaviour and feeling" (p. 70) and resulted in a state of emotional detachment. If detachment is viewed as a defense, as Bowlby viewed it, then what is excluded from consciousness? In my view, experiences of the lost, abandoned, terrified, alone, and enraged child have been sequestered, and dissociated from the rest of consciousness in detachment.

Dissociation of attachment need

Dissociation is "ubiquitous in psychopaths" (Meloy, 1988, p. 151). But, unlike a kind of self-structure that may divide and preserve parts of the self for later development, as in dissociative identity disorder (DID) or masochism (see Howell, 2013), a deeper, grosser, less remediable kind of dissociation characterizes psychopaths—that of attachment need itself (Howell, 1996). This makes them "outsiders to love."

The dissociative personality structure of the psychopath

Unlike that of dissociative disorders, the dissociation in psychopathy tends to be ego-syntonic. In my view, the structure of dissociated self-states in relation to each other and to the whole personality vary in different personality disorders (Howell, 1996, 2003). For example, in masochism, attachment-oriented self-states are executive, ascendant, and conscious, whereas aggressive and rageful self-states are dissociated. In psychopathy and more aggressive and malignant narcissism, I suggest that attachment-oriented and needy self-states are dissociated from the usually conscious aspects of self, which are aggression- and power-oriented. The psychopath's inner world is populated with internalized predator–prey relationships (Meloy, 2001b) in which the predator is idealized, whereas in the outer world the predatory behavior is interpersonally rationalized.

From a psychodynamic, structural perspective, Kernberg (1975, 2001) views psychopathy (or antisocial personality disorder, in his terms) as a subdivision of narcissistic personality disorder (NPD), itself a subcategory of borderline personality organization (BPO). Neither psychotic nor neurotic, BPO includes lower-level character disorders, and is characterized by characteristic defenses. The first of these, splitting, which Kernberg (1984) called "a primitive form of dissociation" (p. 13), is related to the other five: projective identification, denial, devaluation, omnipotence, and primitive idealization. It is difficult for a person who consistently relies on splitting or dissociation (without significant ameliorative help) to learn from experience on an emotional level because the emotional state of mind that needs to learn keeps disappearing from consciousness.

Another view of splitting is as an outcome of relational trauma, with an etiological core of "identification with the aggressor" from a Ferenczian standpoint (Ferenczi, 1949; Howell, 2002, 2005, 2014). Ferenczi wrote of how the terrified and overwhelmed abused child becomes hypnotically transfixed on the aggressor's wishes and behavior, automatically identifying procedurally and by mimicry rather than by a purposeful and defensive identification with the aggressor's role.

Unable to assimilate the events into narrative memory, the child goes into a trance-like state in which the source of the danger, in this case the abuser, is held in focus intently, but in a depersonalized and derealized way. In this process, the abuser's behavior, including facial expression, posture, and words are automatically mimicked as embodied simulation (Gallese, 2009) and procedural enactment (Lyons-Ruth, 1999).

I have previously described (Howell, 2002) how the result is at least two highly incompatible self-states involving the child's relationship to the caregiver, two dominant internal relational positions of victim and abuser. Thus, "splitting" may be quite similar to state switches in dissociative identity disorder. However, as primarily an affective switch, it is a partial dissociation. The alternation of these self-states contributes to the hallmark "stable instability."

The aggressive, abusive self-states, which embody the rage, contempt, and omnipotence, may arise as procedural, imitative, dyadic enactments. This way of thinking is consistent with other defenses that Kernberg sees as related to splitting. Omnipotence, which defends against helplessness and dependency, and devaluation, which in turn defends against envy (Kernberg, 1975), both characterize the abuser-identified state, and are usually attitudes with which the abuser treats the victim. Thus, both omnipotence and devaluation become aspects of the self as a result of "identification with the aggressor." Primitive idealization is felt from, and only from, the perspective of the victim-identified state. I have suggested that there are two stages in identification with the aggressor: First, a phase that is an automatic, self-protective act of the organism, including somatosensory mimicking; and, second, a phase in which dissociation becomes an active defense as it maintains the separation of self-states, holding different affects and world-views.

In borderline personality disorder, this fragmentation of the psyche is predominantly reflected in two distinct self-states (or groups of self-states), one aggressive and one attachment-oriented. The alternation between these self-states is the basis of the characteristic stable "instability" of BPD. In contrast, the psychopath's dominant self-state is omnipotent, grandiose, devaluing, and aggressor-identified, a state that must be continually maintained by devaluing others. (Additional identification with the aggressor, in Anna Freud's (1966) sense of active identification with an authority, may also ensue, strengthening the dissociative defense.) Rigidly dissociated from the dominant self-state are victim-identified states of fear, shame, and neediness. Such layers may allow the view of self as victim to serve as self-exoneration for harm done. Psychopaths are well known for declaring themselves to be victims, even the victims of their victims, as well as turning others against their victims. For example, John Gacy the serial killer said, when asked about his murders, "I was the victim. I was cheated out of my childhood" (Hare, 1993, p. 43). Meloy (2001a, p. 16) notes a search study (Hazelwood & Warren, 2000) indicating that some sexual sadists are able to role-play the victim with a consensual partner, suggesting both intra-psychic oscillation and intimate knowledge of the position of victim. (This raises the possibility that experiences of dissociated attachment-oriented self-states may at times intrude into the person's dominant state of mind.)

However, although switches to the fearful, victimized state may appear to reflect an inner reality, they may be feigned. That is, a person may imitate a needy, victim state on the basis of some vaguely remembered past experience of the self, without really feeling it in the moment. Such chameleon-like simulation aids in the exploitation of those vulnerable to wishing to help a victimized other.

In psychopathy, the attachment need remains deeply dissociated because awareness of it would be unbearably terrifying and overwhelmingly disorganizing. The dissociatively split perception of others follows: Others are viewed both as vicious like oneself (justifying exploitation) and also as trusting fools (whom one is delighted to dupe).

Although psychopaths rarely feel guilty and appear to be shameless about themselves as doers of heinous acts, they are often very vulnerable to the humiliation of being rejected or unwanted and can erupt into violence when they sense this. Bearing in mind Meloy's view of the psychopath's early infancy, the violence may in part derive from intense dissociated experiences of the self as shamed. The unbearable state of mind of the lost, abandoned, terrified, and enraged child would be hard to formulate in a circumstance of negligible attachment, in which there is no sympathetic inner other with whom to reference oneself. For the full psychopath, identifying with this shame state would be tantamount to experiencing psychic annihilation all over again.

Dissociated humiliation: being outcast

In her account of Ted Bundy's life, *The Stranger Beside Me*, Ann Rule (1980), who worked across from Bundy on a suicide hotline, notes that he was, at best, an unwanted illegitimate child. His mother traveled away from home to give birth to him and left him in another city for three months. Then she brought him home to live with her parents, as *their* son and *her* brother. Her father, Ted's grandfather, was a maniacal, volatile tyrant, who was also sadistic with animals. The damage was clearly apparent when Ted was three, as indicated in the chilling tale of an aunt who had come to visit. She woke up from a nap to find her body surrounded by knives laid out on her bed, and a smiling child looking up at her. As a young adult, Ted's fiancée, Stephanie, who had long dark hair, parted in the middle, jilted him. Afterwards, he began his killing sprees, mostly picking up young women who wore their hair as Stephanie did.

Meloy (1988, pp. 155–158) describes a case in which intense feelings of humiliated rage were instantaneously elicited by rejection, causing the man to "snap," resulting in a murder by electrocution and strangling. Abby Stein (2004) dissects the case of an extremely sadistic rape and murder, committed jointly by two sexual psychopaths. She traces this to their feeling unwanted and rejected from birth. They "attempted to fill the victim with varied detritus, having the vagina and the uterus double as a garbage can" (p. 11). Stein suggests that the perpetrators must "get back inside" to stem existential panic. Because there has been such unbearable rejection, "only the destruction of the maternal symbol can reinstate separateness and restore homeostasis" (p. 11). These particulars illustrate in the extreme the horrifying results of the dissociation of unendurable shame, such that "the more legitimately terrifying the actual interactions upon which the fantasies are based were, the greater the likelihood that a terror-inspiring resolution will be attempted" (Stein, 2004, p. 15). The scorched narcissism of one of Stein's murderers is stunning in its disconnection. In recalling his response to the victim's threat to call for help by yelling "rape," he stated, "The threat of someone crying rape is pretty hard on a guy" (p. 9). These destructive but "reparative" fantasies and ensuing actions sustain omnipotence and serve as a bulwark against dissociated shame states.

On an individual level, the psychopath is "turning the tables." But on a social level, he revisits on many his own past terrorization in an endless future. Underlying this multiplication of victims is the timelessness of dissociated experience. There will never be enough victims.

The psychodynamics of evil and psychopathy

Meloy (2001b) ascribes some of the motivations for the psychopath's "evil" to "his wish to destroy goodness" (p. 172). In my view, psychopathy is a kind of addiction to the power of destructiveness that involves an overwhelming envy of those who love and are loved, an envy of those who are insiders to love, of those who belong enough to the human collective to embrace the common virtues of a functioning society, such as honesty and good will. The evil in psychopathy originates in a feeling of being an outsider to love, outside the fabric of the social order and emotional world that is shared by others. The psychopath must destroy and rob this emotional bonding that others have. They need to make others like themselves so that they do not have to be so envious. They strive to damage the integrity of others, especially those close to them, and if they cannot do that, to besmirch the others' reputations. Those who are privy to or who have this goodness (e.g., with respect to women, sexuality, alluring goodness, and acceptance) must have it taken from them. They must be made empty, like oneself.

Kernberg (1975), among others, views psychopathy as a subset of narcissism. The grandiose self of Kernberg's narcissist, an amalgamation of the ideal self, real self, and ideal other, defends against dependency.

> In their fantasies these patients identify themselves with their own ideal self-images in order to deny normal dependency on external objects and on the internalized representation of the external objects. It is as if they were saying, "I do not need to fear that I will be rejected for not living up to the ideal of myself which alone makes it possible for me to be loved by the ideal person I imagine would love me. That ideal person and my ideal image of that person and my real self are all one, and better than the ideal person whom I wanted to love me, so that I do not need anybody else anymore."
>
> (p. 231)

Once the fusion of the ideal self, real self, and ideal object images has occurred, it is extremely effective in perpetuating a vicious cycle of self-admiration, depreciation of others, and elimination of any felt dependency.

In my view, the difference between this kind of narcissist and the psychopath hinges on the need to *actively* destroy sources of envy— beyond mere devaluation and omnipotence—to destroy peoples' personal and professional integrity, self-esteem, success, and ability to trust. As Symington (1980) notes, "The term 'psychopath' or 'psychopathic' covers a wide range of observable phenomena but there is one common denominator: the overriding determination to attain certain goals, and *these by flouting the values which the society holds sacred*" (p. 281; emphasis added).

In distinguishing psychopathy from narcissism, Kernberg (2001) notes the absence of guilt and the "practically total absence of a capacity for non-exploitative object relations" (p. 325). Meloy (2001c) articulates further distinctions: 1) aggressive domination as the only way of relating; 2) an aggressive mode of narcissistic repair, e.g., devaluation of others—benign modes of repair, such as the fictional Walter Mitty's fantasies, are absent; 3) sadistic behavior; 4) "the presence of a negative idealized internal object (e.g., taking pride in one's father's criminality)" (p. 193); 5) the lack of a need to justify unethical or criminal behavior; 6) a repetitive, self-reinforcing cycle involving a guiltless delight about duping and "putting one over," a "success" followed by devaluing the other and idealizing the self, thus reinforcing the grandiose self-structure; and 7) paranoia, rather than depression, when under great stress or characterological criticism.

Continuum and taxon

Psychopathy is understandable both in terms of a continuum and as a taxon, a type or category. On the continuum, to be human is at times, in wish and deed and in varying circumstances, to be evil, ruthless, remorseless, and gleefully sadistic. But, in my view, in differentiation from the normal spectrum of ruthless or sadistic behavior and thought that can be regretted and often repaired, the full psychopath is mostly a type, a person bent on destruction of affectional bonds, trust, and socially cohesive ethical customs.

Conclusion

I began this chapter describing an article in a mainstream journal that extolled the benefits of psychopathy—an article that may indicate a dangerous cultural desensitization such that psychopathy could become a dangerous cultural ego ideal. In Western society, we have progressed a long way beyond the dictate of "see no evil, hear no evil, speak no evil" of an earlier time. Yet, the desirability of accepting sadistic, evil, and psychopathic aspects of ourselves in the context of a self, grounded in an ethical moral compass, is vulnerable to an acceptance of these qualities *without* a moral context. What "is" does not logically prescribe what "ought" to be (Kohlberg, 1971).

Acknowledgments

I thank Harvey Schwartz for the suggestion of the phrase "outsiders to love" (personal communication, 2004).

Small parts of this article have been adapted from Chapter 12 of *The Dissociative Mind*.

I am very appreciative and grateful to Sheldon Itzkowitz for his careful reading and helpful comments and suggestions on earlier drafts of this article.

Note

1 Lawrence Kohlberg (1971) formulated a model of moral development based on the achievement of certain developmental milestones that he believed to be universal. Although Kohlberg included the ability to take the role of the other as a crucial aspect of development and provided an explanation of how people formulate moral principles based on an understanding of social good, his highest stages have been criticized as unclear. The achievement of higher morality also required higher intelligence, and did not explicitly derive from attachment. The theory, in many ways a breakthrough, was ultimately never widely accepted.

References

American Psychiatric Association (2013). *Diagnostic and Statistical Manual of Mental Disorders: DSM-5*. Arlington, VA: American Psychiatric Publishing.

Blow, C. (July 17, 2017). Trump savagely mauls the language. *New York Times*, A19.

Bollas, C. (1995). *Cracking up: The work of unconscious experience*. New York, NY: Hill &Wang.

Bowlby, J. (1944). Forty-four juvenile thieves: Their characters and home-life. In J. R. Meloy (Ed.). *The mark of Cain: Psychoanalytic insight and the psychopath* (pp. 35–41). Hillsdale, NJ: Analytic Press.

Bowlby, J. (1980). *Attachment and loss*, Vol. III. New York, NY: Basic Books.

Cleckley, H. (1941/1988). *The mask of sanity*. Augusta, GA: Emily Cleckley.

Dutton, K. (2013). Wisdom from psychopaths: A scientist enters a high-security psychiatric hospital to extract tips and advice from a crowd without a conscience. *Scientific American Mind*, *23*(6), 36–43. doi:10.1038%2fscientificamericanmind0113%2D36.

Ferenczi, S. (1949). Confusion of tongues between the adult and the child. *International Journal of Psychoanalysis*, *30*, 225–231.

Freud, A. (1936/1966). *The ego and the mechanisms of defense*. New York, NY: International Universities Press.

Freud, S. (1920/1955). Beyond the pleasure principle. In J. Strachey (Ed. & Trans.). *The standard edition of the complete psychological works of Sigmund Freud* (Vol. 18, pp. 7–64). London: Hogarth Press.

Freud, S. (1921/1955). Group psychology and analysis of the ego. In J. Strachey (Ed. & Trans.), *The standard edition of the complete psychological works of Sigmund Freud* (Vol. 18, pp. 65–143). London: Hogarth Press.

Gallese, V. (2009). Mirror neurons, embodied simulations, and the neural basis of social identifications. *Psychoanalytic Dialogues*, *19*(5), 519–536. doi:10.1080/10481880903231910.

Hare, R. D. (1993). *Without conscience: The disturbing world of the psychopaths among us*. New York, NY: Simon & Schuster.

Hazelwood, R., & Warren, J. (2000). The sexually violent offender: Impulsive or ritualistic? *Aggression and Violent Behavior*, *5*(3), 267–279.

Henriques, D. (2011). *The wizard of lies: Bernie Madoff and the death of trust*. New York, NY: St. Martin's Press.

Howell, E. F. (1996). Dissociation in masochism and psychopathic sadism. *Contemporary Psychoanalysis*, *32*(3), 427–453. doi:10.1080/00107530.1996.10746961.

Howell, E. F. (2002). Back to the "states": Victim and abuser states in borderline personality disorder. *Psychoanalytic Dialogues*, *12*(6), 921–958. doi:10.1080/10481881209348713.

Howell, E. F. (2003). Narcissism, a relational aspect of dissociation. *Journal of Trauma and Dissociation*, *4*(3), 51–71.

Howell, E. F. (2005). *The dissociative mind*. Hillsdale, NJ: Analytic Press.

Howell, E. F. (2013). Masochism: A bridge to the other side of abuse, revised. *Attachment: New Directions in Relational Psychoanalysis and Psychotherapy, 7*, 231–242.

Howell, E. F. (2014). Ferenczi's concept of identification with the aggressor: Understanding dissociative structure with interacting victim and abuser self-states. *American Journal of Psychoanalysis, 74*, 48–59. doi:10.1057/ ajp.2013.40.

Itzkowitz, S. (2018). Psychopathy and human evil: An overview. *Contemporary Psychoanalysis, 54*(1), 40–63.

Kernberg, O. F. (1975). *Borderline conditions and pathological narcissism.* Northvale, NJ: Jason Aronson.

Kernberg, O. F. (1984). *Severe personality disorders.* New Haven, CT: Yale University Press.

Kernberg, O. F. (2001). Narcissistic personality disorder in the differential diagnosis of antisocial behavior. In J. R. Meloy (Ed.). *The mark of Cain: Psychoanalytic insight and the psychopath* (pp. 315–337). Hillsdale, NJ: Analytic Press.

Kohlberg, L. (1971). From is to ought: How to commit the naturalistic fallacy and get away with it in the study of moral development. In T. Mischel (Ed.). *Cognitive development and epistemology* (pp. 151–235). New York, NY: Academic Press.

Lewis, D. O. (1998). *Guilty by reason of insanity.* New York. NY: Fawcett-Columbine.

Lewis, H. B. (1971). *Shame and guilt in neurosis.* New York, NY: International Universities Press.

Lewis, H. B. (1981). *Freud and modern psychology: The emotional basis of mental illness*, Vol. 1. New York, NY: Plenum Press.

Lewis, H. B. (1983). *Freud and modern psychology: The emotional basis of mental illness*, Vol. II. New York, NY: Plenum Press.

Lynd, H. M. (1959). *Shame and the search for identity.* New York, NY: Routledge.

Lyons-Ruth, K. (1999). Two-person unconscious: Inter subjective dialogue, enactive relational representation, and the emergence of new forms of relational organization. *Psychoanalytic Inquiry, 19*, 576–617. doi:10.1080/ 07351699909534267.

Meloy, J. R. (1988). *The psychopathic mind: Origins, dynamics, and treatment.* Northvale, NJ: Aronson.

Meloy, J. R. (2001a). Introduction to section I. In J. R. Meloy (Ed.). *The mark of Cain: Psychoanalytic insight and the psychopath* (pp. 3–24). Hillsdale, NJ: Analytic Press.

Meloy, J. R. (2001b). The psychology of wickedness: Psychopathy and sadism. In J. R. Meloy (Ed.). *The mark of Cain: Psychoanalytic insight and the psychopath* (pp. 171–179). Hillsdale, NJ: Analytic Press.

Meloy, J. R.. (2001c). Introduction to section II. In J. R. Meloy (Ed.). *The mark of Cain: Psychoanalytic insight and the psychopath* (pp. 183–204). Hillsdale, NJ: Analytic Press.

Meloy, J. R., & Meloy, M. J. (2002). Autonomic arousal in the presence of psychopathy: A survey of mental health and criminal justice professionals. *Journal of Threat Assessment, 2*(2), 21–33. doi:10.1300/J177v02n02_02.

Piven, J. S. (2007). Terror, sexual arousal, and torture: The question of obedience or ecstasy among perpetrators. *Discourse of Sociological Practice, 8*(1), 1–21.

Rice, M. E. (1997). Violent offender research and implications for the criminal justice system. *American Psychologist, 52*(4), 414–423. doi:10.1037/0003066X.52.4.414.

Rule, A. (1980). *The stranger beside me.* New York, NY: Signet.

Sagan, E. (1988). *Freud, women and morality: The psychology of good and evil.* New York, NY: Basic Books.

Sayrafiezadeh, S. (August 27, 2017). Two lessons in prejudice. *New York Times*, A9.

Schimmenti, A., Passanisi, A., Pace, U., Manzella, S., Di Carlo, G., & Caretti, V. (2017). The relationship between attachment and psychopathy: A study with a sample of violent offenders. *Current Psychology, 33*(3), 256–270. Retrieved from https://link.springer.com/article/10.1007/s12144-014-9211-z.

Schore, A. (2003). *Affect regulation and the repair of the self.* New York, NY: Norton.

Stein, A. (2004). Fantasy, fusion, and sexual homicide. *Contemporary Psycho-analysis, 40*(4), 495–518. doi:10.1080/00107530.2004.10747241.

Stone, M. (2018). The place of psychopathy along the spectrum of negative personality types. *Contemporary Psychoanalysis, 54*(1), 161–182.

Symington, N. (1980). The response aroused by the psychopath. *International Review of Psycho-Analysis, 7*, 291–298.

Verona, E., & Vitale, J. (2006). Psychopathy in women. In C. J. Patrick (Ed.). *Handbook of psychopathy* (pp. 415–436). New York, NY: Guilford Press.

Chapter 3

Sexual desire, violent death, and the true believer

J. Reid Meloy

When Omar Mateen slaughtered 49 people in the Pulse nightclub in Orlando on June 12, 2016, his act conflated three primitive fears and desires: sexual penetration, murderous violence, and the Manichaean belief that others are either good or evil. Although rarely contemplated, we were brought face to face with these largely unconscious conflicts through the acts of one young man, armed with an assault rifle and a semi-automatic pistol, whose behaviors vexed the public: he killed homosexuals, yet may have been homosexual himself; he was married and the father of a little boy—the traditional definition of male fecundity and fatherhood—yet killed other young people near his age with their own reproductive desires; and he pledged allegiance to the Islamic State which espouses a militant Sunni ideology, at war with the Shi'a Muslims for centuries: a 1,300-year conflict that originated over the question of whether or not direct lineage through procreation would define religious leadership (Aslan, 2006; FBI transcript at www.justice.gov/opa/pr/joint-statement-justice-department-and-fbi-regarding-transcript-related-orlando-terror-attack). Focusing on the psychodynamics among these contradictory and primitive states of mind may help us understand such individuals.

The theoretical frame

The theoretical frame for this analysis is built upon a structural and object relations model (Fairbairn, 1943; Jacobson, 1964; Kernberg, 1975, 1976, 1980, 1984, 1992, 1998; Klein, 1957), which, in turn, embraces Freud's (1920/1955) monumental theories of the sex drive and the death drive. These theories, especially the death drive, contradict a more optimistic view of human nature: if it were not for trauma, aggression would not be such a ubiquitous human issue. Whether it is the lone-actor terrorist[1], or state-sanctioned violence, the drive to existential destruction—in this context, the desire to kill and often to be killed—cannot be ignored. The Freudian theory of the closely associated sex and death drives, moreover, is consistent with neurobiological investigations of the amygdala, the almond-shaped "threat sensor" deep within the limbic system, which activates and regulates whenever biological survival is paramount (sexual arousal, a reaction to a threat) and dynamically relates to the pre-frontal cortex (Kiehl, 2006; Van der Kolk, 2015), possibly putting the neurological brakes on more primitive impulse. It is also consistent with mammalian research concerning the existence of two biologically distinctive modes of violence: predatory and affective (Meloy, 2006; Siegel & Victoroff, 2009; Siever, 2008). Predatory violence in all mammals finds its evolutionary genesis in the desire to hunt and kill and has been described as "coldblooded" (Declercq & Audenaert, 2011) or emotionless, whereas affective violence finds its evolutionary genesis in defense against an imminent threat and is impulsive and intensely emotional, often experienced as "defensive rage" (Siegel & Victoroff, 2009). None of us would be here if our ancestors did not do both exceedingly well.

When we move, however, from evolutionary adaptation to terrorism—the killing of noncombatants for political purposes—a psychoanalytic understanding of the internal world of the terrorist must shift from neurotic or normal personality organization to borderline or psychotic personality organization (Kernberg, 1975). Here again, contemporary non-psychoanalytic research obliquely supports our psychodynamic theories: Corner and Gill (2014) found in a sample of 119 lone-actor terrorists that they were 13.49 times as likely to have a major mental disorder than a matched sample of terrorists embedded in a group. In a follow-up study, Corner, Gill, and Mason (2016) found prevalence rates of schizophrenia, delusional disorder, and autism spectrum disorder much higher in the lone-actor terrorists than the group-based terrorists and the general population. In our study of the same sample of 111 European and American lone-actor terrorists, we found a prevalence rate of 41% for a diagnosed mental disorder (Meloy & Gill, 2016). However, such descriptive phenomenology—although informative—does not begin to address the structural and dynamic characteristics of lone-actor terrorists.

Kernberg (1975, 1984) theorized these aforementioned levels of personality organization (neurotic, borderline, and psychotic) by focusing on the similarities and differences across identity integration, defensive oper- ations, and reality testing. At the borderline level identity diffusion is apparent, with contradictory aspects of the self and others poorly integrated and kept apart; defensive operations are characterized by the use of generic splitting and other lower-level defenses, such as primitive idealization, pro- jective identification, denial, omnipotence, and devaluation; and reality testing is marked by a confusion as to the origin of internal or external stimuli wherein internal fantasies often override the constraints of external reality.

At the psychotic level of personality organization, identity diffusion is marked by poorly delimited self and object representations, and pos- sibly delusional identifications; defensive operations are similar to the borderline, but primarily protect the individual from disintegration and self object merging; and reality testing is marked by a merging of internal and external stimuli (Acklin, 1997; Kernberg, 1975).

These two predominant levels of horizontal personality organization characteristic of the lone-actor terrorist—borderline or psychotic—are ver- tically defined by a characterological formation that has, at its foundation,

> a pathologically narcissistic self-structure in which primitive modes of thinking predominate. The capacity for forging normal attachments and object relating is seriously impaired, as evidenced by a failure to sustain meaningful relationships with either a partner or peers. Rela- tions with others are narcissistically driven, the lone-actor's self-image fueled by omnipotent and grandiose fantasies whereas he views other people as objects to be denigrated or destroyed. This reflects a primitive, pre-Oedipal internal world in which part object relations predominate. Likewise, primitive affects such as shame, excitement, envy, rage, contempt, and disgust are prominent, whereas more mature affects (e.g., guilt, fear, depression, remorse, empathy, humor, or joy), which involve an appreciation of whole objects and a capacity for actual bonding, are impaired.
>
> This affect regulation and object relating are underpinned by develop- mentally primitive modes of thinking, such as psychic equivalence and teleologic ideation (Fonagy & Target, 1996, 2000, 2007). These are characterized by rigidity, concreteness, simplicity, and certainty, whereas reflective capacity, symbolization, and mentalization are lacking.

Moreover, although the lone-actor terrorist may consciously express ideological rationalization for his targeted violence, his moral outrage is the unconscious projection of personal grievance that defends against deficits in moral reasoning and superego functioning, and in some cases against psychotic decompensation.

(Meloy & Yakeley, 2014, p. 16)

This theoretical formulation somewhat narrows the characterological focus (Freud, 1914/1957); but—for the purpose of this study—a more granular analysis is required to home in on the wishes and fears of sexual desire, murderous violence, and extreme beliefs in the lone-actor terrorist. The question is how the interplay of these conscious and unconscious thoughts, emotions, and desires contribute to an act of targeted violence, usually toward noncombatant strangers.

Sexual desire and the terrorist

The explicit sexuality of lone-actor terrorists has been the third rail of terrorism research; there is no published empirical study that has focused on their sexual behavior. Yet anecdotal contradictions concerning sexual desire abound in the possessions, letters, and activity of the most senior terrorism leaders. Osama bin Laden castigated the exploitation of women in a 2002 "letter to the American people" in which he wrote,

> your nation exploits women like consumer products or advertising tools, calling upon customers to purchase them … you plaster your naked daughters across billboards in order to sell a product without any shame. You have brainwashed your daughters into believing they are liberated by wearing revealing clothes, yet in reality all they have liberated is your sexual desires.

(Shane, 2011)

Yet when he was killed by U.S. Special Forces in his compound in Abbottabad, Pakistan, a considerable quantity of pornographic videos was found in his computer files. He also provided guidance on masturbation to the jihadists in a letter seized during the raid in 2011 but only released in 2017:

another very special and top secret matter—it pertains to the problem of the brothers who are with you in their unfortunate celibacy and lack of availability of wives for them in the conditions that have been imposed on them. ... [A]s we see it, we have no objection to clarifying to the brothers that they may, in such conditions, masturbate, since this is an extreme case. The ancestors approved this for the community.

(Cottee, 2017)

The Egyptian scholar Sayyid Qutb (1951), considered one of the intellectual founders of the Salafist movement and bin Ladenism, was both disgusted and clearly stimulated by the erotic. While studying in the United States (1948–1951), he recorded his sexual observations, which he called the "appearance of the American temptress":

The American girl is well acquainted with her body's seductive capacity. She knows it lies in the face, and in expressive eyes, and thirsty lips. She knows seductiveness lies in the round breasts, the full buttocks, and in the shapely thighs, sleek legs and she shows all this and does not hide it. She knows it lies in clothes: in bright colors that awaken primal sensations, and in designs that reveal the temptations of the body—and in American girls these are sometimes live, screaming temptations! Then she adds to all this the fetching laugh, the naked looks, and the bold moves, and she does not ignore this for one moment or forget it!

Filled with erotic desire, he went on to morally condemn it through a polemical discussion of sex and Americans decadence:

For Americans sexual relations have always conformed to the laws of the jungle. Some Americans philosophize about it, such as one of the girls in the university who once told me: "The matter of sex is not a moral matter at all. It is but a question of biology, and when we look at it from this angle it becomes clear that the use of words like moral and immoral, good and bad, are irrelevant."

In Qutb's mind, American women were the sources of sin and contamination, dirty and dangerous, fortunately only desired by males other than him (Qutb, 1951; Wrye, 1993).

In a much darker and violent behavioral pattern, the Islamic State constructed a religious narrative in 2014 to justify the sexual assault of Yazidi women by young jihadists to satisfy the young jihadists' sexual desires, a "theology of rape." In interviews with 21 women and girls, the revival of sexual slavery as an institution within the Islamic State was documented, following the capture of several thousand Yazidi women, considered unbelievers by IS, on Mount Sinjar, Iraq. Internal policies and memos recorded their justification of sexual violence, but also the elevation and celebration of rape as spiritually sanctified. The rapists, according to the young women, would refer to the assaults as "ibadah" or worship, and would bookend their raping with prayer before and after (Callimachi, 2015). Such acts appear to represent a compromise formation between the strict sexual repression within fundamentalist Islam and the apogee of sexual desire among young males, providing them with a sanctified sexual outlet without violating the tenets of their beliefs. Such a narrative would mitigate shame, the emotional byproduct of sadistic superego precursors in which sexual desire and its expression are not tolerated, always attributed to the behavior of the feminine, and often—if acted upon outside the strictures of marriage—punishable by death of the woman.

We also see the fear of and desire for sex among those terrorists whose ideological framing (Meloy & Gill, 2016) adheres to ethnic nationalism or anti-abortionism, two other belief systems that have resulted in the targeted killing of civilians. Timothy McVeigh, the terrorist who bombed the federal Murrah building in Oklahoma City on April 19, 1995, and killed 168 people, was characterized in this manner by two reporters who extensively interviewed him and scores of others who knew him throughout his life:

> But as McVeigh thought more seriously about death, he found that what truly gnawed at him was missing the opportunity to have a family. McVeigh had always been frustrated in his attempts to connect with women; *his only sustaining relief from his unsatisfied sex drive was his even stronger desire to die* [emphasis added]. As he grew older, the realization that he would be leaving this world without having brought children into it became a preoccupation. It was one of the few things he had failed to fully anticipate when deciding to end his life.
>
> (Michel & Herbeck, 2001, pp. 440–441)

James Kopp, an anti-abortionist terrorist, murdered Barnett Slepian, an American physician who performed abortions, in his home in upstate New York on October 23, 1998. Kopp had a much more regressive and psychotic link to the negation of sexual desire in his identification with aborted fetuses, the unwanted human products of copulation: During the late 1980s and early 1990s Kopp would chain himself to the abortion medical equipment after having taken laxatives so that he would defecate on himself to be like the unborn and experience their helpless containment in the womb prior to their deaths. The chaining became more complicated over time—on at least one occasion it involved a car axle, multiple glues, and a lock and chain around his neck. Once he was wheeled into a clinic in a wheelchair with his legs under a blanket. He had encased them in cement. He did not become a sniper until after the death of his mother (personal communication, A. Robb, December 2016; Risen & Thomas, 1998).

Menninger (1938) was one of the few psychoanalysts to discern the components of eroticism and sexuality among martyrs, albeit today we see a much more aggressive form of martyrdom in the desire to not only sacrifice the self, but to kill others to advance one's cause or belief system (Meloy, 2004, 2011). Menninger identified three unconscious motivations: the flight from the mother, the renunciation of sexuality, and moral masochism—the eagerness with which the martyr would seek suffering and death. I would add a fourth: the idealization of sexual desire in fantasy, no more apparent than in the young jihadist's belief that he would have access to unlimited virgins—notice the emphasis upon purity—in the afterlife *if he dies a violent death* (Meloy, 2004).

At a developmental level for these young men, object relations remain split (Freud, 1938/1964) and partial: the mother, hence all women, are either good or bad objects, and cannot be trusted but only controlled. Yet they sexually stimulate the genitally mature male. There is no integration of the early pleasure and displeasure toward the maternal object into more complex ambivalent feelings, which, in turn, allow for the representation of woman as a desired object, a whole, real, meaningful person who stimulates both affectional emotions and erotic desire. Without whole object representation there is the absence of a capacity for reciprocal love, joy, mutual eroticism, empathy, sympathy, gratitude, anger, guilt, and grieving as a response to loss. Instead, part object-related emotional states predominate: rage, boredom, envy, excitement (both sexual and nonsexual), shame, contempt, disgust, grievance, and sadism—emotions that thrive in a part object world, but are only diminished in intensity with the advent of whole object relatedness. Such developmental progress also requires the parallel path of disidentification with the maternal object, the reduction of symbiotic anxiety (Greenson, 1954, 1968; Wrye,1993) and the emergence of whole representations of the self. These changes, in turn, diminish the need to utilize projection and projective identification (Grotstein, 1981) to blame the female for the penetration desires and fears of the male (Colarusso, 2012).

At a drive level for the lone-actor terrorist, however, sexuality and aggression remain raw and unmodulated. There is no intrapsychic room for the complexities of love and hate (Gabbard, 2000; Kernberg, 1998). Psychological splitting and terrestrial splitting dynamically reinforce each other, most apparent within fundamentalist religions. Women are to be physically kept separate and hidden (at home or under clothing) so in their perceived omnipotence they do not sexually stimulate men who cannot control (modulate) their desires. Thus, they are psychologically split off and kept separate as either good (the idealized and loved woman, often the asexualized mother or sister), or bad (the sexually stimulating, dirty, and feared woman outside the family or religion) object representation. Among anti-abortionist terrorists, rage toward the murderous mother is displaced onto the father-doctor complicit in the death of the unborn and helpless, a source of the terrorist's identification that shifts from the victim (fetus) to the aggressor (assassin) as was evident in the James Kopp case (A. Freud, 1936/1966; Meloy, Mohandie, Knoll, & Hoffmann, 2015).

The evolutionary failure of sexual desire ultimately rests on the failure to form a sexually intimate pair bond, which facilitates psychological generativity (Erikson, 1950) and reproductive success (Dawkins, 1976). In our research of lone-actor terrorists, we found that 84% of the sample (N = 111) failed to form a sexual pair bond from the advent of puberty until their death or incarceration (Meloy& Gill, 2016). This striking finding is not *specific* to lone-actor terrorists, but a likely *sensitive* indicator of their distal risk.

How do such failures dynamically relate to murderous violence?

Violent death

On March 2, 2011, a young Albanian jihadist named Arid Uka attacked a group of American servicemen boarding a bus at the Frankfurt Airport in Germany. Two soldiers were killed and two were severely wounded (Bockler, Hoffmann, & Zick, 2015). Uka's radicalization extended back several years, but most salient to the theory of this study was the triggering event that occurred the evening before the attack. Uka had never had a girlfriend or a sexual relationship, but that evening, as he had before, he visited multiple websites viewing jihadist recruitment videos. Police interviewers concluded that this was the event that resulted in his specific intent to attack American soldiers:

> He came across two videos: one that showed the dead faces of "Islamic martyrs" and one that dealt with female Muslims harmed by U.S. soldiers. Uka said he was not aware that he was watching a radical Islamist propaganda video showing a staged rape scene taken from a Hollywood movie. He was disturbed and not able to return to his daily routine. He could not sleep all night, and even the next morning he still could not get the rape scene out of his head. After staying up, showering, watching TV, browsing the Internet, and eating breakfast with these pictures still in mind, he knew that he had "to do something."
>
> (Bockler et al., 2015, p. 156)

What was his disturbance? What were the "pictures still in mind"? From a behavioral psychology perspective, this is a classical conditioning paradigm between graphic visuals of death and sexual arousal: the death of those with whom he identified, and the sexual aggression of those he believed were his enemies. But how would a 21-year-old man feel, and what desires would be aroused, by viewing such material? Not knowing the rape video was taken from a Hollywood movie at the time, it is parsimonious to think that he was both sexually aroused by the rape scene and furious at what the unbelievers were doing to a Muslim woman; he consciously condemned their behavior, yet was left with an erotic desire that was intolerable to a young man who had no sexual experience, and was constricted by an ideology that provided no outlet for his desires, only guilt, envy, and shame. And the most intense cognitive dissonance was that he likely identified with both the men who were dead martyrs and sexual aggressors. He told the police he had "to do something" to consciously protect the sisters of the faith. On the way to the airport he listened to the following Arabic chant (*nashid*) on his iPod:

> Mother, remain steadfast, I have joined the Jihad. Don't mourn for me and know I have been awakened. The umma has been blinded, but I have been honored. Mother, remain steadfast, your son has joined the Jihad. The umma has been blinded but I have been honored. Mother, remain steadfast, your son has joined the Jihad. The screams became louder, the injuries increased. The unfulfilled duty, I could not find peace. Today I must leave, tomorrow it is too late. Mother, remain steadfast, your son has joined the Jihad. Today I must leave, tomorrow it is too late. Mother, remain steadfast, your son has joined the Jihad.
>
> (Bockler et al., 2015, p. 157)

He found stability in the soothing affect and lyrical chanting surrounding his internal representation of his mother, and he sought release by killing those projective vehicles who carried his sexual desires, the American soldiers. He was also assured of his own martyrdom in fantasy, and his ascension in the storm to take his place with Allah among the *shaheed* (martyrs) that preceded him—a collectivity that he believed would also bring him the sexual pleasures he had never known in the terrestrial world.

Once again, we return to the words of Qutb (1951) written more than a half century earlier:

> Indeed, the American is by his very nature a warrior who loves combat. The idea of combat and war runs strong in his blood. It is evident in his manner and this is what agrees with his history. For the first waves of people left their homelands, heading for America with the intention of building and competing and struggling. And once there, some of them killed others, as they were composed of groups and factions. Then they all fought against the original inhabitants of the land (the red Indians), and they continue to wage a bloody war against them until this very moment. Then the Anglo-Saxons killed the Latinos and pushed them south toward central

and southern America. Then these Americanized people turned against their mother country, England, in a destructive war led by George Washington until they obtained their independence from the British crown.

Predatory or instrumental violence (McEllistrem, 2004; Meloy, 1988; Siegel & Victoroff, 2009; Siever, 2008) was always attributed to others by Qutb, and continues to be a rigidly held belief among today's terrorists, regardless of ideological persuasion. The state of mind of the lone-actor terrorist *always* justifies his violence as a defensive reaction to an imminent threat, despite overwhelming empirical evidence that lone-actor terrorists will engage in offensive acts—that is, predation—against unarmed civilians in the planning, preparation, and implementation of their violence (Gill, 2015).

The capacity for both predatory (offensive) and affective (defensive) violence is an evolved and biologically rooted trait in all mammals; fortunately, most humans do neither. There is even a strong line of research indicating that both modes of violence are more frequently acted upon by psychopathic individuals, rendering this characterological disorder most dangerous (Cornell, Warren, Hawk, & Pine, 1996; Woodworth & Porter, 2002). However, in the context of terrorism, predation is morally driven, and is best understood as a *superego sanctioned homicidal act*, not the valueless, self-absorbed cruelty of the psychopath. There are, of course, psychopathic terrorists, but most terrorists who choose to act against their perceived enemy are committed to both homicide and suicide as a means to advance a particular belief system. And the advancement is almost always done to purify, particularly in the context of religious terrorism. Although purification may be only one goal for violence, it is central to the often paranoid belief that one is surrounded by contaminants and toxins, including women as temptresses, and violence is the means to purify the road to utopia, which is—by necessity—vaguely defined. Purification, in turn, requires the shedding of blood, a sacrifice: something is offered and made holy, but is also destroyed in the process (Jones, 2010)[2]. Such acts may be compelled and even sanctified by cruel and sadistic superego precursors where violent death for both the self and the other is a religious imperative, and certainly contains a sadomasochistic dynamic[3]; the representation of the self is further burnished by the conscious belief that one is an agent or a soldier for an omnipotent power—the narcissistic fusion of the ideal self and the ideal object, noted by Kernberg (1975) in his treatise on the narcissistic personality disorder, but in this context elevated to a theology that rationalizes violence.

This is the dream of the religious warrior (Gibson, 1994), and is often—in the case of lone-actor terrorists—a grandiose and violent compensatory fantasy that serves as an effective retreat from a socially and occupationally blighted life. The finding of a major loss in love or work has been replicated in most lone-actor terrorism studies (Gill, 2015; Horgan, 2014; Horgan, Gill, Bouhana, Silver, & Corner, 2016; Meloy & Gill, 2016), and carries within it the holding of a grievance, rather than the grieving of the loss, which may function as an emotional accelerant for the violence that has long been contemplated (Meloy & Yakeley, 2014). The losses are often experienced as shameful events and also help organize what Terman (2010) calls the "paranoid gestalt" for the otherwise narcissistically sensitive subject drawn to fundamentalist thought.

The structure of fundamentalist belief *in extremis*

Sexual desire and its interplay with violent death go nowhere without regression; they first fuse in fantasy—an incubation period or pathway that may last for weeks, months, or even years (Gill, 2015; Meloy, Hoffmann, Guldimann, & James, 2012)—then they are acted out. In a structured professional judgment instrument to assess risk of lone-actor terrorist violence (TRAP-18; Meloy, 2017; Meloy & Gill, 2016; Meloy, Habermeyer, & Guldimann, 2015), one of the indicators is "changes in thinking and emotion." It is defined as follows:

Thoughts and their expression become more strident, simplistic, and absolute. Argument ceases and preaching begins. Persuasion yields to imposition of one's beliefs on others. No critical analysis of theory or opinion, and the mantra, "don't think, just believe," are adopted. Emotions typically move from anger and argument, to contempt and disdain for others' beliefs, to disgust for the out group and a willingness to homicidally aggress against them. Violence is cloaked in self-righteousness and the pretense of superior belief. Humor is lost. Engagement with others in virtual or terrestrial reality may greatly diminish or cease once the subject has moved into operational space.

(Meloy, 2017, p. 34)

Unpacking this definition, both structurally and dynamically, suggests that the individual either regresses to a borderline level of personality organization, or has been fixated at this level for some time, presenting a recruitment vulnerability to those interested in fostering a belief that the intent to kill both self and others to advance a particular cause is both justified and sanctified. In some cases, the regression or fixation may be at a psychotic level wherein there is a delusional identification with a holy figure or a holy warrior[4].There is also the characterological imprint of pathological narcissism (Kernberg, 1975)[5].

The fundamentalist mindset is critical to this psychological shift, and its generic organizing defense is splitting, or as termed by Strozier and Boyd (2010), the "centrality of binary oppositions[6]." Splitting as a defense in adults is the psychopathological outcome of the normative infant and childhood need to separate objects and pleasure/displeasure feeling states (Fairbairn, 1943; Freud, 1938/1964; Klein, 1957; Grotstein, 1981; and Kernberg, 1975). The predominance of splitting in adulthood is signaled by the tendency, if not conviction, to view the world in stark black-and-white terms, to simplify reality, to eliminate the gray zones, to perceive the self and others as part objects, and a gross failure to empathize with, or understand the inner lives of others—a failure to mentalize (Fonagy & Target, 1996, 2000, 2007).

For the true believer, splitting provides an open door to a moral framework that is absolute and Manichaean; critical analysis is unnecessary and often cruelly punished because it is viewed as heretical, and anxiety is reduced. If in a group context, such confirmatory bias, i.e., the normal human tendency to not let contrary facts interfere with one's beliefs (Kahneman, 2011), will heighten the sense of group safety from others. If more specific, secondary psychological defenses such as introjection, projection and projective identification, denial, omnipotence, and devaluation that are dependent upon splitting come to the fore. Then differences are perceived as a threat, and paranoia and the apocalyptic—the end of the world—may invite violence if the lone-actor terrorist believes that he must be an active player, instead of a passive recipient within such an event.

In one forensic evaluation, a diagnosed paranoid and schizoid man went to a neighborhood grocery store armed with an AK-47 to buy a pack of cigarettes. A police officer drove up as he entered the store, and the man shot and killed the officer, who was still sitting in his car, with multiple rounds from his automatic rifle. He told me that he kept the AK-47 because he believed he would be left behind during the Rapture, and would need to defend himself during the seven years of tribulation in the battle of Armageddon before Jesus returned and ushered in the millennium, a thousand years of peace—his psychologic was dependent on a misreading of the Christian Book of Revelation[7].When I asked him if he had actually joined a paramilitary group, he said, "no, I prefer to be my own fringe group."

The definition of the term "rapture" is an expression of ecstasy or passion, being carried away by overwhelming emotion, to be seized, kidnapped, or raped. It is derived from the middle French word *rapture* and the Latin *raptus* (http://www.etymonline.com/index.php?term = rapture). Within the tribulations of the Apocalypse, those left behind suffer the absence of erotic pleasure. This young man had no history of a sexually intimate pair bond.

The emotional imprint of characterological narcissism in these cases is most apparent in their sensitivity to shame and humiliation. Actual or perceived losses may stimulate such emotion—the public exposure of the self as deficient—which in turn contributes to the formation of a personal grievance toward the humiliating object. This grievance is joined with an apparent moral outrage as the lone-actor vicariously identifies with a suffering group, and then frames his outrage with a Manichaean belief (Meloy, 2017; Meloy & Gill, 2016). Such are the seeds of a lone-actor terrorist event.

The humiliation by the persecutory object is then undone. It is undone not through anger, but through contempt, the moral devaluation of the other, looking down on those who are thought to humiliate. In the internal world of the lone-actor terrorist, the actual contempt for the other is often magnified by persecutory objects that have been introjected and then continuously projected to rid the self, but once again projectively identified with and reintrojected in a borderline state of oscillation that never ceases and always threatens.

If contempt becomes disgust, there is a further path forward. Disgust is a universal emotion, likely an evolved defense to ward off contaminants and purge the environment of toxins with both moral and somatic correlates (Chapman, Kim, Susskind, & Anderson, 2009). It is evident in the psychology of the true believer, the lone-actor terrorist, when he is no longer angry or contemptuous of the unbeliever and no longer fears him, but instead equates the unbeliever with a toxin. The impulse is to be rid of it, to exterminate, to kill. Most people normatively react with disgust to spoiled food, filthy environments, and cockroaches; some to snakes and spiders. Such stimuli do not evoke anger, nor contempt, but disgust and a desire to cleanse, sometimes through violence, so they do not continue to poison (Matsumoto, Hwang, & Frank, 2013, 2017). In a mass psychology context (Hoffer, 1951/2010), the Nazis equated the Jews with vermin and other contaminants, and thus found an emotional accelerant for the Holocaust[8]. Purification takes a step forward if toxins and contaminants are obliterated. There is no longer a need for anger or contempt: For the violent true believer, the lone-actor terrorist, the utopian fantasy moves closer.

Conclusion

I have tried to suggest ways in which sexual desire, violent death, and fundamentalist beliefs *in extremis* can be understood through the psychoanalytic lens of object relations theory, structural deficiencies, and the contribution of the drives. It seems fitting to close with a quote from Eric Hoffer, the author of *The True Believer* (1951/2010). More than a half century ago, he wrote:

> Though they seem to be at opposite poles, fanatics of all kinds are actually crowded together at one end. It is the fanatic and the moderate who are poles apart and never meet. The fanatics of various hues eye each other with suspicion and are ready to fly at each other's throat. But they are neighbors and almost of one family. They hate each other with the hatred of brothers. ... The vanity of the selfless, even those who practice utmost humility, is boundless.

(p. 86)

Acknowledgments

J. Reid Meloy, Ph.D. Sexual Desire, Violent Death, and the True Believer. *Contemporary Psychoanalysis*, copyright © the William Alanson White Institute of Psychiatry, Psychoanalysis & Psychology and the William

Alanson White Psychoanalytic Society, www.wawhite.org, reprinted by permission of Taylor & Francis Ltd, http://www.tandfonline.com on behalf of the William Alanson White Institute of Psychiatry, Psychoanalysis & Psychology and the William Alanson White Psychoanalytic Society.

Notes

1 Throughout this article, the "lone-actor terrorist" will be referred to by the masculine pronoun, "he," because the vast majority of these terrorists are male.
2 Although violent sacrifice is clearly evident among jihadists, it is not limited to Islam. In a decades-long scandal of violent atonement, a charismatic lawyer and Christian evangelical in Britain severely beat numerous adolescent boys for masturbating while attending a boarding school, telling at least one victim that he needed to "bleed for Jesus" (Yeginsu, 2017). Similar symbolism can be found in the images of Christian saints, "born up to paradise and ensconced in the highest heavens where, purified and sinless, they can intercede for others"(Jones, 2010, p. 95). We see this historically in the beliefs among the anti-abortion terrorists (for example, James Kopp, Eric Rudolph, Robert Dear, Paul Hill) wherein the oscillation and balance between homicidal and suicidal intent will vary, yet the assumption of sexual promiscuity as the cause of the desire for an abortion is a steady undercurrent in their thinking.
3 The sadism of the Islamic State jihadists—or more precisely a theater of necro-sadism (Stekel, 1929)—is evident in the Internet postings of beheadings of unbelievers, individually or in groups, and the ritualized monologue that precedes them with the victim on his knees, done to both horrify and fascinate millions of viewers who dutifully flock to the Internet.
4 This became a contentious issue among psychiatric evaluators in the trial of Anders Breivik, a Norwegian terrorist who killed 77 individuals, mostly adolescents, in July 2011: Did he have schizophrenia or a severe personality disorder? Breivik believed he was a contemporary reincarnation of the 12th-century Knights Templar, the special forces of the Christian crusades whose mission was to counter the influx of Islam into Europe (Meloy et al., 2015). The court found that he was neither psychotic nor insane, which pleased Breivik because this meant that the court believed his actions were rational.
5 Such regression can also occur in large groups, even at the nation-state level. I call this "poliregression." See the excellent work of Volkan (2009, 2013) on large-group identity and psychoanalysis.
6 The fundamentalist mindset is composed of dualistic thinking; paranoia and rage in a group context; an apocalyptic orientation; a relation to a charismatic leader; and a totalized conversion experience. The reader is referred to Strozier and Boyd (2010) for a brilliant explication of this complex concept, which is beyond the scope of this article.
7 There are different theories within Christian theology as to the timing of the Rapture in relationship to the second coming of Christ, and whether or not they are separate events. This subject is articulating a pretribulational premillennialist

theory popular in contemporary evangelical Christianity, but note the necessity of "defensive" violence in his statement to me, which actually resulted in the offensive and predatory ambush of a police officer.

8 The Matsumoto line of research (Matsumoto et al., 2013, 2017) has shown that the expressions of anger, contempt, and disgust toward those viewed as contaminants by leaders predicts political violence among their followers.

References

Acklin, M. (1997). Psychodiagnosis of personality structure: Borderline personality organization. In J.R. Meloy, M. Acklin, C. Gacono, J. Murray, & C. Peterson (Eds.), *Contemporary Rorschach Interpretation* (pp. 109–122). Mahwah, NJ: Lawrence Erlbaum Associates.

Aslan, R. (2006). *No god but God*. New York, NY: Random House.

Bockler, N., Hoffmann, J., & Zick, A. (2015). The Frankfurt airport attack: A case study on the radicalization of a lone-actor terrorist. *Journal of Threat Assessment & Management*, *2*, 153–163. doi:10.1037/tam0000045.

Callimachi, R. (Ed.). (2015, August 14). ISIS enshrines a theology of rape. *New York Times*, https://www.nytimes.com/2015/08/14/world/middleeast/isis-enshrines-a-theology-of-rape.html?_r=0.

Chapman, H., Kim, D., Susskind, J., & Anderson, A. (2009). In bad taste: Evidence for the oral origins of moral disgust. *Science*, *323*, 1222–1226. doi:10.1126/science.1165565.

Colarusso, C. (2012). The central masturbation fantasy in heterosexual males across the life cycle: Masturbation fantasies across the normality-pathology spectrum. *Journal of the American Psychoanalytic Association*, *60*, 917–948. doi:10.1177/0003065112459348.

Cornell, D., Warren, J., Hawk, G., & Pine, D. (1996). Psychopathy in instrumental and reactive violent offenders. *Journal of Consulting & Clinical Psychology*, *64*, 783–790. doi:10.1037/0022-006X.64.4.783.

Corner, E., & Gill, P. (2014). A false dichotomy? Lone actor terrorism and mental illness. *Law & Human Behavior*, *39*(1), 23–24.

Corner, E., Gill, P., & Mason, O. (2016). Mental health disorders and the terrorist: A research note probing selection effects and disorder prevalence. *Studies in Conflict & Terrorism*, *39*(6), 560–568.

Cottee, S. (2017, February 1). Osama bin Laden's secret masturbation fatwa. *Foreign Policy*. Retrieved from, http://foreignpolicy.com/2017/02/01/osama-binladens-secret-masturbation-fatwa/.

Dawkins, R. (1976). *The selfish gene*. London, England: Oxford University Press.

Declercq, F., & Audenaert, K. (2011). Predatory violence aiming at relief in a case of mass murder: Meloy's criteria for applied forensic practice. *Behavioral Sciences & the Law*, *29*(4), 578–591. doi:10.1002/bsl.994.

Erikson, E. (1950). *Childhood and society*. New York, NY: Norton.

Fairbairn, W. R. D. (1943). *An object relations theory of the personality.* New York, NY: Basic Books.

Fonagy, P., & Target, M. (1996). Playing with reality: I. Theory of mind and the normal development of psychic reality. *International Journal of Psychoanalysis, 77,* 217–233.

Fonagy, P., & Target, M. (2000). Playing with reality: III. The persistence of dual psychic reality in borderline patients. *International Journal of Psychoanalysis, 81,* 853–874. doi:10.1516/0020757001600165.

Fonagy, P., & Target, M. (2007). Playing with reality: IV. A theory of external reality rooted in inter subjectivity. *International Journal of Psychoanalysis, 88,* 917–937. doi:10.1516/4774-6173-241T-7225.

Freud, A. (1966). *The ego and the mechanisms of defense* (Rev. ed.). New York, NY: International Universities Press. (Original work published 1936).

Freud, S. (1955). Beyond the pleasure principle. In J. Strachey (Ed. & Trans.), *The standard edition of the complete psychological works of Sigmund Freud* (Vol. 18, pp. 7–64). London, England: Hogarth Press. (Original work published 1920).

Freud, S. (1957). On narcissism: An introduction. In J. Strachey (Ed. & Trans.), *The standard edition of the complete psychological works of Sigmund Freud* (Vol. 14, pp. 73–102). London, England: Hogarth Press. (Original work published 1914).

Freud, S. (1964). Splitting of the ego in the process of defense. In J.Strachey (Ed. & Trans.), *The standard edition of the complete psychological works of Sigmund Freud* (Vol. 23, pp. 271–278). London, England: Hogarth Press. (Original work published 1938).

Gabbard, G. (2000). Hatred and its rewards: A discussion. *Psychoanalytic Inquiry, 20,* 409–420. doi:10.1080/07351692009348897.

Gibson, J. (1994). *Warrior dreams: Paramilitary culture in post-Vietnam American.* New York, NY: Hill & Wang.

Gill, P. (2015). *Lone actor terrorists: A behavioural analysis.* London, England: Routledge.

Greenson, R. (1954). The struggle against identification. *Journal of the American Psychoanalytic Association, 2,* 200–217. doi:10.1177/000306515400200202.

Greenson, R. (1968). Disidentifying from mother: Its special importance for the boy. *International Journal of Psychoanalysis, 49,* 370–374.

Grotstein, J.(1981). *Splitting and projective identification.* New York, NY: Jason Aronson.

Hoffer, E. (2010). *The true believer.* New York, NY: Harper Perennial Modern Classics. (Original work published 1951).

Horgan, J. (2014). *The psychology of terrorism* (2nd ed.). New York, NY: Routledge.

Horgan, J., Gill, P., Bouhana, N., Silver, J., & Corner, E. (2016). Across the universe? A comparative analysis of violent behavior and radicalization across three offender types with implications for criminal justice training and education [Monograph]. *Award No. 2013-ZA-BX-0002*. Washington, D.C: National Institute of Justice, Office of Justice Programs, U.S. Department of Justice.

Jacobson, E. (1964). *The self and the object world*. New York, NY: International Universities Press.

Jones, J. (2010). Eternal warfare: Violence on the mind of American Apocalyptic Christianity. In C. B. Strozier, D. M. Terman, J. Jones, & K. Boyd (Eds.), *The fundamentalist mindset: Psychological perspectives on religion, violence, and history* (pp. 91–103). New York, NY: Oxford University Press.

Kahneman, D. (2011). Thinking, fast and slow. New York, NY: Farrar, Straus & Giroux.

Kernberg, O. (1975). *Borderline conditions and pathological narcissism*. New York, NY: Jason Aronson.

Kernberg, O. (1976). *Object relations theory and clinical psychoanalysis*. New York, NY: Jason Aronson.

Kernberg, O. (1980). *Internal world and external reality*. New York, NY: Jason Aronson.

Kernberg, O. (1984). *Severe personality disorders: Psychotherapeutic strategies*. New Haven, CT: Yale University Press.

Kernberg, O. (1992). *Aggression in personality disorders and perversions*. New Haven, CT: Yale University Press.

Kernberg, O. (1998). Aggression, hatred, and social violence. *Canadian Journal of Psychoanalysis*, *6*, 191–206.

Kiehl, K. A. (2006). A cognitive neuroscience perspective on psychopathy: Evidence for paralimbic system dysfunction. *Psychiatry Research*, *142*, 107–128. doi:10.1016/j.psychres.2005.09.013.

Klein, M. (1957). *Envy and gratitude*. New York, NY: Basic Books.

Matsumoto, D., Hwang, H., & Frank, M. (2013). Emotions expressed by leaders in videos predict political aggression. *Behavioral Sciences of Terrorism & Political Aggression*. https://doi.org/10.1080/19434472.2013.769116.

Matsumoto, D., Hwang, H., & Frank, M. (2017). Emotions and intergroup aggressive cognitions: The ANCODI hypothesis. *Aggressive Behavior*, *43*, 930–107. doi:10.1002/ab.21666.

McEllistrem, J. (2004). Affective and predatory violence: A bimodal classification system of human aggression and violence. *Aggression & Violent Behavior*, *10*, 1–30. doi:10.1016/j.avb.2003.06.002.

Meloy, J. R. (1988). *The psychopathic mind*. Northvale, NJ: Jason Aronson.

Meloy, J. R. (2004). Indirect personality assessment of the violent true believer. *Journal of Personality Assessment*, *82*, 138–146. doi:10.1207/s15327752jpa8202_2.

Meloy, J. R. (2006). The empirical basis and forensic application of affective and predatory violence. *Australian & New Zealand Journal of Psychiatry*, *40*, 539–547. doi:10.1080/j.1440-1614.2006.01837.x.

Meloy, J. R. (2011). Violent true believers. *FBI Law Enforcement Bulletin*. Retrieved fromhttps://leb.fbi.gov/articles/perspective/perspective-violent-truebelievers.

Meloy, J. R. (2017). *Terrorist radicalization assessment protocol (TRAP-18) manual 1.0*. Toronto, Canada: Multi-Health Systems.

Meloy, J. R., & Gill, P. (2016). The lone actor terrorist and the TRAP-18. *Journal of Threat Assessment & Management, 3*, 37–51. doi:10.1037/tam0000061.

Meloy, J. R., Habermeyer, E., & Guldimann, A. (2015). The warning behaviors of Anders Breivik. *Journal of Threat Assessment & Management, 2*, 164–175. doi:10.1037/tam0000037.

Meloy, J. R., Hoffmann, J., Guldimann, A., & James, D. (2012). The role of warning behaviors in threat assessment: An exploration and suggested typology. *Behavioral Sciences & the Law, 30*, 256–279. http://onlinelibrary.wiley.com/doi/10.1002/bsl.999/abstract doi:10.1002/bsl.999.

Meloy, J. R., Mohandie, K., Knoll, J., & Hoffmann, J. (2015). The concept of identification in threat assessment. *Behavioral Sciences and the Law, 33*, 213–237. pdfs.semanticscholar.org/7795/fb47a482f66cd4df3c843c2bd018d9bac8e5.pdf.doi:10.1002/bsl.2166.

Meloy, J. R., & Yakeley, J. (2014). The violent true believer as a "lone wolf": Psychoanalytic perspectives on terrorism. *Behavioral Sciences & the Law, 32*(3), 347–365.

Menninger, K. (1938). *Man against himself*. New York, NY: Harcourt Brace.

Michel, L., & Herbeck, D. (2001). *American terrorist*. New York, NY: Regan Books.

Qutb, S. (1951). "The America I have seen": In the scale of human values. Retrieved from https://archive.org/stream/SayyidQutb/The%20America%20I%20have%20seen_djvu.txt.

Risen, J., & Thomas, J. (1998). *Wrath of angels*. New York, NY: Basic Books.

Shane, S. (2011, May 13). Pornography is found in Bin Laden compound files, U.S. officials say. *New York Times*. Retrieved from www.nytimes.com/2011/05/14/world/asia/14binladen.html.

Siegel, A., & Victoroff, J. (2009). Understanding human aggression: New insights from neuroscience. *International Journal of Law & Psychiatry, 32*, 209–215. doi:10.1016/j.ijlp.2009.06.001.

Siever, L.(2008). Neurobiology of aggression and violence. *American Journal of Psychiatry, 165*, 429–442. doi:10.1176/appi.ajp.2008.07111774.

Stekel, W.(1929). *Sadism and masochism* (Vols. 1–2). New York, NY: Liveright.

Strozier, C., & Boyd, K. (2010) The apocalyptic. In C. Strozier, D. Terman, & J. Jones (Eds.), *The fundamentalist mindset* (pp. 29–37). New York, NY: Oxford University Press.

Terman, D. (2010). Fundamentalism and the paranoid gestalt. In C. Strozier, D. Terman, & J. Jones (Eds.), *The fundamentalist mindset* (pp. 47–61). New York, NY: Oxford University Press.

Van der Kolk, B. (2015). *The body keeps the score*. New York, NY: Penguin.

Volkan, V. (2009). Large group identity, international relations and psychoanalysis. *International Forum of Psychoanalysis*, *18*, 206–213. doi:10.1080/08037060 902727795.

Volkan, V. (2013). *Enemies on the couch*. Durham, NC: Pitchstone.

Woodworth, M., & Porter, S. (2002). In cold blood: Characteristics of criminal homicides as a function of psychopathy. *Journal of Abnormal Psychology*, *111*, 436–445. doi:10.1037/0021-843X.111.3.436.

Wrye, H. (1993). Erotic terror: Male patients' horror of the early maternal erotic transference. *Psychoanalytic Inquiry*, 13, 240–257. doi:10.1080/0735169930 9533936.

Yeginsu, C. (2017, March 4). Dozens say Christian leader made British boys "bleed for Jesus." *New York Times*. Retrieved from www.nytimes.com/2017/ 03/04/world/europe/britain-mansion-child-abusearchbishop-canterbury.html.

Chapter 4

The place of psychopathy along the spectrum of negative personality types

Michael H. Stone

The *Diagnostic and Statistical Manual of Mental Disorders* (DSM), has sometimes been called, half in earnest, half in jest, the psychiatrist's Bible. In the domain of personality disorders, the DSM can, alas, make no claim to biblical inerrancy. This shortcoming is particularly noticeable in the area of *negative*—or as we experience them, disagreeable—personalities. Personality is our window to the world, through which we greet others, through which others come to know us, and through which we judge ourselves.

The spectrum of negative personality

Given the wide range of negative personality traits and types it is useful to place them, insofar as possible, along a continuum or spectrum, from the least disturbing and dangerous to those at the other end, representing the most disagreeable and most dangerous. The DSM is not organized in this manner, and indeed the entire array of "personality disorders" mentioned therein is composed only of a hundred or so descriptors. Not all of these descriptors are actually personality *traits* in the strict sense of the term. The identity disturbance, mood fluctuations, suicidal acts, and impulsive behaviors that are often seen in patients with borderline personality, are symptoms, not traits. A table depicting a spectrum of negative personality, with severity increasing as one moves from left to right, is shown in Table 4.1.

Table 4.1 The Spectrum of Negative Personality

Negative Traits	Severely Negative Traits	Severe NPD, PPD	Malignant Narcis-sism	ASPD	Psychopathy	Psychop-athy with Violence	Sadistic Personal-ity Traits	Sadism with Terrorism
Abrasive et al.: see list below	Aggres-sive et al.: see list below		See descrip-tion below	(PCL-R score low to ~ 20)	Non-violent/ socio-pathic		See list below	

The table includes:

- **Negative traits—some examples:** abrasive, argumentative, "cad," contemptuous, deceitful, discourteous, envious, imprudent, insolent, meddlesome, prejudiced, quarrelsome, tactless, unsympathetic, vindictive.
- **Negative traits of a severer degree—some examples:** aggressive, amoral, bellicose, bigoted, brutal, cruel, grudge-holding, jealous, malicious, predatory, vengeful, scheming, slanderous, tyrannical, unscrupulous.
- **Malignant narcissism:** represents a confluence of narcissistic and antisocial traits, along with aggressive and paranoid tendencies; often with accompanying sadistic tendencies. In contrast to antisocial personality proper, there may still be the capacity for loyalty and concern for others (often: those in one's business, political, criminal, or terror-istic group). Some leaders of sadistic gangs or terroristic groups may exhibit this disorder (Kernberg 1992, pp. 77–78).
- **Sadistic personality traits:**
  - Uses physical cruelty or violence to establish dominance in relationships
  - Humiliates or demeans people in the presence of others
  - Treats or disciplines someone under his control with unusual harshness (e.g., a child, student, prisoner, patient)
  - Amused or takes pleasure in the psychological or physical suf-fering of others (including animals)
  - Lies for the purpose of harming or inflicting pain on others
  - Is fascinated by violence, weapons, martial arts, injury, or torture

- ○ Gets people to do what he wants by frightening them (through intimidation or terror)
- ○ Restricts the autonomy of people with whom he has a close relationship, e.g. will not let spouse leave the house unaccompanied.

These sadistic traits have not been solely for the purpose of sexual arousal (as in the paraphilia of sexual sadism). These sadistic attributes appeared in DSM-3R (1987); the diagnosis depended on the presence of at least four of the above eight attributes.

- **Psychopathy:** the diagnosis is based on the criteria of Robert Hare and his colleagues (1990), where a score may range from 0 to 40. Scores of 30 or more define clear-cut psychopathy; scores from 15 to 29 equate with "some psychopathic traits." Psychopathy in the absence of violence is sometimes called, colloquially, "sociopathy" (as in the case of the Ponzi scheme stockbroker, Bernard Madoff). "Psychopathy," as a term, usually (but not necessarily) connotes the presence of violent behaviors as well.

At the "mild" end of the spectrum, I locate the less disagreeable and dangerous negative traits. It is worth noting that our species (as with all mammalian species) is more alert to what may harm us than to what is pleasing. Our vocabulary is accordingly much richer in negative traits than in positive ones. I had earlier compiled a list of 500 "negative" personality traits, followed by 101 "positive" traits (Stone, 1993, pp. 101–106).

With respect to amenability to psychotherapy, the spectrum points to an inverse relationship: the further along the spectrum toward the psychopathy/sadism end that a person belongs to, the more guarded the prognosis, from a clinical standpoint. At the furthest extreme, where violent forms of psychopathy and marked sadism with terrorism are situated, therapy and corrective measures of any sort will almost never succeed.

I place *narcissistic* and *paranoid* personality disorders at the milder end of the spectrum, although actually both disorders contain subtypes that vary considerably with respect to treatability and also to their potential for social harm. In the DSM-IV (1994) description of narcissistic personality disorder for example, only five (or more) of the nine characteristics are required for the diagnosis. This means there are 256 combinations that fulfill the criteria. A person who has a grandiose sense of self-importance and requires excessive admiration, for example, is less worrisome than someone who is arrogant, exploitative, and lacking in empathy. The latter combination is suggestive of psychopathy. By the same token, persons exhibiting paranoid traits will vary in treatability and in potential danger-ousness according to whether they show the more serious attributes, such as grudge-holding, pathological jealousy, and readiness to counterattack if "slighted." Persons committing mass murder, who belong of course to the dangerous end of the spectrum, usually show those three characteristics; almost all are male (Stone, 2015).

In the middle portion of the spectrum is a personality disorder that combines some traits of both narcissistic and antisocial personalities (ASPD), as described by Kornberg (1992) under the heading of *Malignant Narcissism*. Prominent here, as in ASPD, is a lack of "capacity for loyalty and concern for others." Some persons with malignant narcissism will be found in the ranks of ruthless businessmen, higher-ups in criminal groups, and extremists in certain political and terrorist organizations. Those with a penchant for violence would belong more properly to regions of the spectrum further toward the extreme end.

Although ASPD was often considered "worse" than malignant narcissism, the definitions in DSM have been confusing and have allowed for excessive latitude in the domain of aberrant personality that they purport to cover. The definition of ASPD in the most recent iteration of DSM-5 (2013) lays emphasis, over and above "failure to conform to social norms, and deceitfulness," on such traits as low empathy, manipulative-ness, callousness, and hostility (including vengeful behavior). In this respect, the DSM describes ASPD in a way that comes closer to the definition of psychopathy developed by Hare, Harpur, Hakstian, Forth, Hart, and Newman (1990) and explicated further by Hare and Neumann (2008). But the original versions of ASPD were not developed to be of particular use in forensic settings, i.e., in the prisons or forensic hospitals. As Gacono and Meloy (2012) have pointed out that, in forensic settings ASPD is considerably more common than psychopathy: perhaps only a fourth of the inmates in a prison population will meet criteria for psychopathy, whereas almost all will meet ASPD criteria. Or, as Séguin, Sylvers, and Lilienfeld (2007) point out, the overlap between psychopathy and ASPD, although substantial in prisons, is "asymmetrical" (p. 190). The reason: most incarcerated prisoners meet criteria for ASPD (70–80%) whereas only 15–25% meet PCL-R[1] (Psychopathy Checklist-

Revised) criteria for psychopathy (cf., also Hare, 2003). Psychopathy as defined by the criteria of Hare or David Cooke et al. (Cooke & Michie, 2001) is thus a tighter concept than ASPD and has greater prognostic value vis-à-vis subsequent recidivism. As Robins's (1978) follow-up research showed, most antisocial children do not become antisocial adults. Also, many young adults with ASPD "burn out" as they enter their 40s: they commit fewer offenses, begin to lead responsible lives, and no longer meet ASPD criteria. There is an analogy here with border-line personality disorder (BPD). One might call this the *miracle of maturation*. A high proportion of BPD patients, as they enter their 30s or 40s, achieve a state of either remission or even clinical recovery; they no longer meet DSM criteria for BPD. Myelination in the frontal lobes completes around age 25; cerebral mechanisms fostering self-control are now stronger than the limbic system's tendency to impulsivity (Stone, 2017b). This "ageing out"—encountered in many with BPD or ASPD—tends not to occur among psychopaths. Because there is no separate description for psychopathy in DSM-5, the concepts of ASPD and psychopathy, albeit interrelated (yet conceptually separable), are simply lumped together under the heading of "ASPD." Here we will treat the two entities as separate regions along the spectrum, with psychopathy being closer to the far end of the negative personality spectrum.

Psychopathy or sociopathy?

Thus far, I have said nothing about sociopathy. There are those who refer to *psychopathy* and *sociopathy* as synonyms. For others, the terms are not synonymous, but there is disagreement about the differences. Sociopathy, for some, is akin to a milder form of psychopathy, a sort of psychopathy-lite, where the basic characteristics are the same but the person does not engage in violent acts. The Ponzi scheme manipulator, Bernard Madoff, who bilked people out of billions of dollars, never assaulted anyone, never even keyed a car. But at his trial, Judge Denny Chin called Madoff a "psychopath" who was "extraordinarily evil" (*New York Times*, June 29, 2011). Psychologist David Lykken (1995) would have called Madoff a "sociopath."

In their discussion of psychopathy, Verona and Vitale (2006) distinguish between the antisocial adolescent boys *with* a history of early-onset conduct problems from comparable boys *without* that history: the former tend to show higher levels of callous–unemotional personality traits, worse impulse control, and a greater diversity of criminal behaviors (Moffitt, 2003). Furthermore, the early-onset boys are more apt to be labeled "psychopaths" as they reach adulthood. Another comparable type is the "life-course/persistent" antisocial person described by Moffitt et al. (Moffitt, 2007; Moffitt & Caspi, 2001; Moffitt, Caspi, Harrington, & Milne, 2002). Persons fitting these descriptions are often identified in adolescence, the condition stemming from neurodevelopmental abnormalities discernible already in childhood but continuing into later life. Presumably genetic factors are responsible as underlying causes. In contrast, there is the (more common) adolescence-limited antisocial individual—originating in adverse social processes, but desisting when adulthood is reached. Growing up burdened by marked disadvantages contributes, as Lykken (1995) suggests, to the development of the "hostile" sociopath—who feels rejected by the community and unable to succeed according to its rules. He sees the "aggressive" sociopath as one who has grown up reveling in the sheer dominance over others: a person "of the streets" usually, becoming a rapist, a mugger, or some other sort of violent criminal. As for the "dissocial" sociopath, Lykken refers to persons of essentially normal temperament and psychology who are members of a subculture at odds with the surrounding majority culture. Examples are the Mafiosi, European gypsies, and what he calls "ghetto guerillas" who have been raised to regard the larger society as an "occupying foreign power" (p. 29).

Another way of dealing with the controversy concerning psychopathy and sociopathy is to speak of *primary* versus *secondary* psychopathy—the latter covering the same ground as what others are calling sociopathy. These terms also mirror what others allude to when referring to innate (or inborn/genetic) psychopathy versus a similar picture arising from extremely adverse environmental experience. I have previously used the term "acquired" psychopathy as the equivalent of the "secondary" type—where brutalization by parents during one's childhood, or other extremely adverse life events, seemed the likeliest causes for a psychopathic development that did not derive from any known prenatal factors (Stone, 2009, p. 131).

Wittgenstein said in his *Tractatus logico-philosophicus* (1955) that the meaning of a word is its usage. What are we to make, then, of the word "sociopathy"? There is no universally agreed-upon usage; instead, a bewildering variety of usages. Thus, *sociopathy* may be a synonym for *psychopathy*. Or an environmentally derived form of antisocial personality. Or a nonviolent form of psychopathy. Or a phenomenon among certain members of a disfavored cultural outlier group who are "anti" the rules of the dominant social group, but fairly normal in their interactions within their own culture. Perhaps the one commonality running through the various and conflicting definitions is this: sociopathy is a less violent, less dangerous, more environmentally based, and (usually) less treatment-resistant form of antisocial behavior than what tends to get placed under the rubric of *psychopathy*. Viewed from this perspective, it might have been more accurate for Judge Chin to have called Madoff a "sociopath" because of his having been raised in an upper-middle-class family where there was no abuse or neglect—and with enough capacity for intimacy to have married and raised children. But the staggering degree of financial damage he inflicted on the people he duped perhaps elevated him into the ranks of the psychopath, even though his PCL-R score would be too low to qualify as a psychopath by strict forensic standards.

ASPD and psychopathy from an epidemiological standpoint

ASPD, by virtue of its inclusion within DSM-5 and because its definition is weighted toward behavioral abnormalities, has been easier than psychopathy to assess in epidemiological surveys. Lifetime prevalence for ASPD has been estimated as varying from about 1% to 2% in the general population (Lenzenweger, Lane, Loranger, & Kessler, 2007; Troll, Jahng, Tomko, Wood, & Sher, 2010). Psychopathy has been studied mostly within criminal populations (including prisoners); estimates regarding its occurrence within the general population are more difficult to assess, because such estimates require evaluation by instruments like the 20-point Psychopathy Checklist or the 13-point assay of Cooke (Cooke, Michie, Hart, & Hare, 2004). Coid, Yang, Ullrich, Roberts, and Hare (2009) conducted a survey on a household population in Great Britain using the PCL-Screening Version. The prevalence of psychopathy was 0.6%, and correlated with younger age, male gender, suicide attempts, violent behavior, homelessness, and imprisonment. Their impression was that psychopathy affects less than 1% of the household population, granted that it is considerably higher among prisoners. Patients admitted to forensic psychiatric hospitals are less apt than prisoners to show psychopathy—perhaps only 3% (Douglas, Ogloff, Nicholls, & Grant, 1999)—which is in accord with my experience at the Mid-Hudson Forensic Hospital in New York State. In other studies, as Werner, Few, and Bucholz (2015) note, about 1% or slightly more in the general population are in the range of "potential psychopathy" (Neumann & Hare, 2008).

Ogloff (2006) introduces a useful word of caution, addressing what he regards as a diagnostic conundrum. Focusing on the *International Statistical Classification of Diseases*, 10th edition (ICD-10), he points to the confusion among the descriptions of ASPD, psychopathy, and what in ICD-10 is called "Dissocial Personality Disorder." ASPD, he remarks, overidentified people with offense histories (as applicable to supposedly 50–80% of prisoners), whereas only 15% might meet the criteria for psychopathy. Dissocial personality has more affective features—such as unstable interpersonal relationships, egocentricity, a failure to learn from experience, comorbid depression and anxiety, and concomitant abuse of alcohol and drugs. This description is nearer to some of the "softer" forms of sociopathy, especially among those individuals in whom background factors were primarily those of parental conflict and harsh inconsistent parenting.

Further confounding the efforts to assay the epidemiology of negative personality is the existence of what Hare (1993) has referred to as the "white-collar psychopath." Hare offers vignettes of certain men, often highly successful in the business world, who use their "charm, deceit, and manipulation to gain the confidence of [their] victims" (p. 103). Hare adds that these men often belong to one of the more privileged professions (lawyers, physicians, politicians, investment counselors) in whom we are prone to place our trust. Most people are warier of the men who try to sell them fake Rolex watches on Fifth Avenue—but even they make the occasional sale. We designate all of these men as con-artists; that is, "confidence men" who take advantage of our confidence in their trustworthiness. An example would be the higher-ups at the energy company Enron that defrauded investors and was brought down in 2001. Several of its officers, Kenneth Lay, Jeffrey Skilling, Andrew Fastow—initially lauded for their financial prowess—were subsequently convicted and served sentences (Jackson, 2002). Hare (1998) speaks of psychopaths as "intra-species predators who use charm, manipulation, intimidation, and violence to control others and to satisfy their own selfish needs" (p. 196).

There is widespread agreement that the ratio between males and females is even more lopsided for psychopathy than for ASPD (Paris, 1998). In prison populations, however, although males outnumber females considerably, the proportion of females who meet PCL-R criteria is only modestly less than the proportion of males (Verona & Vitale, 2006). Certain subgroups of prisoners are either exclusively male (men committing serial sexual homicide, i.e., "serial killers") or are almost so (mass murderers). About 90% of "serial killers" are psychopaths. Among mass murderers, 97% of whom are male, 10% in my series were psychopaths (Stone, 2015)—most of the others were disgruntled men with a paranoid cast to their personality. Writing from a neuroscience perspective, Annett Schirmer (2013) points to the marked difference in aggression between men and women. In the United States, she notes, men are 10 times as likely to commit murder as are women, and five times as likely to receive correctional supervision, such as imprisonment (p. 598). Likewise, men are much more numerous among the ranks of psychopaths who manifest what Hecht, Berg, Lilienfeld, and Letzman (2016) call "proactive," as opposed to "reactive" aggression. Proactive, in effect, means behaving aggressively "on purpose" rather than in response to some threat. Proactive psychopaths are similar to what Navarro (2014) calls "predators"—psychopaths who the author (a retired FBI special agent) characterizes as having only one goal: exploitation. Navarro offers many examples, including some from experience as an FBI officer: all involve men for whom "life has no stop signs" (p. 129). Navarro's first example concerns his encounter while arresting a burglar: the man's cold stare unnerved the officer, even though he was taller than the burglar and was able to handcuff him without difficulty. Yet Navarro felt frightened, as though he were in the presence of evil. His experience mirrors my experience years ago when I testified in California on behalf of the true-crime author Joe McGinnis. McGinnis was being sued by the former Green Beret officer/physician Jeffrey MacDonald for not sharing royalty monies and for daring to call MacDonald "antisocial" and "narcissistic." Already a prisoner, MacDonald was there in the courtroom, his feet shackled, but staring at me from his attorney's desk 20 feet away—with the "thousand-yard stare" that

I felt was so unnerving and fear-inspiring that I had to excuse myself briefly to use the bathroom. The other forensic psychiatrist who testified the day before also had the same experience (and also had to use the bathroom). Navarro also mentioned the case: MacDonald had stabbed to death his pregnant wife and two little daughters after the wife returned home unexpectedly and found him molesting their five-year old daughter. It was my encounter with MacDonald (Navarro called him "cold as ice") that led to my preoccupation with the topic of evil—and ultimately to my becoming the host of Discovery Channel's program *Most Evil*, where I went around the country interviewing serial killers, mass murderers, and other particularly predatory killers (cf. Stone, 2009).

Is personality immutable?

If we focus on the main attributes of personality, there is a general impression that these attributes—once they solidify in early adult life—remain pretty much "as is" over time, such that other people recognize us (and continue to recognize us) throughout the life-span. However, although we have already noticed that many persons exhibiting "adolescent-onset ASPD" drop much of their antisocial ways just as many persons with BPD enter a state of clinical remission, or even recovery, as they mature during their 30s and 40s (Stone, 2017a), there is a general impression that psychopaths, especially those with the most marked degree of predatory behaviors, are not only resistant to treatment but do not "age out" over the years. Also, the maturation—and mellower socialization—that typically accompanies our growing older may not be the only factor influencing the duration of psychopathic traits over the years. David Cooke (1998), writing about sociocultural and cross-cultural factors, cites Lykken's observation that children who are hard to socialize will emerge as sociopaths unless they experience highly competent parenting, whereas temperamentally easy children will emerge as well-socialized even if reared by incompetent parents (p. 269). In cultures where aggression is strongly discouraged, such as among the Mennonites and the Amish, antisocial and psychopathic disorders are seldom noted. This, in comparison to the surrounding American culture where there has often been a celebratory attitude toward violence and lawlessness—as in the admiration of Wild West folk heroes like Billy the Kid and Jesse James. Culture can apparently contribute either to the early extinction or to the prolongation of antisocial and psychopathic tendencies.

Of the defining traits of psychopathy, certain ones seemed more resistant to change over the years than others. In their 2006 essay on the "successful" psychopath, Hall and Benning write that those individuals notable for "fearless dominance," but not particularly prone to "impulsive antisociality," are apt to be the high-functioning noncriminal (or at least nonincarcerated) type of psychopath. These are the ones from more advantage socioeconomic and educational backgrounds: men like Madoff, the Enron executives, or businessmen who avoid serious trouble with the law. Traits like impulsivity or novelty-seeking do tend to diminish as one ages.

In any case, our tendency to believe in the steadfastness of personality throughout life has recently been called into question by the results of an unusually long (63-year) follow-up study of personality stability. Using data of personality traits collected in 1947, Harris, Brett, Johnson, and Deary (2016) reevaluated some 174 respondents 63 years later. They found enduring stability in one trait: *stability of mood*, and a near-significant stability in *conscientiousness*.

As for the enduring or "immutable" quality of psychopathy as a personality disorder, my impression is based on personal interviews of several serial killers on Death Row and material from over 800 "true crime" biographies of murderers, many of whom meet the criteria for the "serious"—exploitative/callous/predator—type of psychopath. For the most part, the predatory psychopathic men (and a few women) in this large group show no remorse and often denial of the crimes for which they were (rightfully) convicted. They lend the air of immutability of personality that surrounds the concept of psychopathy.

Sadistic personality

Sadism, which take sits name from the Marquis de Sade (1992; 1995; Francine du Plessix Gray, 1998), has as its chief feature the taking of pleasure in the physical suffering of others (including animals). De Sade was sent to a Jesuit *lycée*, where he was subjected to severe corporal punishment—most especially flagellation. He later became obsessed with subjecting others (mostly women) to humiliation and suffering via rape and beatings. There is no "first" sadist, but the first-century Roman emperor Caligula (12–41 CE), can serve as a good example. Until his assassination in 41, he was feared and hated for boasting of sex with other men's wives, and for killing just for amusement—including the sexual torture of men and women (Suetonius, 1997). In some cases, a sadist inflicts extreme psychological, rather than physical, suffering.

There are often childhood precursors to sadism. In my survey of 166 serial killers (men committing serial sexual homicide), a sadist named Arthur Shawcross, besides bedwetting and fire-setting, took pleasure in smashing squirrels with mallets and burning cats alive. There were another eight men who also sadistically murdered animals and set fires, including David Berkowitz, the "Son of Sam," and the "Moors Murderer," Ian Brady. One of the cruelest serial killers, Mike DeBardeleben, wrote a manifesto about his sadistic personality, in which he said,

> The central impulse [of sadism] is to have complete mastery over another person, to make him/her the helpless object of our will. ... And the most radical aim is to make her suffer. Since there is no greater power over another person than that of inflicting pain on her.
>
> (Hazelwood & Michaud, 2001, p. 88)

Serial killers often present as juvenile delinquents (with ASPD), emerging in their 20s as psychopaths—but with a decidedly sadistic streak, and can be placed in the intersection-region of ASPD, Sadistic Personality and Psychopathy (see Figure 4.1).

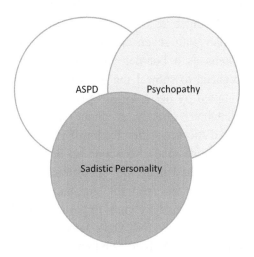

Figure 4.1 Antisocial, psychopathic, and sadistic personalities: overlapping concepts (persons diagnosed with any one of these three personality disorders often show some attributes of one or both of the other two).

As an adolescent, Ted Bundy was a "Peeping Tom" and antisocial; the murders began when he was in his 20s. Devoid of empathy or remorse, he raped and tortured his victims. The same picture is noted in David Brown (aka Benjamin Nathaniel bar Jonah)—who killed a girl during his early years, then kidnapped and raped boys when he was 18, and spent a dozen years in Bridgewater, before relocating to Montana—where he kidnapped, murdered, and cannibalized one known 10-year-old victim and several others.

There are many more sadistic persons, including sadistic killers, than the rare serial killers. There are even sadistic female murderers. Among the men, there are single killers like Dr. John Hill—who killed his wife via septicemia by injecting feces into her veins so as to be free to marry his mistress—and there are multiple killers like Dale Pierre— who, robbing a record shop in Utah, tied up the five people in the shop, raped the women, and forced all five to drink Lysol, killing three and maiming two for life. There is no "worst case" of sadism, just as there is no bottom to human depravity.

The women in the near-to-the-bottom of sadistic torture are fewer— but there are several notable examples. Jessica Schwarz, a Florida truck driver, tortured her 10-year-old stepson by doing such things as forcing him to eat a roach if he did not scrub the kitchen floor sufficiently, eat his supper from a bowl on the floor next to the kitty litter, or make him shout outdoors "I am a liar, I'm no good"—before finally drowning him in the family pool (Rothgeb & Scott, 2005). Fifty years ago, Gertrude Baniszewski, a woman with seven children and no money, took in 15-year-old Sylvia Likens as a boarder while her parents were traveling. Baniszewski commenced to subject the girl to a series of degrading tortures—perhaps prompted by her envy of Sylvia being beautiful, whereas her 19-year-old daughter, already pregnant, was unattractive (Dean, 2008). Among the sadistic acts: after feeding Sylvia disgusting food that she then vomited, Gertrude made her scoop up the vomit and eat it. She called Sylvia a "whore" and made her masturbate in front of her boys with a Coke bottle. Later she beat the girl and pushed her down the stairs; at one point she burned Sylvia's fingertips with a cigarette. The girl was kept naked and rarely fed. Days later, Gertrude took a heated sewing needle and branded Sylvia's abdomen with the words "I am a prostitute and proud of it," then taunted the girl that now no one would want to marry her. Finally, Sylvia was strapped naked to a bed where she starved to death. Both Jessica Schwarz and Gertrude Baniszewski can be placed in the intersection-region of Figure 4.1: those whose personalities partake simultaneously of antisocial, psychopathic, and sadistic attributes.

There are, to be sure, some persons with sadistic personality who make those close to them miserable (via humiliation, unjustified scolding, bigoted remarks, and the like) but have not engaged in overt antisocial acts or the predatory behaviors of the unequivocal psychopath. But in the true-crime literature, sadism, when present, is often of an extreme form; ASPD and psychopathy are usually discernible as well. Examples are legion, but here I will mention just one: the self-styled prophet of an unorthodox Mormon cult—Jeff Lundgren—already had a history of antisocial and psychopathic traits before he became more widely known as a cult leader (Stalter-Sassé & Widder, 1991). He insisted that his two dozen or so adherents give him all their money. When one of the families began to sense he was a corrupt leader, they defected—but not before he lured them to his farm headquarters. Lundgren then tricked the couple and their three children to come one at a time to the barn (made into a slaughterhouse), accompanied by his still-faithful follower, Ron Luff, who I later interviewed in prison. Once in the barn, Lundgren shot each one to death, dumping their bodies into a pit. The remaining members of the cult escaped to another state. While there, Lundgren, tiring of his wife, carried on an affair with another man's wife. Lundgren punished his wife, when she complained, by forcing her to suck his penis—on which he had spread his feces. Sadism of these extreme forms can serve as an introduction to the topic of "evil," because those disposed to commit acts (often involving torture) that we designate as evil belong to the outermost edge of personality "negativity."

When personality disorder elicits the reaction of "evil"

To invoke once again Wittgenstein's clarification that *the meaning of a word is its usage*, the contemporary meaning of "evil" is less freighted with overtones of religious and philosophical thought; instead "evil" has become an emotional word that people use when confronted with the actions of another person or group that evokes horror, revulsion, shock, and fright. We hear of some monstrous act, something heinous—such as an atrocity that has caused unspeakable pain and suffering. Our face scrunches up, we wince, our jaw may drop—and we say, "That was horrible … that was evil!"

We must distinguish between sadistic *acts* and sadistic *personality*. Some persons have committed solitary acts of unimaginable cruelty in response to some life crisis, but their personality on a day-to-day basis would not be characterized as "sadistic." Others behave in a demonstrably sadistic manner throughout their lives. An example of a sadistic *act* is that committed by China Arnold. Born in Dayton, Ohio, in 1980, she had a baby girl (it is not clear by whom) and was living with Terrell Tally. In 2005, Arnold put the baby in a microwave, killing the child with the high temperature and thermal burns. Sentenced to life in prison without parole, she told a cellmate that she killed the baby because she feared Tally would leave her once he found out he wasn't the baby's father. Some thought she killed the baby because it was Tally's child and he had cheated on her, so that was his punishment. The forensic pathologist, Dr. Russell Uptegrove, when examining the corpse, was hesitant to consider whether the baby had been microwaved rather than burned in some other manner: "It was so heinous to think of that," he said, "I couldn't convince myself it was a real possibility" ("Drunken mom microwaved baby," *New York Daily News*, March 2, 2010).

As for sadistic *personality*, the most convincing example—by virtue of its long duration and its most monstrous and disturbing aspects—is that of David Parker Ray (Glatt, 2002). What makes Ray's case all the more shocking is his outward normality—a man who could be affable and charming to his wives (there were four) and his two children, and who worked as a mechanic and later as a park ranger. He was considered charismatic and well-liked. But underneath the surface, Ray was consumed with sadistic sexual fantasies—to the point where he could not achieve erections unless accompanied by fantasies of killing women. It is interesting that it was his father, not his mother, who was abusive and cruel to Ray during his childhood years. In his 30s, Ray began to kidnap and torture women, sending them, after the torture, to Mexico, and selling them into sexual slavery. Using his engineering skills, he built a sound-proofed torture chamber in a mobile home (which he called his Toy Box) in New Mexico—filled with devices for immobilizing and torturing women. A daughter by his third marriage, Glenda Ray, helped capture potential women victims, but his main accomplice was a woman from a highly dysfunctional family, Cindy Hendy—who I later interviewed. Hendy, whose own mother was promiscuous and who never knew her father, was a surprisingly eager participant in Ray's torture of women. Once a woman was captured and lured to the Toy Box, she was bound and hoisted via chains to the top of the mobile home/torture chamber; she was then forced to listen to long recordings Ray had prepared of the sexual tortures she was about to endure. Ray was an accomplished artist and draughtsman who would make numerous drawings of the women and the torture devices to which they would be subjected. To reproduce the contents of Ray's recording would be too lengthy—and too disturbing. I have provided one of the opening paragraphs. Bear in mind that the verbal exposition of the exquisite and degrading tortures to which the women were about to suffer may well have been more excruciating psychologically than the physical tortures that were about to take place.

> Now you are obviously here against your will, totally helpless, don't know where you're at, don't know what's gonna happen to you. ... You're very scared and pissed off. You've already tried to get your wrists and ankles loose, and know you can't. ... You probably think you're gonna be raped and you're fuckin sure right about that. Our primary interest is what you've got between your legs. You'll be raped thoroughly and repeatedly in every hole you've got. Because basically you've been snatched and brought here for us to use as a sex slave. ... You're not gonna like it a fuckin bit. But I don't give a rat's ass about that. ... You're gonna be kept naked and chained up like an animal to be used and abused anytime we want to, any way we want to.

Ray and Hendy were finally arrested in 1999 after they had tortured and killed (according to Hendy) some 60 women, burying their bodies in the surrounding New Mexico desert. No body has ever been recovered. Oddly, Ray's PCL-R score—20—is compatible with only "psychopathic traits"; Hendy's score of 32 would define her clearly as a psychopath—in addition to her being a person with sadistic personality. Hendy had been raised without a father (apart from step-fathers who sexually abused her) and with a promiscuous mother who neglected her. She became a willing accomplice of Ray's, participating actively in torturing his victims. When I interviewed her in prison, she was remarkably cold and callous, without a trace of remorse.

The prolonged tortures to which Ray and Hendy subjected their women victims had some of the qualities of terrorism—partly via Ray's recorded preview of what was about to happen to them. But this was terrorism under wraps: the outside world was unaware, until one of the victims was able to escape and tell the authorities. Large-scale terrorism, such as the kind launched by Islamic jihadists since the time Ayatollah Khomeini deposed the Shah of Iran—and especially since 9/11—has awakened interest as to what kind of persons, and what kind of personalities, carry out terroristic acts. Some of the more notable recent terrorists appear to have markedly rageful and sadistic attributes, and psychopathic traits as well—to the point where it becomes tempting to lump them altogether as a special variety of negative personality at the most dreadful end of our spectrum.

To clarify the points I have been making thus far, concerning the division of the spectrum of negativity into a number of compartments, beginning with mutable ASPD and culminating in the "worst of the worst"—where evil resides—I offer the following vignettes.

Mutable antisocial personality

A fitting example of antisocial personality in the absence of clear-cut psychopathy is that of Stanley Tookie Williams. Born in Louisiana in 1953 to a black woman of 17, a stern and devout Baptist, Stanley grew up without a father. His mother moved with him to Los Angeles six years later. He soon got into street fights and was often bullied by bigger boys. By 12 he was carrying a switchblade. Stanley became part of a gang that engaged in considerable violence and theft. At 16 he was arrested for stealing a car and was sent to a juvenile reform center. While there, he began weight-lifting, emerging at 19 as an immensely strong body-builder, able to bench-press 500 pounds. He became the leader of a prominent gang, the West-Side Crips, with the avowed goals of eliminating all competing gangs and protecting local people from both smaller gangs and police brutality. Stanley studied sociology at a local college and subsequently lived a double life as a gang-leader and youth counselor. Stanley had dabbled in glue-sniffing and marijuana use since the age of 12, but now began using the highly addictive PCP. In service of supporting his drug habit he became violent, and in 1979 killed one person in a convenience store and then three people in a motel, while stealing money for PCP. This led to his arrest for felony murder, and a death-penalty sentence. He was sent to San Quentin's Death Row. At first, he committed a number of assaults against guards and other inmates. But over time, he transformed, educated himself further, and wrote books urging young blacks and others to avoid falling into the life of gangs and violence that had ruined his life. He, and the many people who now began to champion his cause, argued for clemency on the grounds of his redemption and remorse. Because of his books and of his rejection of violence, he was even nominated for the Nobel Peace Prize. Yet, although many thousands of supporters petitioned for clemency and abolition of the death penalty, Williams was executed in 2005.

Psychopathic with violence

In their biography of their stepfather, Lori and Cindy Hart (2016) sketch the life of Donnie Rudd—a story of bizarre and unimaginable complexity. Born in 1942 in a small town, he became a lawyer and moved with his first wife, Louann—and their four children—to the Chicago area. He became a prominent patent attorney for Quaker Oats. The Rudds befriended a neighboring family, John and Dianne Hart and their four children. Ultimately Donnie charmed Dianne into a clandestine affair and eventually Dianne insisted on divorcing John. The two rejected spouses, John and Louann, united in their grief, became friendly, and a plan evolved where the couples would swap spouses. John would marry Louann, and Dianne would marry Donnie. Their houses were united through a newly cut door, and the Hart children become "Rudds," and vice versa. Months later, Dianne learned that Donnie was spending time with his 19-year-old legal assistant, Noreen Kumeta, whom he secretly married. Telling Dianne he was on a clandestine mission for the CIA, Donnie traveled to another state, intending to end the "unofficial marriage." He took out a big insurance policy on Noreen, and one month later she died. It was reported that she and Donnie had an accident while driving. A car sideswiped theirs and Noreen's door swung open, tossing her out and causing fatal head injuries. Donnie collected $200,000 in insurance money and then persuaded Dianne to go through with their original plan to marry. Out of her acute loneliness, Dianne agreed. Donnie then became a star as a condominium lawyer, promising clients big settlements that never materialized. There were lawsuits and he went bankrupt. A female client whom he had promised a near-million-dollar settlement sued him. (He had lied to her about the "delay" in getting her money, saying he was getting treatments for a nonexistent kidney cancer.) The client was later murdered. Because of the lawsuits, he was disbarred as an attorney and he (and Dianne) left for Texas. Dianne died shortly thereafter of breast cancer. Five months later, Donnie married a fourth time—to Mary Bret. She soon discovered his fantastical lies—such as having won the Congressional Medal of Honor in Vietnam (where he had never been). They divorced and a few months later, on the same day his last divorce came through, he married yet again, to Emma Leising. That marriage also ended in divorce. By now his chronic lying and deceptiveness led the daughter of the third wife, Dianne, to convince the police to look into the "accidental" death of Noreen and to the hitherto unexplained murder of the woman who was his client—as crimes committed by Donnie. When Noreen's body was exhumed, it was found that she had been bludgeoned to death by blows to her head with a heavy object. Donnie Rudd was convicted of that murder, and jailed. At that time, he was also suspected of murdering the client. He pleaded not guilty and told the police yet another lie: that he had colon cancer. Rudd was shown at last to be an unregenerate—and a murderous—psychopath, who lied as glibly at age 75 as he had done all his life.

Psychopathy with violence and sadism

George Woldt was born in South Korea in 1976 to an American soldier and his Korean wife, Song-Hui. At first, she doted on her son, but she was a psychotic woman: paranoid and given to marked mood swings. Later, she became violent and abusive toward George, who was also physically abused by his violent, alcoholic father. The family eventually settled in Littleton, Colorado. Because of the abusiveness, George left home at 17, and quickly impregnated his girlfriend. He had multiple female sexual partners, who he called "bitches"—an attitude that reflected his withering hatred of women. He was preoccupied with absolute control over women, and nurtured brutal rape fantasies. Lucas Salmon, a shy young man his age, was still a virgin, and hoped George would show him the ropes about sex. George ensnared Lucas into becoming an accomplice to the rape of a stranger. With George at the wheel, they drove a car until they came upon a young woman, Jacine Gielinski, as she was returning home. Grabbing her from behind, they forced her into the car. George proceeded to rape her; then it was Lucas's turn. Unable to get erect at first, he masturbated till near ejaculation, then inserted, and quickly reached orgasm. His years of virginity now behind him, the plan then proceeded to the next step: killing the woman to hide evidence of the crime. But they were incredibly clumsy: they cut Jacine's throat at the wrong angle, which led only to massive bleeding, then stabbed her repeatedly in the chest and finally strangled her till she died. George then stuffed mud into the girl's vagina, thinking—in his ignorance—this would eliminate any semen that could be tested for DNA. When a passerby who heard or observed something suspicious notified the police, the pair were immediately arrested. Because of the torturous and prolonged nature of the murder, with grossly depraved indifference to the victim's life, the jury voted the death penalty for both. George, viewed as the primary perpetrator, was considered "sadistic, narcissistic, and psychopathic."

Evil as soul murder

The further along the spectrum of negative personality we proceed, ending with persons who embody the attributes of *narcissistic*, *psychopathic*, and *sadistic*, the more often we will encounter examples that horrify and elicit from us the reaction "That was *evil!*" There is, however, another approach to the concept of evil that is highly relevant, and that comes from the field of philosophy. The contemporary British philosopher Roger Scruton (2017), for example, regards, as a paradigm of evil "the attempt or desire to destroy the soul of another, so that his or her value and meaning are rubbed out" (p. 138). In particular, the one who tortures "is using the body to dominate another's first-person being and delighting in the ruin and humiliation that can be brought about through pain" (p. 139). Scruton's definition is particularly applicable to instances, as we saw in the last clinical example above, of rape. This crime involves, in Scruton's words, the "triumph over the other's subjectivity, a delight in wresting sexual pleasure from an unwilling donor" (p. 64). This definition is mirrored in the manifesto, cited above, by the serial killer Mike DeBardeleben. He made chillingly clear that the essence of evil lies in the simultaneous dehumanization of, and infliction of pain on, the victim. At the farthest end of the spectrum of negative personality, we confront—in acts of evil—the horrors I have described and the nullification of another human being.

Acknowledgments

Michael H. Stone, M.D. The Place of Psychopathy Along the Spectrum of Negative Personality Types. *Contemporary Psychoanalysis*, copyright © the William Alanson White Institute of Psychiatry, Psychoanalysis & Psychology and the William Alanson White Psychoanalytic Society, www.wawhite.org, reprinted by permission of Taylor & Francis Ltd, http://www.tandfonline.com on behalf of the William Alanson White Institute of Psychiatry, Psychoanalysis & Psychology and the William Alanson White Psychoanalytic Society.

Notes

1 The Psychopathy Checklist-Revised (PCL-R), designed by Hare (2003), is a 20-item assessment tool used to evaluate the presence of psychopathic traits among individuals in high-security psychiatric units, prisons, and other forensic settings.

References

Coid, J., Yang, M., Ullrich, S., Roberts, A., & Hare, R. D. (2009). Prevalence and correlates of psychopathic traits in the household population of Great Britain. *International Journal of Law Psychiatry, 32*, 65–73. doi:10.1016/j.ijlp.2009.01.002.
Cooke, D. J. (1998). Cross-cultural aspects of psychopathy. In T. Millon, E. Simonsen, M. Birket-Smith, & R. D. Davis (Eds.), *Psychopathy: Antisocial, criminal and violent behavior* (pp. 260–276). New York, NY: Guilford Press

Cooke, D. J., & Michie, C. (2001). Refining the concept of psychopathy: Toward a hierarchical model. *Psychological Assessment, 13*, 171–188. doi:10.1037/10403590.13.2.171.

Cooke, D. J., Michie, C., Hart, S. D., & Hare, R. D. (2004). Reconstructing psychopathy: Clarifying the significance of antisocial and socially deviant behavior in the diagnosis of psychopathic personality disorder. *Journal of Personality Disorder, 18*, 337–356. doi:10.1521/pedi.2004.18.4.337.

Dean, J. (2008). *House of evil.* New York, NY: St Martin's Press.

Diagnostic and statistical manual of mental disorders (4th ed.). (1994). Washington, DC: American Psychiatric Press.

Diagnostic and statistical manual of mental disorders (5th ed.). (2013). Washington, DC: American Psychiatric Press.

Douglas, K. S., Ogloff, J. R. P., Nicholls, T. L., & Grant, I. (1999). Assessing risk for violence among psychiatric patients: The HCR-20 violence risk assessment scheme and the psychopathy checklist-screening version. *Journal of Consulting and Clinical Psychology, 67*, 917–930. doi:10.1037/0022-006X.67.6.917.

du Plessix Gray, F. (1998). *At home with the Marquis de Sade.* New York, NY: Simon & Schuster.

Gacono, C. B., & Meloy, J. R. (2012). Assessing antisocial and psychopathic personalities. In J. N. Butcher (Ed.), *Oxford handbook of personality assessment* (pp. 567–581). New York, NY: Oxford University Press.

Glatt, J. (2002). *Cries in the desert: The shocking true story of a sadistic torturer.* New York, NY: St Martin's Paperbacks.

Hall, J. R., & Benning, S. D. (2006). The "successful" psychopath: Adaptive and subclinical manifestations of psychopathy in the general population. In C. J. Patrick (Ed.), *Handbook of psychopathy* (pp. 459–478). New York: Guilford Press.

Hare, R. D. (1993). *Without conscience: The disturbing world of the psychopaths among us.* New York, NY: Pocket Books.

Hare, R. D. (1998). Psychopaths and their nature: Implications for the mental health and criminal justice systems. In T. Millon, E. Simonsen, R. D. Davis, & M. Birket-Smith (Eds.), *Psychopathy: Antisocial, criminal, and violent behavior* (pp. 188–214). New York, NY: Guilford Press.

Hare, R. D. (2003). *Manual for the revised psychopathy checklist* (2nd ed.). Toronto, ON: Multi-Health Systems.

Hare, R. D., Harpur, T. J., Hakstian, A. R., Forth, A. E., Hart, S. D., & Newman, J. P. (1990). The revised psychopathy checklist: Reliability and factor structure. *Psychological Assessment, 2*, 338–341.doi:10.1037/1040-359 0.2.3.338.

Hare, R. D., & Neumann, C. S. (2008). Psychopathy. In P. Blaney & T. Millon (Eds.), *Oxford textbook of psychopathology.* New York, NY: Oxford University Press.

Harris, M. A., Brett, C. E., Johnson, W., & Deary, I. J. (2016). Personality stability from age 14 to age 77 years. *Psychological Aging, 31*, 862–874. doi:10.1037/pag0000133.

Hart, L., & Hart, C. (2016). *Living with the devil: A family's search for the truth in the face of deception, infidelity, and murder.* (n.p.) Authors.

Hazelwood, R., & Michaud, S. G. (2001). *Dark dreams: Sexual violence, homicide, and the criminal mind.* New York, NY: St Martin's Press.

Hecht, L. K., Berg, J. M., Lilienfeld, S. O., & Letzman, R. D. (2016). Parsing the heterogeneity of psychopathy and aggression: Differential associations across dimensions and gender. *Personality Disorder, 7,* 2–14. doi:10.1037/per0000128.

Jackson, B. (2002). Enron execs hid losses, made millions. Retrieved from http://edition.cnn.com/2002/LAW/02/02/enron.report/index.html.

Kernberg, O. F. (1992). *Aggression in personality disorders and perversions.* New Haven, CT: Yale University Press.

Lenzenweger, M. F., Lane, M. C., Loranger, A. W., & Kessler, R. C. (2007). DSM-IV personality disorders in the National Community Survey Replication. *Biological Psychiatry, 62,* 553–564. doi:10.1016/j.biopsych.2006.09.019.

Lykken, D. T. (1995). *The antisocial personalities.* Hillsdale, NJ: Lawrence Erlbaum Associates Publishers.

Marquis de Sade, D. A. F. (1992). *The misfortunes of virtue and other early tales* (D. Coward, Trans.). New York, NY: Oxford University Press.

Marquis de Sade, D. A. F. (1995). *Les oeuvres.* Edition established by Michel Delon. Paris, FR: Gallimard/Bibliotèque de la Pléiade.

Moffitt, T. E. (2003). Life-course persistent and adolescence-limited antisocial behavior: A ten-year research review and research agenda. In B. B. Lahey, T. E. Moffitt, & A. Caspi (Eds.), *Causes of conduct disorder and juvenile delinquency* (pp. 49–75). New York, NY: Guilford Press.

Moffitt, T. E. (2007). A review of the research on the taxonomy of life-course persistent versus adolescence-limited antisocial behavior. In D. J. Flannery, A. T. Vazsonyi, & I. D. Waldman (Eds.), *The Cambridge handbook of violent behavior and aggression* (pp. 49–74). New York, NY: Cambridge University Press.

Moffitt, T. E., & Caspi, A.(2001). Childhood predictors differentiate life-course persistent and adolescence-limited pathways among males and females. *Development and Pathology, 13,* 355–375. doi:10.1017/S0954579401002097.

Moffitt, T. E., Caspi, A., Harrington, H., & Milne, B. (2002). Males on the life-course persistent and adolescence-limited antisocial pathways: Follow-up at age 26. *Development and Pathology, 14,* 179–206. doi:10.1017/S0954579402001104.

Navarro, J. (2014). *Dangerous personalities.* New York, NY: Rodale Books.

Newmann, C. S., & Hare, R. D. (2008). Psychopathic traits in a large community sample: Links to violence, alcohol use, and intelligence. *Journal of Consulting & Clinical Psychology, 76,* 893–899. doi:10.1037/0022-006X.76.5.893.

Ogloff, J. R. (2006). Psychopathy/antisocial personality disorder conundrum. *Australian and New Zealand Journal of Psychiatry, 40,* 519–528. doi:10.1080/j.1440-1614.2006.01834.x.

Paris, J. (1998). A biopsychosocial model of psychopathy. In T. Millon, E. Simonsen, M. Birket-Smith, & R. D. Davis (Eds.), *Psychopathy: Antisocial, criminal and violent behavior* (pp. 277–287). New York, NY: Guilford Press.

Robins, L. N. (1978). Sturdy childhood predictors of adult behavior: Replications from longitudinal studies. *Psychological Medicine, 8,* 611–622. doi:10.1017/S0033291700018821.

Rothgeb, C., & Scott, S.(2005). *No one can hurt him anymore.* New York, NY: Pinnacle Books.

Schirmer, A. (2013). Sex differences in emotion. In J. Armony & P. Vuilleumier (Eds.), *The Cambridge handbook of human affective neuroscience* (pp. 591–610). New York, NY: Cambridge University Press.

Scruton, R. (2017). *On human nature.* Princeton, NJ: Princeton University Press.

Séguin, J. R., Sylvers, P., & Lilienfeld, S. O. (2007). The neuropsychology of violence. In D. J. Flannery, A. T. Vazsonyi, & I. D. Waldman (Eds.), *The Cambridge handbook of violent behavior and aggression* (pp. 187–214). New York, NY: Cambridge University Press.

Stalter-Sassé, C., & Widder, P. M. (1991). *The Kirtland massacre.* New York, NY: D. I. Fine Publishing.

Stone, M. H. (1993). *Abnormalities of personality: Within and beyond the realm of treatment.* New York, NY: W. W. Norton.

Stone, M. H. (2009). *The anatomy of evil.* Amherst, NY: Prometheus Books.

Stone, M. H. (2015). Mass murder, mental illness, and men. *Violence and Gender, 2,* 51–86. doi:10.1089/vio.2015.0006.

Stone, M. H. (2016). Long-term course of borderline personality disorder. *Psychodynamic Psychiatry, 44*(4), 449–474. doi:10.1521/pdps.2016.44.3.449.

Stone, M. H. (2017a). Borderline personality disorder patients 25 to 50 years later, with commentary on prognostic factors. *Psychodynamic Psychiatry* (In press). doi:10.1521/pdps.2017.45.2.259.

Stone, M. H. (2017b). Psychotic homicide offenders. In J.Stuart & L. Mellor (Eds.), *Homicide: A forensic psychology casebook* (pp. 187–203). New York, NY: CRC Press.

Suetonius, G. (1997). Lives of the caesars (J. C. Rolfe, Trans.). Cambridge, MA: Loeb Classical Library.

Troll, T. J., Jahng, S., Tomko, R. L., Wood, P. K., & Sher, K. J. (2010). Revised NESARC personality disorder diagnoses: Gender, prevalence, and comorbidity with substance dependence disorders. *Journal of Personality Disorders, 24,* 412–426. doi:10.1521/pedi.2010.24.4.412.

Verona, E., & Vitale, J. (2006). Psychopathy in women. In C. J. Patrick (Ed.), *Handbook of psychopathy* (pp. 415–436). New York, NY: Guilford Press.

Werner, K. B., Few, L. R., & Bucholz, K. K. (2015). Epidemiology, comorbidity, and behavioral genetics of antisocial personality disorder and psychopathy. *Psychiatric Annals,* April 1. doi:10.3928/00485713-20150401-08.

Wittgenstein, L. (1955). *Tractatus logico-philosophicus.* Abingdon: Routledge & Kegan Paul.

Chapter 5

The perpetrators

The receivers and transmitters of evil

Valerie Sinason

The only thing necessary for the triumph of evil is for good men to do nothing.

Attributed to Edmund Burke, yet first said by J. S. Mill, 1867

He was a brilliant dad, really.

Daughter of British serial killer Fred West, 1995

Ordinary people, simply doing their jobs, and without any particular hostility on their part, can become agents in a terrible destructive process. Moreover, even when the destructive effects of their work become patently clear, and they are asked to carry out actions incompatible with fundamental standards of morality, relatively few people have the resources needed to resist authority

Stanley Milgram, 1974

The apple does not fall far from the tree.

Old proverb

Introduction

For nearly a decade the British public were haunted by the murders and torture committed by Fred West (1941–95) and his second wife Rose. West was a serial killer in the UK who committed at least 12 murders with Rose. One of his daughters explained that together her parents killed 30 people, something West himself had also said to police (Zoie O'Brien, 2018). West was able to evade the police for some time but once he was in custody, he showed the police where some of the bodies were buried—under the patio of his house. West hanged himself in prison on January 1, 1995 while awaiting trial. His wife was convicted of murder and child abuse and maintained she was victimized by West. Between them, Fred and Rose had eight children who were physically and sexually abused; two of them were murdered. The family home also contained a torture chamber.

Outside of war atrocities, serial killers are often thought of as the epitome of the perpetration of evil. How had these two troubled individuals perpetrated such evil acts? Where did they come from?

Rose West was born to a depressed mother and a violent schizophrenic father who abused her and had a sexual relationship with her younger brother. She met Fred at a bus stop when she was 15 and he was 27.

Fred was one of eight children; six survived, born to disciplinarian farm-worker parents. He reported he was sexually and physically abused by them. Both Fred and Rose had problems with school and learning. After marriage Rose worked as a prostitute while Fred watched. Allegedly Rose encouraged Fred to abuse their daughter Anna Marie, whom she also abused. Sadly, Rose's father would visit her at her marital home and abuse her.

"He was a brilliant dad, really," said Mae, a daughter, then 23 years old, in an interview with the *Independent* (Aitkenhead, 1995). "Well, apart from he wouldn't leave you alone. But you could have a good old laugh with him. You would never think he was a murderer." Of Rose she explained:

> "She's more like a normal mum, now. Which is a shame, because she's locked up." It's such a pity, she says, that her mother's five grandchildren will all grow up with their gran in prison, because Rose liked children so much.
>
> (Aitkenhead, 1995)

In looking at the high number of Adverse Childhood Experiences (ACES) the Wests had experienced, perhaps what is surprising is that only a minority of childhood victims of trauma act as receivers and transmitters in such an extreme way. Browne (1993) is one of the few criminologists whose research results show that only one in four of those victimized become a victimizer. The majority manage the pain, shame and humiliation they have experienced on their own without passing it on. Nevertheless, the 25% who do become victimizers and perpetrators are responsible for the largest amount of generational transmission of trauma, committing illegal offences that hurt others.

A "new normal" is created in families where there is accepted and sustained psychopathology in the form of sexual disturbance, sadism and criminality. Even where there is a private awareness that what is happening is wrong, the victim learns to accommodate to what is happening in order to survive (Sinason, 1996). Hence the daughter of an incestuous and serial killer father can say he is a great dad because attachment, accommodation and normalization make it so. And looking back at Fred and Rose West's childhoods we can see how boundaries were broken for them from the start. Indeed, following the impact of an internalized death wish (Sinason, 1986) or an infanticidal attachment (Kahr, 1993, 2007) or literal rather than symbolic attachment (Sachs, 2017) we can see how re-enactments are inevitable without external support, treatment or extra capacity for resilience.

Lloyd De Mause (1974), an American psycho-historian, declared that the history of childhood was a nightmare from which we were only just beginning to recover. Around the world in the twenty-first century, except in a few small pockets of liberal democracies, children can be physically abused by adults under the legal right of "justifiable chastisement" for punishment with no right or recourse to any justice. Indeed, with total obedience being demanded of children in many countries around the world and political, personal, religious and moral directives enforced without choice, they remain, as a group, the world's largest number of slaves. The relentless and inevitable passing on of cruelty is the price the world pays for its silence and complicity. Remove the concept of "evil" from its religious associations to a more secular conceptualization and we find a clear grouping of internal and external clusters that allow perpetrators to re-enact (de Zulueta,1993) which Baron-Cohen (2011) has usefully categorized under the heading of non-empathy.

For nearly four decades I have been working with perpetrators suffering with intellectual disabilities, dissociative disorders and/or forensic profiles including rape, incest, child rape, murder, racist attacks and alleged assassinations (Sinason, 2008, 2012, 2017, 2018). Sadly, many of these people transformed from victims to victim-perpetrators. Despite this, I have yet to meet a single individual who I would consider to be intrinsically evil. However, the states of mind (often dissociated) in which their heinous crimes are committed are extremely frightening and chilling.

Andrew (pseudonym), a man with a severe intellectual disability, was kidnapped and abused as a baby. He was also abused by his parents and older brother. He was obsessed with the idea of kidnapping a baby left outside a shop in a pram. He hated the mothers who left their baby vulnerable like that and wanted to punish them by stealing and hurting their baby. He also hated his baby-self for being so vulnerable. Identifying with both the kidnapper and his abusing mother allowed him a way out of his terror of being hurt. He could identify with the aggressor and feel the excitement of hurting the baby that his mother and his kidnapper had experienced.

Isaac Brown (pseudonym), also a man with a severe intellectual disability (Sinason, 2012), was found as a baby, almost dead in a dustbin. He was detained in hospital under the Mental Health Act (sectioned) for attempting to strangle babies and expressed a wish to marry a little boy or kill him. What became tragically clear in therapy was that, for him, infanticide and pedophilia were a defense against incest. He considered that anyone, male or female, who was 12 years older than him could be the parents who threw him away. Therefore, the only recourse was to marry someone very little. His hatred for his discarded child-self was expressed by murderous wishes to other small children who wanted a mother or missed their mother.

Almost every appalling and obscene action committed that I have been able to examine comes from a predetermined cluster of internal and external obstacles that can be triggered and obstruct any capacity to empathize or reflect. Similarly, even the rare individual who might have no internal redeeming feature can only achieve their acts of perpetration because of the active or passive collusion of others. Hitler, an international embodiment of evil, was a physically abused child, one of only two siblings out of the six born who survived infancy. His father was violent, and his mother was a powerless third wife. His failure to enter art school and family conflict over his career wishes pushed him into poverty. When struggling to survive it was Jewish patrons who bought his paintings and a Jewish doctor who could not keep his mother alive. These issues were to be used by social groups that found a home and use for his rage.

No dictator or adult or child who inspires and perpetrates evil actions arrived into such a position alone. Internal resilience, nature of attachment patterns, socio-political conditions, levels of empathy, adverse childhood situations, fear, obedience and hierarchy all have an impact on outcome. The bystander, someone who does not become involved when someone else needs help, can be more responsible for the transmission of evil being unchecked than the sadistic or psychopathic individual. Clarkson (1963) underlines this point by speaking of the "non-innocent bystander". Usually, the victims and victimizers are the smallest category while the bystander is the largest.

The act and transmission of evil is only too real and must not be minimized (Grand, 2010). Like other colleagues, I have sometimes fallen into the error of finding theory and understanding an omnipotent defense against the unbearable actuality of evil. Coming as it does as a terrible solution that is beyond words, evil unites the victim-perpetrator, the victim and the non-innocent bystander with its contagious deadness. In seeking vengeance and punishment rather than justice, victims, their families, legal systems and whole countries can spread the toxin. State murder continues. Honor killings. Fascist theocracies. Trafficking. The moral defense (Fairbairn, 1952), self-injury where the victim (usually the child) takes on the badness of the perpetrator, creates a situation where "the masochist feels like a criminal, and the psychopathic sadist feels like a victim" (Howell, 1996), only replenishing the hunger that cannot be assuaged.

I have looked into the dead empty eyes of those who tell me they will remain lonely in the most terrible way because no-one except their victims and perpetrators can truly understand the loneliness of the mental state they had to enter, the internal wasteland of those who became a thing, a non-person and felt impelled to repeat and find their own thing—spreading evil. In children's homes and prisons, I have also seen the blood-hungry excitement that roars as a defense against terror and spreads evil.

An unwilling perpetrator

An 85-year-old German Jewish refugee, Beatrice, came for a consultation. She had a life-threatening cancer and wanted to think about some complex past problems before she died. She had been a distinguished French lecturer until her retirement and had then continued to conduct regular salons to discuss French literature and politics. She had no living family.

Her refugee background was painfully familiar. Before the round-up to the concentration camps in Germany, her mother had been a political writer and her father a publisher. Although intellectually libertarian in some ways, her parents had high and hard standards for their two daughters and were particularly emphatic on manners and dress. Beatrice loved school and it was clear that a high-level educational career was expected of her and her younger sister.

She was, it emerged, only 13 when the family was sent to a concentration camp. After the nightmare of their journey and arrival, and just as they were being divided according to gender, her younger sister started weeping uncontrollably. She was shot dead and, in fighting to turn back to reach her, her father was shot too. Frozen into silence she and her mother were separated. What she had witnessed from those first hellish moments and right through until her rescue were the extremes of human evil.

Coming as a refugee to the UK as a 17-year-old, without any living family or friends, she demonstrated remarkable resilience. She eventually learned English working as a cleaner, then as a domestic in an Anglo-French Jewish home where she was encouraged to take language lessons and further exams. She undertook professional training, found residential work and then became manager of a residential home for unwanted traumatized children. After six months of managing the home she had what she believed to be a psychotic breakdown. Resigning from the job she then re-educated herself as a French teacher and an unbroken career followed. She never married but had long-term loyal friendships.

As she had grown older and weaker and more in touch with mortality fears, she was forced to reacquaint herself with old terrors. She was now experiencing flashbacks and was terrified to leave her home. Just coming for a consultation in broad daylight to a place near her home was exhausting. However, it was not the concentration camp she was forced into that reappeared in her dreams, but the one she partially, temporarily and unintentionally created. In a children's home.

As a house manager she was triggered by the hope in the children's eyes on visiting days and the subsequent despair of those children whose parents did not visit. She dressed the ones with visitors in nice clothes so they could feel proud during the visits and denigrated savagely the children who had no visitors. The worst part of her memory was that she had forced children who cried into wearing the clothes of a child who had died while living at the home, and then beat them for crying.

The narrative grew deeper. When she herself was taken to see her mother, she went with a sudden gleam of hope in her eyes that she could still remember, a hope that had survived despite all the sights she had seen. She saw her mother in the distance and wanted to run to her but was held back. She did not want the same fate as her father. Nor could she scream and cry and be killed like her sister. She froze at what she witnessed. Her mother was being held roughly by a man, Dieter, a fellow prisoner she knew. To their side was a young camp guard, Ernst, pointing his gun at her mother. There was a moment when her mother looked at her. A second that lasted a lifetime. Her elegant mother now skeletal and dressed in rags. Her gleam of hope meeting her mother's terror, her mother's incapacity to help her, her incapacity to help her mother. A moment that haunted her and would last for decades.

At a sign from Ernest, Dieter began to punch and kick her mother viciously. She fell to the ground before Ernst finally shot her. Beatrice was marched back. Her world was now totally changed.

When she was released and at the point of dying of starvation, she already understood that Dieter would have been killed if he did not attack her mother. She felt his position was no different to her father's. Dieter had family who might just survive the war. And she knew that Ernst, the young Nazi guard who shot her mother, was aware that he too would be killed if he did not do what was ordered. Indeed, she saw them as twins that history had placed on opposing sides but subject to the same evil. Dieter found ways of providing a cube of chocolate for Beatrice and, later, work that allowed her the possibility of survival. He wanted to atone. Beatrice had forgiven him: "It was the law of the animal world. Eat or be eaten, kill or be killed."

To my knowledge, no-one in this sequence was a sadist, a psychopath, an innate torturer or a cruel person. And yet evil acts were perpetrated, re-enacted and co-constructed through the terrible fear each carried.

Beatrice could not bear the sight of children hoping to see their parents. It did not matter if they had mad hope and their parents would never come, or if their parents really were coming. Both states painfully reminded her of her own traumatized child-self. She also could not bear the sounds of crying children because it reminded her of her sister's murder.

Indeed, at one level, Beatrice behaved in that "mad" period like a pedophile. A pedophile is not someone who "loves" children in a perverted way. A pedophile is really someone who hates children through a projection of the hated child-self onto suitable other children—like Isaac Brown. Projection of the hated vulnerable child-self and an identification with the abuser is what mainly fuels pedophilia.

Beatrice was also like the infanticidal mother who murders her baby because she cannot bear its crying. Such mothers are described as "evil monsters" who "do not care". The problem is that they care too much because their own crying child-self is haunting them on the inside and outside.

The look that passed between 13-year-old Beatrice and her mother before her mother was killed was indeed like Ferenczi's confusion of tongues (1932) in which a terrible attachment is created through suffering. "The precocious maturity of the fruit that was injured by a bird or insect" (Ferenczi, 1932, p. 165).

In our work Beatrice and I agreed that the look that passed between her and her mother, through no fault of theirs, was one in which the child received the terrible final agonies of the parent and could not filter it. She hated her mother for this in the same way that child observers of domestic violence hate their mothers for forcing them to see that a mother cannot protect herself or her child. But this hatred is twinned with guilt because hatred is combined with ambivalent love. We can only guess at the unbearable turmoil expressed in her mother's eyes as she gazed at her child in "smart clothes" and with a gleam in her eye.

I never met the actual Dieter, but I have met many like him, male and female, including child soldiers and child alters of people whose DID [dissociative identity disorder] showed signs of being created deliberately. Ferenczi saw such children as experiencing confusion, fragmentation and loss of confidence in their own selves, all being heightened when incest or violent physical abuse occurred. To survive, the child takes in the badness and is consumed by it. This is what Fairbairn (1952) brilliantly termed the "moral defense."

As Clarke (2012, p. 204) explains

> The child seeks to purge his objects of their badness by taking this badness upon himself and is rewarded by the sense of security that an environment of good objects confers. However, this outer security is purchased at the price of inner security as his

ego is henceforth left at the mercy of a band of internal persecutors. The bad objects the child internalizes are unconditionally bad and, since the child has internalized them, and thus identifies with them, then he is unconditionally bad. In order to be able to redress this unconditional badness the child internalizes his good objects, and the nurturing aspects of his/her caregivers which assume a super-ego role.

Being made to helplessly witness something violent and/or sexual involving adults is something that occurs through all kinds of abuse, from domestic abuse to child soldiers. Survivors of extreme abuse have also spoken of a ritual in which a child is deliberately made to witness a murder so that the pain is transmitted into them through their eyes in the hope the adult will then not feel what they have done.

Beatrice was able to achieve some resolution before the pain from her cancer took over. She could even laugh when I quoted Philip Larkin's famous poem "This be the verse" to her. The poem concludes with the observation that as man hands misery on to man "don't have any kids yourself." Beatrice had not. What she had lived through made her feel unsafe having children. There are other survivors who can be more attached to life and the ongoingness of being. Despite the significant impact of trauma, each person has their own individual capacity for resilience and ways of coping.

"I went mad," she said.

> The children reminded me of myself. They kept hoping they would see a parent, but their parents had all died or rejected them. They weren't yet hardened and hopeless. You could see that gleam of longing in their eye. I could not bear it. I wanted to poke their eyes out. I dressed them so beautifully when someone did come. But it broke the hearts of all the unwanted ones. And I could not bear their crying. I got flashbacks of my sister crying and being shot for it, and then my father being murdered. Tears, for me, were like bombs. The home unravelled me and all the work I had done. I cannot forgive myself for shouting at the children and even hitting them.

She then hesitantly and with great pallor explained:

You see, I was finally allowed to see my mother, in that place. My hair was combed, and I was put in something new. I did not think why. I just so wanted her to see I was still a good tidy girl because it mattered to her. But they had deliberately taken me to watch her be killed. Just to hurt her more. I did not matter.

She went white and silent.

I went back and put on the dead clothes of a friend who had died. Somehow, I went mad in that home. It made me see what I could not bear to remember. I wanted to silence their crying. I could not bear their noise. But they wouldn't be quiet. They were too upset, and I lost it. I lost it. I was back with a murdered sister, father and mother.

None of the staff in the children's home reported her damaging behavior. This shocked her. It was she herself who recognized her dysfunctional behavior and resigned. She pointed out that for the staff, even in her mad state, she was on the whole a less abusive head than the previous one who assaulted the children regularly.

In the UK physical punishment of children has now been forbidden in schools but is still allowed in the home, unlike in most of Europe. Internationally, adult violence as an outcome of transmission of generational trauma from assault on children is proved. Ironically, one of the most brilliant researchers in this field, Professor David Finkelhor, is from the USA, where in many states the legal status of corporal punishment in the school and home by adults makes for toxic outcomes (2008). Indeed, he has created an umbrella term, "Developmental Victimology," for all the many forms of child victimization.

Obedience, from my experience, is one of the key constituents of the need to perpetrate, especially when joined with fear. It was obedience and fear that were behind the actions of Dieter and Ernst. To be at risk of annihilation, a nothing, a disposable nothing, especially when one's own life is at stake, means it is better to become the other, the torturer. It is too unbearable to inhabit the mind and body of the attacked one. Additionally, to be forced to annihilate another, the potential victim must be stripped of his/her humanness and perceived as a "thing".

Milgram and obedience

Stanley Milgram conducted some memorable experiments that have been replicated many times over and have a significant and painful place in our understanding of human behavior and evil.

As I have written elsewhere (Sinason, 2008), with the trial of Eichmann causing enormous international publicity and rethinking of Nazi war crimes, Milgram was influenced by the groundbreaking work of New York philosopher and immigrant Hannah Arendt. In writing her famous concept of "the banality of evil" Arendt (1963) stated that Eichmann was not a sadist but a bureaucrat. This dovetailed with Milgram's concerns around obeying orders and the ethical, moral and philosophical issues involved. He devised an experiment, which showed conclusively how 65% of people would obey an order which went contrary to their views on the importance of human dignity and care if a "researcher/authority figure" told them to.

While the evil of obeying orders was easiest to examine when looked at retrospectively at Nazi atrocities, there was little social capacity for taking the same concept forwards to Guantanamo Bay, Abu Ghraib, "rank abuse,", the speed of the Rwandan genocide, cannibalism in Bosnia, honor killings, all of which point to the centrality of obedience in the social and religious psyche. Lloyd De Mause (1974) is one of the few psychoanalytic historians to endorse this, backed by the work of crusading psychoanalysts such as Alice Miller, who addresses the issues of beating, submission and obedience in childhood.

A perpetrating female alter in a man with a DID proudly said her name was Evil. She proudly announced it spelled out "live" back to front. And she could live through anything, all the electric shocks and beatings and rapes that made other people cry or die or give up. And she was so good at managing this that now the important people who did all this had let her be the punisher. She had a belt and a knife, and she knew how to administer the electric shocks and the cuts in the right places too. It was fun.

> I would like to change my name, like you said, to something nicer. But when I put the knife in, my scars just close as if it never happened to me. And when they scream and I say they are nothing, no thing, no body, I know I am a somebody. I have a face. I do the talking. And they are silenced.

In considering perpetrators as the receivers and transmitters of evil I could have focussed on sadism (Sinason, 2018) or infanticidal attachment in perpetrator alters with DID (Sachs, 2017; Sinason, 2018) or the impact of religious concepts of evil on cult perpetrators. However, the tragic eyes of Beatrice, an involuntary perpetrator, haunted me and in the end the obviousness, if not the banality, of evil filled my mind. Our mass media use the non-psychological term "monster" when examining heinous crimes. This allows the delusion that we only need to catch a monster for all evil to end forever, like the war that will end all wars. Fred and Rose West were once babies who were failed. Accepting the resilience of survivors who do not re-enact the cruelty they experienced does not absolve us of responsibility for those who are not able to stop offending. By examining evil and how it is perpetuated we have more of a possibility of a humane society that reduces its numbers of non-innocent bystanders.

References

Aitkenhead, D. (December 17, 1995). I'm so like my dad, says Stephen West. *The Independent*. Retrieved from www.independent.co.uk/news/uk/home-news/im-so-like-my-dad-says-stephen-west-1526097.html.

Arendt, H. (1963). *Eichmann in Jerusalem: A report on the banality of evil.* New York, NY: Viking Press.

Baron-Cohen, S. (2011). *Zero degrees of empathy.*London: Penguin.

Browne, K. (1993). Violence in the family and its links with child abuse. In C. J. Hobbs and J. M. Wynne (1995) (Eds.), *Bailliere's clinical paediatrics* (pp. 149–165). London: Bailliere Tyndall.

Clarke, G. S. (2012). Failures of the moral defence in the films *Shutter Island, Inception* and *Memento*: Narcissism or schizoid person disorder? *International Journal of Psychoanalysis, 93*, 205–212.

Clarkson, P. (1963). *The bystander: An end to innocence in human relationships.* London: Whurr.

De Mause, L. (1974). *The history of childhood.* New York, NY: Psychohistory Press.

De Zulueta, F. (1993). *The traumatic roots of destructiveness/from pain to violence.* London: Whurr.

Fairbairn, W. R. D. (1952/1981). *Psychoanalytic Studies of the Personality.* London: Routledge and Kegan Paul.

Ferenczi, S. (1909). Introjection and transference. In *Sex in psychoanalysis* (pp. 35–57). New York, NY: Basic Books.

Ferenczi, S. (1955). Confusion of tongues between adults and the child. In *Final contributions to the problems and methods of psychoanalysis* (pp. 156–167). London: Hogarth Press. (Original work published 1932).

Finkelhor, D. (2008). *Child victimization*. Oxford: Oxford University Press.

Grand, S. (2010). *The reproduction of evil*. New York, NY: Routledge.

Howell, E. F. (1996). Dissociation in masochism and psychopathic sadism. *Contemporary Psychoanalysis*, *3*, 427–455.

Kahr, B. (1993). Ancient infanticide and modern schizophrenia: The clinical uses of psychohistorical research. *Journal of Psychohistory*, *20*, 267–273.

Kahr, B. (2007). The infanticidal attachment. *Attachment: New Directions in Psychotherapy and Relational Psychoanalysis Journal*, *1*(2), 117–132.

Larkin, P. (2001). "This be the verse," from *Collected Poems Philip Larkin*. New York, NY: Farrar Straus and Giroux.

Milgram, S. (1974a). *Obedience to authority: An experimental view*. New York, NY: HarperCollins.

Milgram, S. (1974b). The perils of obedience. In *Harper's Magazine*, December, abridged and adapted from *Obedience to Authority*.

O'Brien, Z. (September 17, 2018). Fred West's daughter fears her serial killer father had more than 30 victims as she reveals she's kept her son in the dark about his grandparents and their sickening crimes. MailOnline. Retrieved from www.dailymail.co.uk/news/article-6175191/Fred-Wests-daughter-fears-serial-killer-father-30-victims.html.

Sachs, A. (2017). Through the lens of attachment relationship: Stable DID, active DID and other trauma-based mental disorders. *Journal of Trauma and Dissociation*, *18*(3), 319–339.

Sinason, V. (1986). *Mental handicap and the human condition*. London: Free Association.

Sinason, V. (1996). From abused to abuser. In C. Cordless and M. Cox (Eds.), *Forensic psychotherapy: Crime, psychodynamics and the offender patient* (pp. 371–382). London: Jessica Kingsley.

Sinason, V. (2004). Learning disability as trauma [PhD thesis]. St Georges Hospital Medical School Library.

Sinason, V. (2008). From social conditioning to mind control. In A. Sachs and G. Galton (Eds.), *Forensic aspects of DID*. Forensic psychotherapy monograph series (pp. 167–185). London: Karnac.

Sinason, V. (2012). Infanticide and paedophilia as a defence against incest. In J. Adlam, A. Aiyehbusi, P. Pleinot, et al. (Eds.), *The therapeutic milieu under fire* (pp. 175–186). London: Jessica Kingsley.

Sinason, V. (2017). Dying for love: An attachment problem with some perpetrator introjects. *Journal of Trauma and Dissociation*, *18*(3), 340–355.

Sinason, V. (2018). Sexual sadism in ritual abuse: The dilemma of the perpetrator. In A. Seghal (Ed.), *Sadism: Psychoanalytic developmental perspectives* (pp. 51–75). London: Karnac.

Chapter 6

The Other within

White shame, Native American genocide

Sue Grand

My awareness of collective racial shame began during a visit to Prague. I was standing in the Spanish synagogue in the Jewish ghetto. Awed by the Moorish beauty of this synagogue, I was chilled by its history. Case after case held Jewish artifacts, plundered by the Nazis. Sacred objects, purged of the living hands that once held them. Then shipped across Europe, to be displayed in a museum, once the Final Solution was complete. After the triumph of the Reich. For the gaze of a purified, Aryan race. I am imagining them, gazing at my extinction: blue-eyed, blond, unknowing, unthinking. Reading informational plaques that re-write my extermination. We would simply vanish into Aryan modernity.

Standing in the Spanish synagogue, I think about genocide and extinction, about who writes the history of atrocity. I am haunted, but I am innocent. Then, memory and history crack open. Suddenly, I am an adolescent, looking at another display under glass. I am looking at the Indian displays and dioramas at the Museum of Natural History in New York City (NYC). What, precisely, am I seeing? Life-size, three-dimensional portraits of hunters and gatherers. An enormous stuffed buffalo, ancient pottery, primitive tools, loin cloths, beaded leather, feather headdresses, peace pipes, artifacts of burial. For us, as children, these dioramas were alluring portals to a mythic past. They were realistic and yet magical, sealed and enclosed, but surely possessed of some hidden door—we wanted to get inside them, and time travel to the "wild west". Intriguing and primitive, these still-life Indians were figural archives of ancient knowledge, spiritual links to the natural world. They were formidable warriors, sensual and cruel, powerful, fearless, both noble *and* savage. They were the precursors to white modernity, barefoot trackers lost to NYC pavement. They were the legendary ghosts of "our" pre-history. None of us actually knew a "real Indian"; they had simply vanished with time.

In the Spanish synagogue I am having dual vision. I am here, now, imagining Aryans looking at *my* extinction. And I am reading informational plaques that re-write the Indian extermination. I am brown-eyed, blond, unknowing, unthinking, oblivious. Gazing at these still-life hunter/gatherers, everything seems pastoral, and then, simply, not. Times changed, the buffalo disappeared. At one moment, I was just standing there in my Jewishness, looking at plundered silver candlesticks, prayer books, menorahs. I was certain about the locus of Good and Evil, and I knew which side I was on. But then, my perspective and my identity shift. The Nazi intention refracts white American mythology, and I am no longer sure who or what I am, or where Good and Evil reside, or what racist lives inside me, or what moral axis I am living in. Imagining Aryan eyes on *my* bones, I discover myself, looking through *Aryan* eyes *at* Native American bones. My persecuted *Jewishness* flips into a predatory American *whiteness*, and there is an all-seeing Native American eye on that whiteness. I am suffused with shame. *On whose soil have I made my home?*

Shame as revelation

My innocence is lost. As Layton (2015) suggests, my collective self has multiple identity markers, and two of them really are exactly what is visible and received: American and *white*. White: my Jewishness is slippery; my skin is marked by predation. My life is inscribed with multiple historical legacies in which I am both a victim of destruction *and* a collusive agent in the destruction of others. Shame awakens me to this complexity; it is a being-seen, in a first encounter with alterity (see Wilson, 1987). In this condition, the "vanished" Indian Other possesses his own gaze and penetrates my white blindness. I have looked through my "Aryan" eyes; I have been seen in that look, and shame refers to a failure of my own ego ideals (Wurmser, 1987). But I am in agreement with Lynd (1958): this shame can also be a call to fulfill those ideals.

In the reckoning with genocidal history, collective racial shame can have a paradoxical effect. This shame can feel persecutory, it can reify subject–object splits and moral categories; it can readily collapse into violence, denial, and vengeance, and turn us *away* from knowing the Other.

But it also encodes the voice of this Other; it can be a call to conscience, an awakening to social pathologies. In its more problematic form, shame seems to divide the sacred and the profane; it certainly imagines that the clean do not shit; it denies the ordinary human-ness of our humanity. It obscures the messiness of inter-subjectivity and ethics. It conjures a cold, unforgiving eye upon us. It vacates our world of empathy and self-compassion, and makes us want to hide from the Other.

But collective shame also anticipates movement: from moralism to ethics, from solipsism to I–Thou conversation, from denial to collective responsibility. All of this is inspired by an emergent Other, possessed of an all-seeing eye on our transgressions. To be seen by this eye: this can feel like an exposed, all-consuming badness; a sense of radical nakedness in relation to radical scrutiny. But as Lynd theorized back in 1958, shame is not simply an exposure of unwanted aspects of self. Shame disrupts our societal roles and false values—because it introduces us to another perspective that is outside of us. In the arena of race, then, collective white shame can rearrange the field of perception, and produce a crack in memory and history, when the Other has been "vanished" as white America has vanished the Indian. When we are exposed to the eye of the vanished Other, when we allow ourselves to experience our own "deserved shame" (Watkins, 2016) about cultural evil, that shame allows "our moral sense to tune in to the beacon of goodness and justice" (Lebron, 2013, p. 7). This can inspire us towards the depressive concern and restorative justice that moved so many veterans to protect the recent protests at Standing Rock.

Creative shame and the restoration of history

Psychoanalysts have tended to emphasize the sheer destructiveness of shame—as a toxic form of splitting and projection, a cruel and dangerous affect. Thus *shame* would seem to *reduce* our capacity to make amends for our own destructiveness. But does it? In this chapter I am suggesting a more nuanced understanding of shame as *affect*, *inter-subjective process*, and *cultural commentary*. I am complicating shame's toxicity by highlighting shame's *creative moment*: that breach in our white blindness that permits us to see the Other, *whom we could not see before*. As many analysts (Kohut, 1977; Wurmser, 1987; Leighton, 2004; Orange, 2010, etc.) have noted, shame can inflame the disintegrating self, incite aggression, and destroy the human links that we are seeking to restore. I am certainly *not* an advocate of this kind of shame. But as Watkins (2016), Lebron (2013), and Braithwaite (1989) suggest, there is an ethical call embedded in our retrieval of our own "deserved shame". When we cringe before the all-seeing eye, it can be a first order of engagement with the marginalized Other. We start to imagine another mind to converse with. As Lewis puts it, "The 'me' emerges in distinction from the 'other' … it is the eye of the other in me who beholds my transgression" (Lewis, 1995, p. 92). If we can acknowledge shame and mitigate its inflammation, the Other outside can become increasingly visible. And this visibility enables us to query cultural evil and our collusion with that evil. This shift is potentiated as the *I* (eye) of the oppressed perceives, externalizes, and separates from its oppressor (Gaztambide, 2017). Now, as Benjamin (1988) describes it, there is, "a new possibility of colliding with the outside and becoming alive in the presence of an equal other" (p. 221).

To defeat this dialogic possibility, psychopathic regimes often construct seamless insularity for the dominant, so that this visibility is occluded. In her work on "white fragility" DiAngelo (2006) describes these formidable white arrangements: radical forms of exploitation and segregation that foreclose all encounter with our racialized Other. In such radical segregation, there is no hope of finding our way towards reparative guilt. Reparative guilt is predicated on our proximity to the wounded Other, and it is predicated on our wounded Other seeing *us*. Reparative guilt is threatening, and de-stabilizing, for racist regimes; it is precisely why oppression is hidden from view. When this concealment reaches its apex, the master narrative is almost seamless. This is precisely what whiteness achieved with the "vanishing" of the American Indian. In this mythic vanishing, there was no agentic destruction. Shame cannot rupture our insularity or expose our agency. Ambivalence cannot be evoked; and reparative guilt is pre-empted before it can arrive.

The American genocide has been an exemplar of this malignant cultural condition; it has produced a seamless, non-reflective, collective white narcissism. Whenever we are in this cultural condition, we need to be startled by an outside that is outside of us. Repair cannot begin with depressive concern and reparative guilt. It must begin with the rupturing gaze of wounded otherness. If we are not psychopathic, and if we have a way to tolerate the induced shame, history will begin to penetrate us. It can feel toxic to experience what Watkins (2016) refers to as our "deserved shame". But if we hold each other well enough in the first shock of this mortification, that zone can become facilitative of racial justice.

The question, for me, then is *not* how we *avoid* experiencing *creative shame*. It is how we contain, empower, and decode this together, within a shared sense of tragic complexity, and an understanding of our flawed human goodness. This allows us to resist participation in psychopathic structures. Without this containment, we can get locked down into persecutory systems of *malignant shame*. There, we will try to put our shame back into the Other, reproducing their sense of "*undeserved shame*" (Watkins, 2016) in escalating systems of cruelty. To affirm creative shame while we mutually contain shame's potential for savagery: this is our collective challenge. To face this challenge, we need to understand this: creative shame is not a stable state or individual capacity. It is an intersubjective *moment* in a fast-moving inter-subjective *process—a process that readily becomes toxic*. We need to greet creative shame in a spirit of compassion, so that we don't slide into malignant shame. This empathic reception is not false forgiveness; it does *not* obscure our transgressions *or* the emergent subjectivity of the Other. Rather, it restores our humanity, so that we can begin the movement towards restorative justice.

For me, this collective responsibility began in the Spanish synagogue. Once, I was riveted by those displays at the Museum of Natural History. I wanted those still-life Indians to come alive. Suddenly, in Prague they came alive with a vengeance. They have continued to rupture my white blindness, and they have called on me to know history. This history is terrible; it is myth-busting; it keeps reawakening my collective racial shame. I have come to know this: I am one of the persecuted, and I am implicated in the persecution of others. Some of my Jewish-American forebears bought and sold human beings (see Jordan, 1995) in their quest for wealth and whiteness. And after Prague, the Holocaust will be forever linked to the Native American genocide, which Hitler actually praised for its inspiration (Stannard, 1992; Sterba, 1996; Coates, 2014). As Sterba notes (1996), our atrocities certainly rivaled Hitler's, and our "manifest destiny" became his *Lebensraum*.

Strategies of racial disappearance

Ever since the incident in Prague I have been thinking about racial guilt and racial shame and genocidal vanishing. I am thinking about the differential structures of racial subjugation; the differential myths that sustain these structures, and ways they evoke/suppress our deserved shame and guilt. In the United States, black slavery and indigenous extermination were twinned; they were parallel, inter-dependent regimes for constructing white wealth. But they also had distinctive arrangements of visibility and/or vanishing; I believe that these arrangements have bearing on our capacity for collective shame or guilt.

The enslavement of Africans, the extermination of the Indians: these systems were both clearly genocidal. At the first European contact, it is estimated that the Native population in the territorial United States was 5 million. By 1890 there were 248,000 (Bruyneel, 2007). The number of African slaves who died during the middle passage is estimated in the *millions* (see Sterba, 1996), without accounting for their deaths *in* slavery. In the colonial era, both peoples were enslaved by Europeans for trade and free labor.[1] Both were starved, tortured, and rapidly worked to death.[2] Beginning in the 1600s, settlers in Rhode Island engaged in the trans-Atlantic slave trade, exchanging Native captives for African slaves. As Gallay (2009) put it, "both Indians and Africans were depicted as savage heathens" (p. 3).

But by the eighteenth century, our home-grown genocides bifurcated into divergent pathways. These pathways overlapped, converged, and exacerbated each other;[3] but they differentially constructed racial presence and racial absence. With regard to this differential project, George Washington put it rather succinctly: "the gradual extension of our Settlements will as certainly cause the Savage as the Wolf to retire; both being beasts of prey tho they differ in shape" (as cited in Saunt, 2005, p. 17).

The differential math of genocide

Africans arrived on this continent stripped of everything except their labor. Indigenous peoples would be exploited for labor, but also for skills, resources, and land. For settler imperialism, both redness and blackness became subservient to whiteness; they both had to absorb malignant projections, and justify white dominance. But, over time, this dominance required the visibility and controlled proximity/distance of "whites" and "blacks". On the east coast, in the eighteenth century, the plantation sugar economy expanded. This economy relied on vast infusions of slaves. The Native population was already decimated by slavery, extermination, starvation, and disease. But African slaves were constantly being replenished. By the eighteenth and nineteenth centuries, skin color was raced, and slavery was raced as *black*. African slave labor didn't entirely replace Native slave labor in the territorial United States, but by that era, another genocidal project became more salient with the Native population: that is, the land and dominance to be gained from their extermination and/or removal.[4] Thus, African American slavery was grounded in proximal castes of whiteness and blackness. Native American extermination became a divine mission of westward expansion and Indian absence. To build the U.S. economy, "redskins" had to "vanish" from the landscape of whiteness.

And such is the perversity of racism: once slavery was raced as black, the historical truth of Native American slavery *vanished* from white guilt and white consciousness. Of course, throughout our history, to be black is also to be disappeared and murdered. Jim Crow, convict labor, lynching, mass incarceration, police shootings—these atrocities are acts of disappearance. But before and after the Indian Removal Act of 1830, U.S. wealth has been grounded in the regulated *presence of* whiteness and blackness, and in Native American "vanishing". Whiteness has always extruded blackness but whiteness has not written blackness into an extinct, distant past. Indeed, whiteness has claimed superiority through its opposition with blackness. But after the eighteenth century, land seizure required the disappearance of "redskins".

"Redskins" were further sequestered from whiteness by master narratives about American origination. These narratives tell us that Europeans "discovered" America; that US civilization began with European settlement. They tell us that *we* created modernity, that this modernity was an essential Good,[5] and that Indians were unable to adapt and assimilate, thereby writing *themselves* out of existence. As O'Brien (2010) notes, local histories of nineteenth-century New England were regularly identifying the "last Indian".[6] This narrative of disappearance was mythologized in James Fennimore Cooper's "American masterpiece", *The Last of the Mohicans*. Disappearance through a failure of adaptation: this myth is thoroughly contradicted by historians. The indigenous population was extraordinarily adaptive to its colonizers (see Miles, 2005; Saunt, 2005; Gallay, 2009; O'Brien, 2010; Dunbar-Ortiz, 2014). Nonetheless, those who survived extermination, cultural annihilation, and disease were forced to march, starving, and nearly naked in the snow, to the barren "Indian territory" west of the Mississippi. Most of them died on this "trail of tears".

White settlers were infinitely inventive in their practices of extermination and erasure. Those Indians who somehow remained in physical proximity to whiteness were often re-inscribed as not-really-Indian. Here, there is a stunning, predatory differential between the twin genocides. In African American slavery the one-drop rule was used to define blackness. As white masters raped slave women, questions arose about the condition of the children. Did they follow the condition of the slave mother, or that of the master father? If they followed the father into whiteness, these children would gain their freedom. With the one-drop rule, slave states determined that just one drop of blackness disqualified these children from claiming whiteness, thus protecting the slave economy from the financial losses of manumission. Through rape, the one-drop rule of African slavery actually *increased* the number of black slaves, while sustaining the (relative) visibility of blackness to whiteness. But the Native American predicament operated in reverse: a drop of whiteness was used to eradicate "redness", although redness could never acquire the full privilege of whiteness. In the official narrative, "real Indians" were only the "full bloods" who always maintained traditional practices. In most land treaties (all of which were broken), only these "full-blooded Indians" held land rights. But, of course, over centuries of slavery, rape, accommodation, and assimilation, Native Americans had engaged with white settlers and black slaves and black freemen. There were inter-cultural penetrations; cultural transformations; inter-cultural kinship networks; mingled DNA; and the destruction of indigenous land, culture, and economies, and therefore fewer "full bloods" living traditional lives. Since only "full bloods" had land rights, then most Indians could be expelled from their land.

Here we can see the differential math of white wealth and of racial subjugation: black slaves are multiplied by their one-drop rule, while the Indian population is subtracted through its inverse. When Native Americans did assimilate and adapt, their "semi-whiteness" disqualified them as "real Indians". Reading history, one has the impression of an unseen psychopathic hand arranging all this madness. All of these strategies constructed and sustained the myth of the "vanishing Indian", as Native peoples were regulated out of their own identity and existence.

This myth recast genocide as evolution: redskins just seemed to fade away into White Homo Erectus.[7]

It is no accident, then, that centuries later, U.S. psychoanalysis has been silent about this atrocity, and its traumatic legacies. In the twenty-first century, mythic narratives keep erasing atrocity and writing the Indian out of existence. Certainly, with the exceptions of Apprey (2003); Gump (2000, 2010) Alan Bass (2003), and Grand (2014), psychoanalysts have barely attended to African American slavery. But we have attended not at all to the Native American genocide. This absence in psychoanalysis parallels the void in our national narrative. Where Native American trauma should be inscribed, there is only an *absence without commentary*. This mirrors the problem of *who* is writing on psychoanalysis and what culture, and region, of the United States that they are writing within. White psychoanalysts of the urban northeast live in some proximity with anti-black racism; many white analysts are addressing that racism (Altman, 2000; Suchet, 2007; Grand, 2014). But—and this is a terrible admission—for analysts in the urban northeast, Indians can seem archaic and so absent that they can't even elicit this white racial address. This psychoanalytic silence perpetuates our national myth.

To break up this myth, we need these moments of creative shame. White presence, Indian absence: this was not about evolution. It was about centuries of warfare, rape, starvation, and enslavement; disease; broken treaties; laws that forbid Indians from hunting, trapping, and fishing on their own land; land theft; narrowing racial laws; the purposeful slaughter of the buffalo and provision of smallpox-infected blankets; and the maddening switchbacks through which whites defined the "blood quantums" of "real Indians". And this absence is not about innocent white settlers under attack by savage warriors. This is a history of asymmetrical violence, of white predators, and of Native American victims. As Dunbar-Ortiz (2014) points out, the colonialists *always* addressed indigenous tribes with practices of total extermination, using atrocities against civilians that were previously unknown to indigenous warfare. Contrary to our national mythology, scalping was invented *by* white settlers; Indian scalps were sold for profit, and celebrated as conquest.[8] Prior to Andrew Jackson's ascent to the White House, his "troops fashioned reins for their horses' bridles from skin stripped from the Muskogee bodies" (Dunbar-Ortiz, 2014, p. 99).

Souvenirs from these corpses were given as gifts and the mutilated bodies were referred to as "redskins" (Dunbar-Ortiz).

In all of this malignancy we obscured indigenous protest:

> Why should you take by force that from us which you can have by love? Why should you destroy us, who have provided you with food? What can you get by war? … You see us unarmed, and willing to supply your wants, if you will come in a friendly manner, and not with swords and guns, as to invade an enemy.
>
> Wahunsonacock, Powhatan, 1609

Refusing gratitude and denying their own dependency on Native resources and generosity, whiteness clamored about "manifest destiny". White greed moved west with ethnic cleansing, erasing indigenous culture, be-fouling and stealing the land, removing survivors to remote and unwanted land. And insofar as whiteness did have proximity to its victims, whiteness kept extruding its "deserved shame" (Watkins, 2016) into the imago of the "drunk Injun".

Slaves and masters: transmissions of shame and malignance

Throughout all of this predation, white dominance kept sundering the natural alliances that could have defeated it. In our early history, Africans and Indians were enslaved, starved, tortured, and persecuted *together.* Their alliance would have been formidable. But American wealth has always been grounded in a divisive hierarchical system of "vanished Others", of those who have been raced, classed, and gendered into subjugation, exploitation, antagonism, and mistrust. All arranged in layers of relative privilege, colonized by scarcity, written and divided by the master narrative, so that unity and resistance are weakened. It's all here, in this terrible history.

In the colonial era, the French, Spanish, and British were in contest for dominance, all of them enlisting Native warriors, commanding them with threats and promises, seducing them with European goods and weapons, enlisting them as partners in commerce and as slavers, exploiting their prior inter-tribal conflicts, so that inter-tribal alliances are in continuous flux.[9] In every region, each tribe was its own nation with distinct language, culture, economies, region, and religion. There were no *Indians* until European presence made "them" into *redskins*. From the beginning, Europeans persecuted these nations as one, even as they exploited their pre-existing rivalries and alliances. The effect was bewildering, and solidarity was belated. Indian Confederacies could not be formed until the indigenous population was being decimated, and diverse nations recognized themselves as the annihilated Other, raced by Europeans as *redskins*:

> Brothers – my people wish for peace; the red men all wish for peace; but where the white people are, there is no peac̲e̲ for them ... The white men ... do not think red men sufficiently good to live ... Brothers – if you do not unite with us, they will first destroy us, and then you will fall an easy prey to them. They have destroyed many nations of red men because they were not united, because they were not friends to each other. Brothers – we must be united, we must smoke the same pipe; we must fight each other's battles. Tecumsah, Swanee. Approximately 1790.
>
> (Nabokov, 1999, pp. 97–98)[10]

Persecution and colonization always seem to arouse our mutual terror and our hatred; this condition seduces, violates, starves, and degrades us; it pits us against one another in gradations of privilege, objectification, survival, and abjection. Who is a subject? Who is disposable? Predatory conquest is brilliant and incisive: it perceives, and foments, our rivalries, competitions; our cravings for wealth, status, dignity, security, and inclusion. In these conditions, we can all become agents of the machine that is destroying us. We can commit what I have called the "bestial gesture of survival" (Grand, 2000), dehumanizing those who are suffering the same fate.

Divide and conquer: U.S. wealth is a historic register of this obscenity, and most of us have been implicated in it. If Indian resistance was much less violent than whiteness imagines, it is not always innocent. Native peoples were both slavers and the enslaved. There were slaving tribes who captured other tribes, entering into commercial arrangements with the very colonists who would subsequently enslave these Indian slavers. While Africans were being kidnapped by Africans in Africa, for European shipment to American colonies, Indians were being captured by Indians, for European shipment to the Caribbean colonies, to Canada, to the Great Lakes region, and from the south to the north in the territorial United States (Gallay, 2002; Newell, 2009; Snyder, 2010; Rushforth, 2012).[11]

On our shores, Indians were enslaved *with* Africans, and they formed familial bonds. Insofar as African slaves and Native peoples sustained their alliances, they effectively threatened the genocidal regime. The Tuscararoa provided sanctuary for escaped black slaves, and formed an underground railroad as early as the 1600s; the earliest slave revolt was jointly mobilized by Native and African slaves in NYC, in 1708 (Miles, 2009). The Seminoles of Florida welcomed fleeing black slaves, formed kinship systems, became fierce warriors of resistance, and were renown as the "undefeated tribe" (see Henson, 1849; Brooks, 2002; Saunt, 2005; Hill, 2009; Miles, 2011; Krauthamer, 2013). But according to Saunt (2005) and Miles (2005), alliances between black slaves and Native peoples seem sparse. And when these alliances occurred, white dominance could read its future defeat. During the Civil War,

> some ten thousand men in Indian Territory, made up of Indigenous volunteers, along with African Americans who had freed themselves and even some Anglo-Americans, engaged in guerrilla warfare against the Confederate Army. They fought from Oklahoma into Kansas, where many of them joined unofficial Union units that had been organized by abolitionists who had trained with John Brown years earlier.
>
> (Dunbar-Ortiz, 2014, p. 136)

Throughout our history, white wealth has been endangered by such solidarity, and it has splintered all of these alliances. Throughout United States history, poor whites and ethnic immigrants have been lured into false consciousness by the promise of wealth and whiteness (Williams, 1998). Black slaves and Native tribes were divided by racial hierarchies, the racing of slavery, and by the false promise of Indian survival if they assimilated to white "civilization". The resulting divisions between redness and blackness were exacerbated by laws that criminalized sanctuary of fleeing African slaves (Miles, 2005; Krauthamer, 2013).

The pressures of indigenous survival undermined alliances between these two persecuted peoples. Nonetheless, Miles, Snyder, Saunt, and Gallay all conclude that Native peoples did share some culpability in the African

American genocide, much as my own Jewish ancestors of the fifteenth and sixteenth centuries participated in the trans-Atlantic slave trade (Jordan, 1995). Until about the mid nineteenth century, Africans were enslaved *with* Native peoples. Throughout the southeast, northeast, and Indian Territory, Indians had been stripped of the resources that defined and sustained them; but, like all of us, they could also be lit up by the greed that lit up their colonizers. These tribes owned, and traded in, black slaves. According to these historians, Indians had a significant role in the domestic slave trade, even as they formed bonds of kinship and mingled DNA (Miles, 2005; Saunt, 2005; Snyder, 2010).

And by the late seventeenth century, colonists had established their contradictory "one-drop rules" for Africans and Indians. They had "bizarre blood-quantum requirements claiming that Native identity 'dissolves' with intermarriage … (colonists) began recasting indigenous people as 'colored', 'mulatto', 'French'—anything but 'Indian'" (Senier, 2014, p. 2). Blackness was, as always, at the lowest rung of the caste system, and, given the one-drop rule of *African* slavery, blackness could *never* attain *either* redness *or* whiteness. For a Native person to be labeled "colored" or "mulatto" or kin with blackness: this could further dilute Native American identity and land claims. It would distance them forever from any entry into "white civilization". And to have one-drop of blackness: this was to be at risk for being sold into black chattel slavery. Native American survival would increasingly require the affiliation with whiteness and the corresponding disavowal of blackness.

In all of these ways, the white incursion broke apart the natural alliances that would have defeated it, and mutual antagonisms were intentionally inflamed. Black Indians often found themselves doubly abased and vanished, by both whiteness and redness, existing at the marginalized nexus of this complicated history. Blackness *could* be absorbed into Indian kinship systems, but only if this blackness was denied and vanished. But southeast Native tribes[12] would also acculturate, and accrue wealth and status by establishing plantations, enslaving blacks, and repudiating black kin.[13] Some Native planters enslaved *their own black kin* (Saunt, 2005; Miles, 2011; Krauthamer, 2013).[14] Free families of African descent continued to live in Indian nations (Snyder, 2010). But, as Dunbar-Ortiz (2014) notes, Indian tribes were continually assessing where, and with whom, they were most likely to survive and retain culture and land rights. Sometimes this assessment made for what seems, now, like very strange bedfellows. Some southeast tribes[15] would fiercely oppose abolition, support the Confederacy in the Civil War (also Minges, 2004; Saunt, 2005), and resist emancipation in Indian Territory even after the war was lost. Fleeing slavery, blacks often encountered re-enslavement as they sought sanctuary in Indian Territory. The resulting alienation and animus has haunted generations;[16] it splintered familial bonds *and* political alliances.[17,18] Recently, there is an effort to repair this legacy, and to recognize the black Indian.

Flawed human goodness: redeeming our shame

Throughout U.S. history, security, wealth, and dignity have been linked to the Holy Grail of whiteness. That whiteness has always been predicated on persecution, scarcity, division, and extermination. Any genocide that lasts centuries is not going to be a pure story. In this history, there *are* some *very* clear lines between Good and Evil; between perpetrators and their innocent victims. But in these conditions, we don't know what we, ourselves, would do. The complexity of this history can further bewilder our "deserved" and "undeserved" shame; it can make us more resistant to knowing history. Most of us cannot escape from bias and greed, from collusion, from the exigencies of terror and hunger and survival, or from the prejudicial myths written by master narratives.[19]

To resist racist regimes we need to find a way to restore the human bonds that genocide seeks to destroy. But to speak to the Other, the all-seeing eye of shame must be softened by another kind of vision. This is a compassionate sight that sees our flawed human goodness, and allows us to witness our own ignorance and welcome the stranger. Even though we are not yet purged of our prejudice. This is a form of the "radical hope" that Lear (2006) found in the dream of Plenty Coups. This radical hope has been passed through the ages; it is the story told by Josiah Henson, in his encounter with the Native American stranger,[20] as he flees African American slavery:

> We were instantly on the alert as we could hardly expect them to be friends. The advance of a few paces showed me they were Indians, with packs on their shoulders; and they were so near that if they were hostile, it would be useless to escape … they looked at me in a frightened sort of way for a moment and setting up

a peculiar howl, turned round, and ran as fast as they could ... what they were afraid of I could not imagine, unless they supposed I was the devil whom they had perhaps heard of as black. ... my wife was alarmed too, and thought they were merely running back to collect more of a party, and then to come and murder us, and she wanted to turn back. ... as we advanced, we could discover Indians peeping at us from behind the trees and dodging out of our sight. The chief ... soon discovered that we were human beings ... and now curiosity seemed to prevail. Each one wanted to touch the children who were shy as partridges ... a little while sufficed to make them understand what we were, and whither we were going and what we needed; and as little, to set them about supplying our wants, feeding us bountifully, and giving us a comfortable wigwam for our night's rest. The next day, we resumed our march ... they sent some of their young men to point out the place where we were to turn off and parted from us with as much kindness as possible.

(Henson, 1849, pp. 53–54)

Acknowledgments

Sue Grand, Ph.D. The Other Within: White Shame, Native American Genocide. *Contemporary Psychoanalysis*, copyright © the William Alanson White Institute of Psychiatry, Psychoanalysis & Psychology and the William Alanson White Psychoanalytic Society, www.wawhite.org, reprinted by permission of Taylor & Francis Ltd, http://www.tandfonline.com on behalf of the William Alanson White Institute of Psychiatry, Psychoanalysis & Psychology and the William Alanson White Psychoanalytic Society

Notes

1 O'Brien (2010) notes, for example, that the Pokanoket in Cape Cod were enslaved in 1614.
2 Gallay estimates that before 1715, approximately 30,000–50,000 Native people were taken as slaves by the British.
3 Most notably in the arena of African American slavery. In the eighteenth century, Native Americans had a considerable role in African American slavery. See Krauthamer (2013).
4 Jackson passed the Indian Removal Act in 1830.
5 This mythology is ongoing. David Brooks (*New York Times*, September 25, 2015, A35) writes in "The American Idea": "America was settled, founded

and built by people who believed they were doing something exceptional ... American was defined by its future, by the people who weren't yet here and by the greatness that hadn't yet been achieved ... once the vast continent was settled the United States would be one of the dominant powers of the globe."

6 Even now, there seem to be ongoing disputes about this firsting and lasting. In 1996, the 8,500-year-old skull of "Kennewick Man" was discovered in Washington, and claimed as Caucasian. Native Americans said that these were the bones of their ancestors, and tried to reclaim Kennewick Man for burial. Lawsuits contested repatriation. Recently, Danish scientists settled this dispute over identity and history: they conclusively determined that Kennewick Man is most closely linked to Native Americans (C. Zimmer, *New York Times*, June 19, 2015). Nonetheless, repatriation is still in doubt.

7 See Miles, 2005; Saunt, 2005; Gallay, 2009; Newell, 2009; Snyder, 2010; Senier, 2014.

8 The term "redskin" originated as a descriptor of the wounded craniums of these scalped bodies (see Dunbar-Ortiz, 2014).

9 Cited in Wilson, J. (1998). *The Earth Shall Weep*, p. 43. New York: Grove Press. Also, for example, in their effort to dominate South Carolina, the British attack French-allied Choctaws, and also attack the Apalachee to strike at the Spanish. The Chickasaws switch alliance from the French to the British, and take native slaves for the British (Gallay, 2002). In the King Philips War (1675–1676), New England colonists went to war with their allies—Mohegan and Pequot—against Wampanoags, Narragansetts, Nipmucs, and others. For Native Americans, there were 5,000 casualties (Gallay, 2009).

10 By the mid eighteenth century, the capture, and sale, of Native slaves decreased east of the Mississippi as tribes formed confederacies and refused large-scale slaving (Gallay, 2009).

11 Native slavery was officially outlawed in the mid eighteenth century, but it continued.

12 These tribes included the Choctaws, Chickasaw, Cherokee, and Creeks. Miles (2009), traces Native American plantation slave practices through the Cherokee family of Shoe Boots, and the Cherokee Van family (Miles, 2011). Krauthamer (2013) highlights these practices of the Choctaw and Chickasaw in Indian Territory.

13 According to black slave narratives, conditions varied—often Indian masters were described as more humane. See Minges, 2004.

14 The Choctaws did not develop slave codes until after removal. But later, their laws would forbid marriage with African Americans, and prohibited black slaves from learning to read or own firearms, in disturbing mimicry of white masters (Snyder, 2010).

15 The Choctaw, Chickasaw, Cherokee, Creek, and even the Seminoles (Krauthamer, 2013).

16 With the Dawes Act of 1887, federal land allotments are determined by "blood quantums", with "full blood" Indians receiving the largest allotments, and former black slaves the smallest (Krauthamer).

17 See Stolberg, *New York Times*, July 7, 2015, p. A1. The trans-generational legacy of this complexity persists: in the recent controversy about

removing the Confederate flag flying above the South Carolina capital, a white conservative wanted to erect a monument to a Cherokee chief who became a Confederate general (Pitts, *New York Times*, July 10, 2015, p A16.). To this day, there are tensions between Native tribes and "black Indians" (Saunt, 2005; Miles, 2011).

18 By contrast, Northern Creeks actually anticipated the 13th Amendment, abolishing slavery, granting freed slaves equal tribal status in September 1863 (Saunt, 2005).

19 As Snyder put it, "rather than a one-way monologue crafted by the white elites, the language of race was a dialogue shared by whites and Indians and shaped by the violent intimacy of the Southern border wars. New articulations of race blended with – and complicated – older notions of Native identity. Challenging colonialism, Indians drew on their experiences with 'Virginians' to craft a racial ideology underpinned by nativism" (2010, p. 172).

20 Northern Ohio, tribe unknown.

References

Altman, N. (2000). Black and White thinking: a psychoanalyst reconsiders race. *Psychoanalytic Dialogues*, *10*, 589–605.

Apprey, M. (2003). Repairing history: reworking transgenerational trauma. In: *Hating in the First Person Plural*. Ed.: D. Moss. New York: Other Press, pp. 3–29.

Bass, A. (2003). Historical and unconscious trauma: racism and psychoanalysis. In: *Hating in the First Person Plural*. Ed.: D. Moss. New York: Other Press, pp. 29–45.

Benjamin, J. (1988). *The Bonds of Love*. New York: Pantheon Press.

Braithwaite, J. (1989). *Crime, Shame, and Reintegration*. New York: Cambridge University Press.

Brooks, J. F. (2002). *Captives and Cousins: Slavery, Kinship and Community in the Southwest Borderlands*. Chapel Hill: University of N. Carolina Press.

Bruyneel, K. (2007). *The Third Space of Sovereignty: The Postcolonial Politics of U.S.–Indigenous Relations*. Minneapolis: University of Minnesota Press.

Coates, T. N. (Jan 16, 2014). Hitler on the Mississippi banks: thoughts on Timothy Snyder's *Bloodlands*. *The Atlantic*, internet.

DiAngelo, R. (2006). My race didn't trump my class: using oppression to face privilege. *Multicultural Perspectives*, *8*(1), 51–56.

Dunbar-Ortiz, R. (2014). *An Indigenous People's History of the United States*. Boston: Beacon Press.

Gallay, A. (2002). *The Indian Slave Trade: The Rise of the English Empire in the American South 1670–1717*. New Haven: Yale University Press.

Gallay, A. (2009). Introduction. In: *Indian Slavery in Colonial America*. Ed.: A. Gallay. Lincoln: University of Nebraska Press, pp. 1–33.

Gaztambide, D. J. (2017). A "psychoanalysis for liberation": reading Friere as an act of love. *Psychoanalysis, Culture and Society*, *22*(2), 193–212.

Grand, S. (2000). *The Reproduction of Evil: A Clinical and Cultural Perspective.* Hillsdale: Analytic Press.

Grand, S. (2014). Skin memories: on race, love and loss. *Psychoanalysis, Culture and Society, 19*, 232–249.

Gump, J. (2000). A white therapist, an African American patient – shame in the therapeutic dyad: commentary of paper by Neil Altman. *Psychoanalytic Dialogues, 10*, 619–632.

Gump, J. (2010). Reality matters: the shadow of trauma on African American subjectivity. *Psychoanalytic Perspectives, 27*(1), 42–54.

Henson, J. (1849). *The Life of Josiah Henson, Formerly a Slave, Now an Inhabitant of Canada, as Narrated by Himself.* Boston: Arthur D. Phelps.

Hill, R. W., Sr. (2009). Rotihnahon:tsi and Rotinonhson:ni: historical relationships between African Americans and the confederacy of the six nations. In: *Indivisible.* Ed.: G. Tayac. Smithsonian. National Museum of the Native American, pp. 99–109.

Jordan, W. D. (1995). Slavery and the Jews: a review of the secret relationship between blacks and Jews: volume one. *The Atlantic.* September, 1995, 1–29.

Kohut, H. (1977). *The Restoration of the Self.* Madison: International Universities Press.

Krauthamer, B. (2013). *Black Slaves, Indian Masters: Slavery, Emancipation, and Citizenship in the Native American South.* Chapel Hill: University of North Carolina Press.

Layton, L. (2015). Beyond sameness and difference: normative unconscious process and our mutual implication in each other's suffering. In: *Psychology and the Other.* Eds.: D. Goodman and M. Freeman. Oxford: Oxford University Press, pp. 168–188.

Lear, J. (2006). *Radical Hope: Ethics in the Face of Cultural Devastation.* Cambridge, MA: Harvard University Press.

Lebron, C. J. (2013). *The Color of Our Shame: Race and Justice in Our Time.* New York: Oxford University Press.

Leighton, J. (2004). The analyst's sham(e): collapsing into a one-person system. In: *Transformations in Self Psychology: Progress in Self Psychology, Vol. 20.* Ed.: W. J. Coburn. Hillsdale: Analytic Press, pp. 169–188.

Lewis, M. (1995). *Shame: The Exposed Self.* New York: Free Press.

Lynd, H. M. (1958). *On Shame and the Search for Identity.* London: Routledge/Kegan Paul.

Miles, T. (2005). *Ties that Bind: The Story of an Afro-Cherokee Family in Slavery and Freedom.* Berkeley: University of California Press.

Miles, T. (2009). Taking leave, making lives: creative quests for freedom in early black and native America. In: *Indivisible.* Ed.: G. Tayac. Smithsonian: National Museum of the Native American, pp. 139–151.

Miles, T. (2011). Of waterways and runaways: reflections on the Great Lakes in underground railroad history. *Michigan Quarterly Review, L*(3), n.p.

Minges, P. (2004). *Black Indian Slave Narratives.* Winston-Salem: John F. Blair.

Nabokov, P. (1978). *Native American Testimony: A Chronicle of Indian–White Relations from Prophecy to the Present, 1492–2000*. New York: Penguin.

Newell, E. M. (2009). Indian slavery in Colonial New England. In: *Indian Slavery in Colonial America*. Ed.: A. Gallay. Lincoln: University of Nebraska Press, pp. 33–67.

O'Brien, J. M. (2010). *Firsting and Lasting: Writing Indians Out of Existence in New England*. Minneapolis: University of Minnesota Press.

Orange, D. (2010). *Thinking for Clinici Ans: Philosophical Resources for Contemporary Psychoanalysis and the Humanistic Psychotherapies*. London: Routledge.

Rushforth, B. (2012). *Bonds of Alliance: Indigenous and Atlantic Slaveries in New France*. Chapel Hill: University of North Carolina.

Saunt, C. (2005). *Black, White, and Indian: Race and the Unmaking of an American Family*. New York: Oxford University Press.

Senier, S. (2014). Introduction. In *Dawnland Voices*. Ed.: S. Senier. Lincoln: University of Nebraska Press, pp. 1–21.

Snyder, C. (2010). *Slavery in Indian Country: The Changing Face of Captivity in Early America*. Cambridge, MA: Harvard University Press.

Stannard, D.E. (1992). *American Holocaust: The Conquest of the New World*. New York: Oxford University Press.

Sterba .J.P. (1996). Understanding evil: American slavery, the Holocaust, and the conquest of the American Indians. *Ethics*, *106*(2), 424–448.

Suchet, M. (2007). Unraveling whiteness. *Psychoanalytic Dialogues*, *17*(6), 867–887.

Watkins, M. (unpublished, 2016). The social and political life of shame in the U.S. Presidential Election 2016. Presented at the Massachusetts Institute for Psychoanalysis, Cambridge, MA.

Williams, P. (1998). The ethnic scarring of American whiteness. In: *The House that Race Built*. Ed.: W. Lubiano. New York: Vintage Books, pp. 253–264.

Wilson, E., Jr. (1987). Shame and the other: reflections on the theme of shame in French psychoanalysis. In: *The Many Faces of Shame*. Ed.: D. L. Nathanson. New York: Guildford Press, pp. 162–194.

Wurmser, L. (1987). Shame: the veiled companion of narcissism. In: *The Many Faces of Shame*. Ed.: D. L. Nathanson. New York: Guildford Press, pp. 64–93.

Chapter 7

American hierarchy

White, "good"; Black, "evil"

Cleonie White

"Three evils"

Some sixty-four years after W. E. B. DuBois' (1903) stunning declaration that "the problem of the twentieth century is the problem of the color line," Dr. Martin Luther King, Jr., the revered leader of the Civil Rights Movement, addressed the inaugural meeting of the National Conference on New Politics. In his speech entitled "The Three Evils of Society" (1967), he identified the driving forces to be interrogated in his time:

> I suspect that we are now experiencing the coming to the surface of a triple-pronged sickness that has been lurking within our body politic from the beginning: that is the sickness of *racism, excessive materialism*, and *militarism* [emphasis added].

Dr. King's observations reflect his knowledge that, as I argue, *Time has a way of keeping us tethered to its now, even as it steals into silence those lived experiences of the past which give meaning to our visions of selfhood.* Dr. King, furthermore, evidenced an uncanny attunement to history's function as *the soulmate of memory.* Indeed, *remembrances* illustrate that, *as the present is issue of the past*, only a return into the dark caverns of history will lend meaning to the constituent evils, the turbulence of our present, perpetrated upon your nation and upon you as private citizen, by the power elite, the political class.

Most of us who actively opposed the winning candidate of the 2016 U.S. presidential elections feel accosted by extreme levels of political chaos which, by design of the tribalist, nationalist, class, who vilify difference, threaten safety, and fuel fears, anxieties, profound sadness, and, often, volcanic rage. How else could Americans have elected to the highest office in the land an alleged sexual molester; a creator of, and adherent to, "alternative truths"; a man best characterized by the conservative columnist George F. Will (2017) as "America's child President ... a sad, embarrassing wreck of a man"?

All it took was a narcissistic, self-absorbed, politically toxic pied piper, eager to antagonize long-festering, racist grievances in our culture; a candidate who gleefully appealed to the baser nature of his supporters. Donald Trump's shameless vitriol, his partisan rhetoric, centered on the mythical construct, *race*; his insistence on framing observed, interpersonal differences as menacing, threatening, and dangerous, succeeded in unleashing White supremacist rage. Race is an American construct—a "shiny" object, if you will—designed to secure economic power for the social elite, while masking the impact of their greed on the lives of disenfranchised citizens, including economically depressed White Americans. *Racism, therefore, is America's evil (s)kin!*

The historic, systematic, demonization of the racialized Other in the name of American greatness is the soup in which Trump's "make America great again" ideology simmers. This equation of American conquest with American greatness—with America's "manifest destiny"—is best captured by John Gast in his patriotic painting, *American Progress* (1872). Through the air-borne body of a spirit-like woman, representing America, Gast depicts American progress, moving from the enlightened East, bringing light—education, technology—to the "dark," "uncivilized" West—to the land masses that Native Americans owned and called home. The destructive impact of this push into uncharted territory is painfully captured by Grand (2018). As Grand informs us, "By the eighteenth and nineteenth centuries, skin color was raced, and slavery was raced as black" (p. 90). Grand exposes the devious, inner workings of the colonialist, White American mind intent on securing economic superiority. Black slavery, Grand (2018) enlightens us, facilitated the vanishment of Native Americans and expansion further west: "White greed moved west with ethnic cleansing, erasing indigenous culture, befouling and stealing the land, removing survivors to remote and unwanted land" (p. 94).

"Hate," Coates (2015) declares, "gives identity ... We name the hated stranger and are thus confirmed in the tribe" (p. 60). Spewing racist, xenophobic, nationalist/isolationist ideology, Trump reinforced his supporters' fantasies that the unlimited power of his presidency would also be theirs. Trump's arrival seemed nothing short of the *Second Coming*—he, the savior of White supremacist power. "Political correctness" seems to have vanished from segments of society. People of color are again experiencing the pain of being Othered and targeted by those who feel entitled/privileged by their whiteness. Increased witnessing to police *lynchings by bullets*, notwithstanding, and infuriatingly brazen in their enacted privilege, many White Americans authorize themselves to police Black bodies and to dial 911 for reinforcement and validation when, repeatedly, any perceived threat to their safety was a figment of their own warped, racist minds. Farzan (2018) reports some of multiple such incidents: Alison Ettel (White) called the police, offended that an eight-year-old girl (Black) was selling lemonade without a permit. A White woman, Teresa Klein, called the police on a crying nine-year-old Black boy, whom she falsely accused of groping her, after (videotape showed) his backpack accidentally brushed against her in a crowded store. Non-European immigrants, most of whom seek refuge from certain death in their countries of origin, are banned at our borders. *And innocence is wrenched from border-crossing infants and young children seeking asylum.* Subjected to expressed, nationalist indignation, these children are robbed of their parents—of their *needs* and rights to secure attachments.

Dr. Christine Blasey Ford captured the nation as she gave persuasive testimony of her alleged sexual abuse at the hands of a powerful White American man, Judge Brett Kavanaugh, seeking Senate confirmation to the Supreme Court. And she was ridiculed—accused of conspiring to destroy the life of an innocent man! The women who identified with and supported her—women demanding justice—were easily reduced to a new political trope: "*MOB!*" The accused, privileged, White male is deemed "proven innocent" by President Trump, who declared that, in this country, the accused is innocent until proven guilty. Really? Really! Consider the "Central Park Five." Five Black and Hispanic teenagers accused of raping a White woman in New York's Central Park. In response to these accusations, Donald Trump purchased full-page newspaper ads—before trial—declaring that "roving bands of wild criminals roam our neighborhoods" and demanding the return of the death penalty (Mueller, Weiser, & Greenberg, 2018). Even after they were exonerated "based on DNA evidence and the detailed and accurate confession of a serial rapist" (Burns, 2016), Trump still refused to acknowledge *their* innocence, insisting that they remain guilty by reason of their false confessions (Burns, 2016).

Assuredly, Trump's position does not wear well on the conscience of White Americans whose conscious engagement with Otherness unfolds in the questioning, "moral third" spaces (Benjamin, 2018) that eschew "me/not me" splitting and promote, instead, "belief in a Third that unifies Us and Them" (Benjamin, 2018, p. 473). But for those of his supporters who have long flown high the banner of White supremacy, Trump's racially exclusionary rhetoric, his fascist ideology, and demonstrated striving toward nationalist authoritarianism, made of him the leader they had long awaited.

Below the Mason–Dixon Line: Jim Crow

The so-called "White backlash" following the 2016 election was "just a new name for an old phenomenon," as Dr. King reflected in 1967. White anxiety peaked following the Civil War and the social justice reforms following the First Reconstruction, which secured the civil and human rights of former slaves. Former slave owners chafed at the loss of the supreme economic and moral power their whiteness had once afforded them and they vowed to reclaim that privilege and restore the glory of their southern states. With the Compromise of 1877 and the election of Rutherford B. Hayes, Federal troops were recalled from deployment in the South. Shortly thereafter, the rights of citizenship afforded former slaves were summarily reversed by the White power elite of the South. Racial discrimination and segregation under newly enacted Jim Crow laws led to some of the most pernicious acts of evil perpetrated against African Americans since the Antebellum South.

New "Black Codes" (Blackmon, 2008; DuVernay, 2016) were written into law designed specifically to limit rights of citizenship, including their freedom of movement—new ways of legislating and enslaving Black bodies. Rigid segregation laws separating Blacks and Whites in all public spheres, and incarceration rates among southern Blacks, soared. This latter arrangement proved a boon to the lagging southern economy, through prisoner leasing for profit. The recent discovery of the remains of sugar cane workers in Texas is clear demonstration of the horrors inherent in this arrangement (Mervosh, 2018). Staples (2018) is brutally honest in exposing the horrific and inhumane working conditions these African American remains revealed the sugar cane workers were forced to endure. As Staples makes clear,

> [t]he dead—some of whom may have been born in slavery—are victims of the infamous convict leasing system that arose after Emancipation. Southerners sought to replace slave labor by jailing African Americans on trumped-up charges and turning them over to, among others, sugar cane plantations in the region once known as the Sugar Bowl of Texas.
>
> (Mueller et al., 2018)

What takes hold in the Jim Crow South, post Emancipation, and has been transmitted across generations, is an uncompromising institutionalization of racism (in housing, education, healthcare, and the law) that renders African Americans far more disenfranchised than their White counterparts. Today's outsized Prison Industrial Complex must be understood as a current iteration of this long history of disenfranchisement for Black citizens (Alexander, 2010/2012). It is this monetizing of Black bodies that is the underbelly of the so-called "school-to-prison pipeline" militantly soldiered by the power elite.

The era of the Civil Rights Movement witnessed the birth of a Second Reconstruction, which succeeded in reversing many of the politically sanctioned, discriminatory laws of the Jim Crow era. But this period, too, from the 1960s onward, has seen its own backlash. Critical social reforms, attacked by angry, White Americans, were categorized as "reverse discrimination" (affirmative action, for example). One need only study recent statistics to see clear links between racist Jim Crow laws and current enactments in the legal system. According to the Southern Poverty Law Center (SPLC, 2014) archives, rates of incarceration continue their unprecedented rise, despite a steady drop in crime rates in the United States. Thus, while the United States has 5% of the world's population, it houses 25% of the world's prisoners. The SPLC reports that, between 1980–2000, some 350,000 to 2.1 million, or 3% of children in the United States, had fathers who were imprisoned. Most disturbing are the statistics from the SPLC which demonstrate that African Americans are incarcerated at *six times* the rate of Whites: although people of color use drugs at roughly the same rate as White people, they are three to five times more likely to be arrested and given longer sentences.

Alexander (2010/2012) captures in stunning detail the ways in which the decisively evil, restrictive, laws of the "old" South, as "a new racial caste system," continue to be ruinous to the lives of African American men:

> The arguments and rationalizations that have been trotted out in support of racial exclusion and discrimination in its various forms have changed and evolved, but the outcome has remained largely the same. An extraordinary percentage of black men in the United States are legally barred from voting today, just as they have been throughout most of American history. They are also subject to legalized discrimination in employment, housing, education, public benefits, and jury service, just as their parents, grandparents, and great-grandparents once were ... What has changed since the collapse of Jim Crow has less to do with the basic structure of our society than with the language we use to justify it ... Rather than rely on race [explicitly], we use our criminal justice system to label people of color "criminals" and then engage in all the practices we supposedly left behind.
>
> (pp. 1–2)

Paradoxically, economically disadvantaged White Americans who, themselves, depend upon these "entitlement" programs for survival, are also placed at risk. But the deeply ensconced images of the dangerous, Black, drug-addict predator and the "welfare queen" of the Ronald Reagan era in effect instill shame, and silence potential White protest against loss of these needed programs. Again, we observe the clever methodology among those with power to manipulate minds, to racialize need, and to "erase" conscious identification with America's class of economic outcasts. Thus, even the poorest of Whites, who rely on welfare to feed themselves and their children, are made to feel, in concert with their White identity, superior to any Black American.

One might very well tag the election of Barack Obama as a backlash to the backlash to the Second Reconstruction. White Americans of conscience and African Americans formed a unified block that voted for change. Yet, paradoxically—unsurprisingly—the vision of a Black President in the White House only stirred hatred among self-identified Nazi-supporting Americans, for whom this was clear signage of their dwindling grasp on economic power and the supremacy of whiteness. Donald Trump popularized the anti-Obama "birther" movement, questioning the legitimacy of the President. The Rev. William J. Barber, II (2016) best describes this aftermath:

> We can't make sense of what's happening in front of us because, somehow, we've failed to see that this has been happening all along ... But inside this long, sad tale about America lies a roadmap for today ... I believe the turmoil we are witnessing around us today is in fact the birth pangs of a Third Reconstruction.

Americans of color bore witness during the eight years of President Obama's leadership to a pernicious rise in *naked* expressions of racism and sanctioning of brutal, deadly force against Black people—by police, teachers, and neighborhood bullies. It continues. It is not hyperbolic to argue that currently observed *freedom of racist speech* emanates from our highest levels of government. Brandishing their Confederate flags, Nazis marched in Charlottesville, North Carolina, shouting, "Jews will not replace us"; one of them drove his car into a crowd and murdered a peaceful protester; and President Trump declared that there were "some very fine people on both sides" (*The Atlantic*, 2017). Additionally, as if not content with his disparagement of his predecessor, Trump has spent his time in office exerting every effort to undo President Obama's legacy by rescinding treaties, attempting to dismantle the Affordable Care Act, and attacking the Obama era's environmental protection laws and agreements (Paris Climate Accord). And, of course, we see what he continues to do regarding immigration and asylum seekers.

"Shadow and Substance"

Although he does not identify the cultural/political world as a specific point of inquiry, I read in Bromberg's (2009/1993, pp. 165–187) writings an urgent, unspoken reach toward dynamic engagement of all spaces, including cultural spaces, within which hope, and creative narratives, are rendered relationally possible. Lending clarification for his choice of "Shadow and Substance" (1993) as the title for his paper, Bromberg writes, "I wish to convey in a single phrase my view of the unconscious as a reality that is 'inside', 'outside', *and simultaneously both*" (p. 166, emphasis added). *Indeed, traumatizing structures of society and traumatized structures of mind are inexorably linked.* The conceptualization of "the social character" by Erich Fromm (1942)—one of our early American psychoanalysts who fled the Nazi regime—holds further relevance in our efforts to understand what motivated the "Trump voter." "The social character," Fromm proposes, "comprises only a selection of traits, the essential nucleus of the character structure of most members of a group which has developed as the result of the basic experiences and mode of life common to that group" (p. 1). In his discussion of the rise of Fascist and Nazi ideology, Fromm offers further clarity:

> the lower middle class reacted to certain economic changes, such as growing power of monopolies and post-war inflation, with an intensification of certain character traits, namely sadistic and masochistic striving; the Nazi ideology appealed to and intensified these traits; and the new character traits then became effective forces in supporting the expansion of German imperialism. In both instances we see that when a certain class is threatened by new economic tendencies it reacts to this threat psychologically and ideologically; and that the psychological changes brought about by this reaction further the development of economic forces even if those forces contradict the economic interests of that class.
>
> (p. 14)

Fromm's argument regarding the intersections of class and power lends support to the theory that economically depressed Trump supporters did vote against their own interests. Following Fromm, we can readily discern the authoritarian candidate's methods of manipulating thought through splitting and "Us/Them" binary constructions focused on gender, nativist, anti-immigrant demagoguery, and most especially, by peddling racist ideology. Particularly on the issue of race, our country has long endured and struggled to negotiate deep wounds that threatened our sense of community and our belonging. But, since the election of President Obama, a malicious odor released into our cultural ethos by political, far-right conservatives has threatened our stability and sense of safety, and has thrust us into frantic searches for community, for country, for family, and for identity.

White fantasy, Black reality, and the unyielding terrors of race

> White, by the way, is not a color. It's an attitude. You're as white as you think you are. It's your choice ... Black is a condition.
>
> (Baldwin, 1968; emphasis added)

Those who voted for Donald Trump were not a homogeneous group. With the help of wealthy, White supremacist radio and cable TV talk show hosts, Trump successfully infected the rage, fears, and anxieties of his disaffected supporters with daily doses of racism, couched in bold accusations against Black and Brown "predators"—dark, monstrous, criminal, threatening! Why did this racist policy—"conquer and divide"—succeed? Here is what bell hooks (2000) proposes: "Racial solidarity, particularly the solidarity of whiteness, has historically been used to obscure class, to make the white poor see their interests as one with the world of white privilege" (p. 5). hooks (2000) continues: "Class matters. Race and gender can be used as screens to deflect attention away from the harsh realities politics exposes" (p. 7). And she goes further. Interrogating more closely our dread of confronting class, hooks (2000) argues that,

> Consumer culture silences working people and the middle classes. They are busy buying or planning to buy. Although their fragile hold on economic self-sufficiency is slipping, they still cling to the Dream of a class-free society [in which] everyone can make it to the top ... They are too afraid to think too deeply about loss. At the end of the day the threat of class warfare, of class struggle, is just too dangerous to face.
>
> (p. 6)

hooks' (2000) position that American culture is *lost in consumption* recalls Dr. King, and reflects the theories of Erich Fromm (1976). Fromm, a Marxist-Socialist, believed that there was much in psychoanalytic theory that was applicable to our understanding of culture and the socio-political world. In his popular contribution *To Have or To Be?* Fromm (1976) investigates, confronts, and impeaches a culture whose trajectory toward success resides in the seduction of its citizens into false beliefs, without concern for the psychological harm wrought upon these very citizens blindly embedded in these illusionist bubbles. Fromm argued that more and more people were being steered by a corporate culture into a state of selfhood defined by consumerism. Their position on the social status ladder is defined by the goods they collect, hoard, and display. So, if *having* defines selfhood, we can only imagine the state of personal, and interpersonal pressure, angst, and conflict that define that life. For, beneath the gathering of goods must reside an abiding dread that these things can be lost. What, then, becomes of one's status in the world? What becomes of one's identity? One's self?

What if we expand Fromm's ideas further to include the consumption of race—particularly whiteness? I argue that the political promise made to Trump voters is not only the possibility of consuming goods, but more potently, *the necessary, and certain consumption of whiteness*. Again, if they are blinded by the promise of whiteness, they fail to discern the fallacy of economic success promised by the very White elite for whom poor Whites, lacking in proper Anglo-Saxon "stock" (Painter, 2011), could never truly be White. Preoccupation with money and consumerism becomes a substitute for the anxiety inherent in the condition of *having to be White* in order to find home within the dominant tribe. From their perspective, they voted against the looming new and frightening reality that *White is the new Black!* What I mean by this is that, as it has been ingrained in their minds that poverty is associated with the Black race, and that *Black* equals *slave*, then the growing decline in their own economic status brings them frightfully into the sphere of Blackness, into loss of freedom, and, therefore, loss of their primary object of consumption—*whiteness*. I argue that a significant portion of working-class, disenfranchised Whites in America feel alienated from themselves as economic victims of the very hoarders of wealth whom they support. So, those who voted in support of a presidential candidate who spewed racial hatred did so in the belief that White supremacy and, therefore, reality as they knew it was at risk. *Skin-is-their-thing—that construct of economy that instantly defines boundaries between self and Other and "secures" continuity of identity.* They voted to secure the illusion that they are White, and that, therefore, they *are*.

But for thinkers such as bell hooks (2000), the race problem in America is unresolvable without concerted effort to address the economy and its debilitating impact on social justice and the constitutional rights of all citizens—across race and gender—to attain economic security and avoid "class warfare" (p. 8). We must, she argues, "challenge classism … and attend to the gap between rich and poor, the haves and have-nots" (pp. 8–9). Erich Fromm argues definitively that modern man's obsession with accumulating *things* equates him—his identity—with the things he feels compelled to accumulate. It is an empty state of *having*, Fromm asserts. *To Have or To Be?* A healthy state of being, Fromm wisely professes, resides in our capacity to free our souls from preoccupation with accumulating things, to reside in harmony with our humanity that silent reflection affords. We feel less isolated in the company of our things; and we arrive at new heights of curiosity about the humanity of the extruded Other when we free our identity from the objects onto which we have projected meaning for our lives. Until our arrival there, though, race and racism mark the everyday of our lives in frightening, destructive ways. The case for the inherent evil of racism is passionately stated by Toni Morrison (2014):

> One of the most malevolent characteristics of racist thought is that it never produces new knowledge. And while racist thought and language have an almost unmitigated force in political and social life, the realm of racial difference has been allowed an intellectual weight to which it has no claim. It is truly a realm that is no realm at all—an all-consuming vacancy that is both common and strange.

Black bodies under siege

The proletariat, the besieged, the rejected—those discarded, hated members of a nation—are, themselves, the very seers of that nation.

Too frequently we are greeted by horrific images of uniforms and dead bodies and protests and riots and military equipment, of scores of human beings dying in their quest for freedom, of borders falling and calls for stronger walls of exclusion to be built. As an identified intellectual sophisticate, you take notice, feel a twinge of sorrow, even, and then you fall into silence. You want to scream an unholy scream because those are *your* people being murdered, *your* people inhaling tear gas, *your* people locked in a war zone, *your* American people exploding in all manner of ways; and you cannot scream out the ungodly pain you feel rising up inside you because somewhere you know that you have been a silent participant in sustaining the very structures that beat their bodies down. And then, unexpectedly, this realization softens you into recognition of the so-called Trump voter as *Subject*. You contextualize this phenomenon of the racially and economically "blinded" poor White voters psychoanalytically. You recognize that they have been shaped psychologically into a rigid belief that their sense of place is located in their identity with whiteness, that this is their place of belonging, that whiteness defines their tribe. You call upon your observing eyes to recognize at least a portion of Trump supporters as more than simple products of internalized hate. Theirs is a dread of annihilation so great that they cannot look, or see, beyond their edge. *Racism is as much the burden of the racist as it is the burden of its victims.*

It *is* the economy! African Americans have always known that—even in moments when they become lost in psychic doubleness. But they've had to defend against racism because nationalist White Americans *refuse to let go of the fantasy of Whiteness, trusting, instead, false narratives fed them by the power elite*: that it is the Dark Other who causes them pain. Nevertheless, despite these desperately held fantasies, these "Trump voter" parents are, like me, complex *subjects*. They, too, are parents of tragedy. *Their* children, too, suffer the terrible consequences of opioid addiction. And, as much as I weep for the mothers of Black men and women killed by official bullets, I weep for the mothers of *these* children, dead from drug overdose. I, also, want to fight against the money-making "Big Pharma Industry" that indiscriminately pollutes their communities with deadly drugs.

Yet this empathy, too, is more complex than it appears. When I imagine the Trump voter, I cannot but see in my memory the savage beatings of now-Congressman John Lewis, the assassination of Dr. King. Nor can I erase from view barbaric images of White Americans posing—energized—at the root of yet another Southern tree, gleefully framing another of its "strange fruit." Lynchings of Black bodies was, for so long, a form of sport—a time of gathering and family celebration. My people were forced to flee. Held hostage to these laws, and yearning for safety of limb and life, African Americans began the exodus from the South—the great migration. Arguing that these mass migrations should be understood as flight from terrorism, Stevenson (2015), founder of the Equal Justice Initiative in Montgomery, Alabama, where the history of lynchings in the South is researched, documented, and memorialized, declares that, "lynching and the terror era shaped the geography, politics, economics and social characteristics of being Black in America during the twentieth century."

As I have argued, this historical shaping of Black experience in America is profoundly linked to the experience and expectations of being White in America. So, in this cultural moment in American life, *time* collapses. Past and present merge. Black women cry out for recognition, Black sons are falling at the hands of descendants of White masters, and something inside you turns to the Black mother left behind—the mother who, not very long ago, as time goes, proudly presented to the world the life just now erased into non-existence with the ease of snuffing out, into smoke, a flame at the tip of a match with a single drop of spit on the fingertips! You are shaken as you grieve with the mother who, that morning, feared to let her son go, warned him not to call attention to himself with his look, his gait, the decibels of his voice. You feel with the mother, who hoped that, if only her son remembered the rituals of his public conduct—which she has taught him every day since he could walk—she might have the blessing of one more time laying her loving eyes upon him. Your mind can't stop itself. You "know why the caged bird sings" (Angelou, 2009). You are overwhelmed with compassion for the lives behind the bodies. And you weep with the mothers of unspeakable loss, who now hold fast to sentimental representations of their loved ones: memories in photographs, in items of clothing, shoes—baby shoes —and other objects of love, scented with the real persons who inhabited those lost bodies. You fight despair, as the soft, soothing voice of your ancestor, *your* Langston Hughes, reminds you to "Hold fast to dreams/ For if dreams die/Life is like a broken-winged bird/That cannot fly" (1926/1994). Against all odds, this is how you dwell in possibility, envision change, stay woke, keep on keeping on.

References

Alexander, M. (2010/2012). *The new Jim Crow: Mass incarceration in the age of colorblindness* (pp. 1–2). New York, NY: New Press.

Angelou, M. (2009). *I know why the caged bird sings*. New York. NY: Ballantine Books.

Atlantic, The. (2017, August 15). Trump defends white-nationalist protesters: "Some very fine people on both sides." Retrieved from www.theatlantic.com/politics/archive/2017/08/trump-defends-white-nationalist-protesters-some-very-fine-people-on-both-sides/537012/.

Atlantic, The. (2017, August 18). Why the Charlottesville marchers were obsessed with Jews: Anti-Semitic logic fueled the violence over the weekend, no matter what the president says. Retrieved from www.theatlantic.com/polit ics/archive/2017/08/nazis-racism-charlottesville/536928/.

Baldwin, J. (1968, August 2). How to cool it. *Esquire*. Retrieved from www. esquire.com/news-politics/a23960/james-baldwin-cool-it/.

Barber, W. J., II. (2016). Speech delivered during a Bible study meeting: Pullen Memorial Baptist Church, Raleigh, NC. Retrieved from https://thinkprogress. org/rev-barber-barber-moral-change-1ad2776df7c/.

Benjamin, J. (2018). "The Wolf's Dictionary": Confronting the triumph of a predatory world view. *Contemporary Psychoanalysis*, *53*(4), 470–488.

Blackmon, D. A. (2008). *Slavery by another name: The re-enslavement of black Americans from the Civil War to World War II*. New York, NY: Doubleday.

Bromberg, P. M. (2009/1993). Shadow and substance: A relational perspective on clinical process. In *Standing in the spaces: Essays on clinical process, trauma, and dissociation* (pp. 165–187). New York, NY: Analytic Press.

Burns, S. (2016, October 18). Why Trump doubled down on the Central Park Five. *New York Times*. Retrieved from www.nytimes.com/2016/10/18/opinion/ why-trump-doubled-down-on-the-central-park-five.html.

Coates, T. N. (2015). *Between the world and me*. New York, NY: Spielberg's & Grau.

DuBois, W. E. B. (1903). *The souls of black folk*. New York, NY: New American Library.

DuVernay, A. (Director) (2016). *Thirteenth* [Documentary]. United States: Forward Movement, Kandoo Films.

Farzan, A. N. (2018). BBQ Becky, Permit Patty and Cornerstore Caroline: Too "cutesy" for those white women calling police on black people? Retrieved from www.washingtonpost.com/news/morning-mix/wp/2018/10/19/bbq-becky-permit-patty-and-cornerstore-caroline-too-cutesy-for-those-white-women-calling-cops-on-blacks/.

Fromm, E. (1942). Character and social process: An appendix to *Fear and Freedom*. Transcribed by Andy Blunden for Value-of-Knowledge site, 1988; Proofed.

Fromm, E. (1976). *To have or to be?* New York, NY: Harper & Row.

Gast, J. (1872). *American Progress*. Oil painting, 12 3/4" x 16 3/4". Museum of the American West, Griffin Park. LA no. 92.126.1, Library of Congress no. 975.075.47. Retrieved from the Archive for Research in Archetypal Symbolism. Retrieved from https://aras.org/sites/default/files/docs/00043AmericanPro gress0.pdf.

Grand, S. (2018). The Other within: White shame, Native-American genocide. *Contemporary Psychoanalysis*, *54*(1), 84–102.

hooks, b. (2000). *Where we stand: Class matters*. New York, NY: Routledge.

Hughes, L. (1926/1994). Dreams. In *The collected poems of Langston Hughes*. New York, NY: Knopf.

King, M. L., Jr. (1967). The three evils of society. Retrieved from www. youtube.com/watch?v=6sT9Hjh0cHM&feature=youtu.be#.

Mervosh, S. (2018). Remains of Black people forced into labor after slavery are discovered in Texas. Retrieved from www.nytimes.com/2018/07/18/us/grave-convict-lease-texas.html?module=inline.

Morrison, T. (2014, May 24). Interview, Hay Festival. *The Telegraph*. Retrieved from www.youtube.com/watch?v=vtJFK_HtlQk&app=desktop.

Mueller, B., Weiser, B., and Greenberg, Z. (2018, July 20). City releases trove of documents in Central Park jogger case. *New York Times*. Retrieved from www. nytimes.com/2018/07/20/nyregion/documents-from-the-central-park-jogger-case-are-released.html.

Painter, N. I. (2011). *The history of white people*. New York, NY: Norton & Co.

Southern Poverty Law Center. (2014). 18 things you should know about mass incarceration. Retrieved from www.splcenter.org/news/2014/12/22/18-things-you-should-know-about-mass-incarceration

Staples, B. (2018, October 27). A fate worse than slavery, unearthed in Sugar Land: Bodies of sugar cane workers recently discovered in Texas reveal grue-some details about the convict leasing system. *New York Times*. Retrieved from www.nytimes.com/2018/10/27/opinion/sugar-land-texas-graves-slavery.html.

Stevenson, B. (2015, February 10). History of lynchings in the south documents nearly 4,000 names. *New York Times*. Retrieved from www.nytimes.com/2015/02/10/us/history-of-lynchings-in-the-south-documents-nearly-4000-names.html.

Will, G. F. (2018, July 17). This sad, embarrassing wreck of a man: Which Repub-licans will stand behind a president who puts Russia first? *Washington Post*. Retrieved from www.washingtonpost.com/opinions/this-sad-embarrassing-wreck-of-a-man/2018/07/17/d06de8ea-89e8-11e8-a345-a1bf7847b375_story.html?utm_term=2d17ecfa5795.

Chapter 8

Sympathy for the devil

Evil, social process, and intelligibility

Robert Prince

"Sympathy for the Devil" (Jagger and Richards, 1968) is a ballad sung in a voice that is simultaneously threatening and seductive. The listener is challenged to name the balladeer whose identity is slowly revealed as he places himself in the center of successive historical traumas. The audience is asked questions which draw them into ambiguities which make their complicity inescapably evident and thus compel their sympathy. Objections to the concept are appropriate. Sympathy for the devil is perverse, perhaps something that could only afflict rock and roll groups and psychoanalysts. If the very idea isn't steeped in evil itself, it must refer first to the concretization of the imaginary and then a denial of the real consequences of evil. The case study that will be presented, that of Adolf Eichmann, is of a perpetrator of deeds so heinous that they threaten to transcend understanding. It is precisely this traumatic effect, the overwhelming of mind, thought, and symbolic functioning, that is shared by victim, witness, and perpetrator. The last is least likely to find redemption, but it is not this that deserves sympathy. The following study rejects both relativistic and absolutist approaches. It struggles with our understanding that the themes that define evil are not only ambiguous and contradictory, but also entangled with each other. No single perspective suffices: the religious, historical, social, moral, epistemological, and finally the psychological are all necessary. Thus, "sympathy" is neither approbation nor identification but an attempt to appreciate the dilemmas faced by the devil.

We can be assured that humankind has a need to both understand evil and to attribute evil to a source. But which need is the more compelling? Much can be articulated about evil, but none of it certain. Do evil people exist, or does evil exist in people? Perhaps evil is an actuality that resides in humans, maybe in nature? Maybe it's no more than a part is a point of view. Are "good and evil" mutually exclusive, or do they coexist? Perhaps one can only be known by the other. Although the existence of "evil" is contentious, the idea of God is more acceptable. Some see that "evil" force standing on its own, concretized as demon. In other views, evil or an evil act is any opposition to the omnipotent will of a Middle Eastern potentate or failure of subservience to any deity that resembles one.

Once the political comes into consideration, it is necessary to think of evil in relation to social structure, as partly constructed, having social referents, social realities, and social functions. For example, for most contemporary Westerners, stoning an adulterer is an evil act arising from barbarous ignorance. But it could also be understood as serving the primary function of creating a way to understand the world or secondarily defending an established belief system, or as serving the group's or social order's need for cohesiveness and survival. Can the "evil" of the suffering imposed on the individual be weighed against the value of preserving a consensus about the rules that govern social behavior? Is one person's—or one culture's—vice another's virtue? Or is the cultural argument a rationalization of the sadism and traumatic background of the individual perpetrator? Or changing focus again, does evil reside, not in any individual, but somewhere in the mob, in group process, or as Freud foreshadowed in *Civilization and Its Discontents* (1930), the inherent conflict between individuals and the social order? Are there any characteristics that are particular to evil? At the very least, political bodies worldwide require violence to enforce order and they ubiquitously represent opponents, internal and external, as "evil" (Armstrong, 2015). The major social and scientific advances and the feats of exploration and discovery of the past two millennia—including those celebrated as heroic—have often been entwined with horrific violence (Harari, 2015). Moreover, evil, or the demonic, serves an important function in the management of prevailing social anxieties either in hysterical form, as exemplified by the Salem witch trials, or in paranoiac form in the persecution of scapegoats.

Susan Neiman (2002) argues that the problem of evil is the "guiding force of modern thought" (p. 2), and that the core of this is making the world intelligible. Neiman contends that modern conceptions of evil begin with the Lisbon earthquake of 1755, which represented "natural evil," insofar as it was visited on a pious Christian nation, one confident that it was free of sin. Thus, it posed a challenge to theodicy, the belief in God's goodness and justice as central to understanding the world. Two centuries later, Leyotard (cited by Hartmann, 1996) would use the metaphor of an earthquake to describe the Holocaust, a human evil so immense it destroyed the measuring instruments by which the world could be known.

Although knowing that evil has historical references to cruelty and suffering, Neiman states that today, "[evil] has come to stand for absolute wrongdoing that leaves no room for account or expiation" (2002, p. 3). She rejects the idea that a particular incarnation of evil is "uniquely paradigmatic." Likewise, she disagrees with the view that "evil has an essential quality that stays constant throughout its manifestations ... and attempts to capture the forms of evil within a single formula run the risk of becoming one-sided or trivial" (p. xiii.). Although Neiman's views are tempered by the awareness of the possibility that the world might contain neither justice nor meaning, threatening our ability to live in it, her epistemological position is sharply contrasted by Martin Heidegger, who is widely accepted as among the most important modern contributors to our thinking about the world. Heidegger forcefully rejected "relativism." Hannah Arendt also drew her concern about the lack of a stable moral center, with a metaphor from Kant—the same philosophical wellspring from whom Arendt drew—that is, "homelessness" (Koonz, 2003, p. 52).

Given Heidegger's influence on contemporary thought, including psychoanalysis, it is remarkable that until relatively recently the relationship of his thought to the Holocaust has been dissociated. Not only did he contribute to the rise of the Nazis by lending them his prestige and respectability, Heidegger's philosophy is concretized in what Koonz (2002) provocatively labels the "Nazi conscience." Koonz identifies the principles of Nazi ideology—the carefully crafted "moral" image of its leaders, and particularly the ideals of racial purity it extolled—as fueling its success. Heidegger was or evolved as an anti-Semite. He saw Nazism as a response to the corruption of modernity, bureaucratization, industrialism, materialism, and scientism—represented by Jews—all of which threatened "authenticity" and thus a loss of being. Because these evils emanated from the Jew, placing the purity of the *Volk*[1] in peril by depriving them of their "authenticity" and the quest for a life worth living (which Heidegger exalted) could morally lead to the conduct of genocide. The application of Heidegger's ideas serve as a caution of the most extreme kind, in that his call for an "ethical responsibility for truth" (quoted by Koonz, 2003, p. 52) represents a search for (to reference Neiman's [2002] term) *intelligibility* gone horribly wrong.

The work of Hannah Arendt further twists and turns in the project of making the world intelligible through making evil intelligible. Arendt was heavily influenced by Kant. She was a Jew who escaped from Germany, was a student of Heidegger's and very briefly his lover. Arendt distinguished herself with her foundational *explorations* of totalitarianism, in which she argued that the rise of totalitarianism had pointed to the existence of a new kind of evil: "absolute evil." Her standing resulted in an assignment to cover the 1960 trial of Adolf Eichmann for *The New Yorker*. Observing him in the Israeli court, she was struck by how small and insignificant this once strutting, terrifying figure seemed as he stood in his glass booth. Most of her conclusions, however, stemmed from close textual study of transcripts from which she interpreted. In contrast to her earlier work, *Eichmann in Jerusalem: A Report on the Banality of Evil* (1962) created a furor that began the modern controversy about the nature of evil.

The acrimonious condemnation of Arendt, so intense that disputes about her book ended friendships, stemmed in part from her thesis that portrayed Jews and the Jewish Councils (the *Judenrat*)—whom Eichmann had used to facilitate deportations—as complicit and culpable. Arendt's inclusion of the *Judenrat* in consideration of guilt was viewed by many as unacceptable, both because it ignored the moral gray areas inhabited by dire contingency and especially in light of the lenience she was presumed to have accorded Eichmann.

Through his role in the extermination of the Jews, Eichmann was easily seen as a personification of Kantian "radical evil," that is, a concept of the innateness of human evil that went beyond mere moral violations to an assault on the categories and standards of morality. However, Arendt (1962) rejected a representation of him as a demonic figure. She painted Eichmann as a diligent mediocrity, someone actually "stupid," shallow, and inarticulate to the point of clownishness. To her, he was noteworthy only in his desire to please his superiors, a hollow functionary who represented the hideous possibilities of the bureaucratic man, the antithesis of Heidegger's ideal. She accepts Eichmann's portrayal of himself as a "cog-in-the machine," writing,

Despite all the efforts of the prosecution, everybody could see that this man was not a 'monster,' but it was difficult indeed not to suspect that he was a clown. And since this suspicion would have been fatal to the entire enterprise [his trial], and was also rather hard to sustain in view of the sufferings he and his like had caused to millions of people, his worst clowneries were hardly noticed and almost never reported.

(p. 55)

Arendt concludes, Eichmann was "not an Iago or a Macbeth" and that "except for an extraordinary diligence and looking out for his personal advancement, he had no motives at all. ... [He] never realized what he was doing" (p. 285).

Arendt's view was consistent with characterizations of other perpetrators as normal humans in extreme situations. Going beyond the mere impossibility of predicting how anyone would behave under similar circumstances, she expressed amazement at who behaved how. Arendt's thesis overlaps with other portrayals of Germans embedded in evil circumstances. For example, Browning (1998) and Friedlander (1997) wrote of "ordinary men" swept up by extraordinary reality into a conformist routine driven by group loyalty or obedience into behavior that may have been actually abhorrent to them. Even after more than a half century of headline-grabbing social/psychological experiments, we may not be far beyond Arendt's amazement at who behaved badly and who behaved well. Nevertheless, the subsequent emergence of details about Eichmann suggests that although *banality*—a term Arendt used in her title, but only once on the last page of her text, and came to regret—might apply to some, it was woefully misleading, particularly regarding Eichmann. The disjunction between Arendt's portrait and descriptions, partly a function of Eichmann's extraordinary ability to deceive and to make others believe him and disbelieve their own perceptions, is essential to the approach this article takes to the problem of intelligibility and evil. The facts are elicited with only great difficulty and even then are subject to an interpretive lens. Deception can represent radical evil when it attacks reality by offering wishes in place of actuality.

Adolf Eichmann, also known as Otto and perhaps Karl, was head of the Gestapo's Department for Jewish Affairs. He was the architect of the murder of 6 million Jews. Able to hide after the Nazi defeat, he was followed to Argentina by his wife and three children; a fourth child was born there. He was aided by, and participated in, a circle of Nazis who—having political hopes—looked longingly back to Germany for a victory of a resurgent right wing over the liberal, centrist parties. This nefarious group was under the protection of the Argentinean dictator, Juan Perón. The search for Eichmann was compromised by various parties who had a stake in allowing him to remain hidden for overlapping and conflicting reasons, including sympathy towards Nazi ideology and keeping the lid on a can of worms. Others wanted him found to scapegoat or to exonerate the guilt of the many, to suppress a genocidal narrative, or to betray him for purposes of furthering postwar political aspirations and geopolitical considerations. Holocaust denial was a particularly important aim of the Argentinean Nazi group; and it was only in this project that Eichmann, who was proud of his role, might have been at odds with them (Stangneth, 2015). In the search for Eichmann, vengeance and justice balanced concerns for political repercussions for all stakeholders. After earlier opportunities to locate him were missed or sabotaged, he was kidnapped in 1960 by the Israeli Secret Service from a hiding place that was almost in plain sight. Despite international uproar over the violation of Argentinean sovereignty, Eichmann was taken to Israel to be put on trial for crimes against humanity.

Contesting Arendt's portrayal of Eichmann's mediocrity and "stupidity," Bettina Stangneth (2015) describes how Arendt fell into the "trap" of his deceptions. The Eichmann Arendt saw in Jerusalem, predominantly through the lens of close study of transcripts of his testimony, wore a "mask." By tracing Eichmann's biography, Stangneth reconstructed the history of his crimes. Utilizing Eichmann's own writings as well as observations by contemporaries (some 1,300 pages of transcribed recordings of interviews with Wilhem Sassen, a Dutch Nazi, and discussions with his Nazi circle in Sassen's Buenos Aires home), Stangneth concludes:

> Eichmann acted out a new role for every stage of his life, for each new audience and every new aim. As subordinate, superior officer, perpetrator, fugitive, exile, and defendant, Eichmann kept a close eye on the impact he was having at all times, and tried to make every situation work in his favor. There was a method to his behavior, as a comparison of the many roles he played will reveal.
>
> (p. xvii)

Arendt's characterizations of Eichmann are belied by descriptions from multiple other sources while he was in power and after. These depict a proud,
grandiose, boastful, unrepentant, overarching, ambitious, self-promoting,
flaunting, devious, conniving, innovative, and rabidly anti-Semitic individual
who behaved in a god-like way. This was in stark contrast to the plodding
bureaucrat portrayed by Arendt. The man who defended himself to the court
in Jerusalem as a minor functionary following the orders of superiors (characterizations that would previously have precipitated one of his rages), he
proudly boasted of his active pursuit of mass murder to his Argentinean
cohort. In Argentina, Eichmann described the joy he had felt at his
efficiency moving Hungarian Jews to their death, his pleasure at being able
to claim credit for the deaths of millions.

Eichmann personally oversaw deportations. Although he never personally tortured anyone, he would typically ask questions at the beginning of
an interrogation, leave, and then return for his answers after the torture
was completed. In contrast to the numb bureaucrat that Arendt conceived,
he didn't "get caught up in the usual bureaucratic formalities" and "had
a talent for organization, and for making possible things that had never
been done before" (Stangneth, 2015, p. 27). He was more than zealous: He
was ferocious in pursuing the aim of extermination; more than unmerciful,
he raged at pleas for mercy. He did not merely take orders as he claimed
in his defense; he furiously opposed orders that would save even a single
Jewish life, even when they came from Hitler himself. He found uncon-
ventional solutions to problems. For example, toward the end of the war,
Himmler complained about the problem of the disposal of bodies. Eichmann conceived the idea of marching prisoners on foot, calling them
"Jew-treks," in the middle of winter, during the last months of the war, to
facilitate the dispersal of corpses over hundreds of miles.

Above all, Eichmann was cunning and manipulative: He mastered
the ability of managing information, lying, creating alibis, and he
excelled at disinformation—for example, creating false pictures by
giving false dates. His "negotiations" with the Jewish community were
always in bad faith. He deceived his victims in order to facilitate their
extermination, but gave up pretense when it had accomplished its aims
and was no longer necessary.

Eichmann's creation of the Theresienstadt concentration camp just
outside of Prague stands as a monument to deception, a symbol of

a domain ruled by Satan, by the most profound manipulation of truth and reality. It was described as a "spa" town where elderly Jews could "retire." It actually served as a transit station to the extermination camps where tens of thousands died of starvation and disease. But, its more important function was to counter the disturbing reports of Nazi atrocities. Just before visits by the Red Cross or other inspectors, houses would be painted, flowers planted, and an orchestra and athletic matches organized. Stangneth (2015) writes:

> The idea that Eichmann and his colleagues could go to such lengths to make an entire town look presentable for just one day, only to return to gruesome normality the next, lay far beyond the powers of the imagination. … Eichmann … created an illusion that rendered the horror almost invisible.
>
> (pp. 37–38)

How does the disparity between the two Eichmanns—the clownish mediocrity Arendt describes and the image that emerges from other sources—illuminate an understanding of evil?

Arendt initially accepted the conclusion of the examining psychologists, who she called the "soul experts," that Eichmann was not mentally ill, at least in the forensic sense of being able to tell right from wrong. Going further, she quotes a psychologist who evaluated Eichmann and found him to be even more "normal" than he was, and a minister who found Eichmann's psychological outlook, his attitude toward his wife and children, mother and father, brothers, sisters, and friends, to be not only normal but "desirable—a man with 'positive' ideas." Arendt thus advances the legitimacy of the dilemma posed by the defense, that in the Third Reich only "exceptions" would have behaved differently and that Eichmann's behavior should be understood in the context of a normal set of responses to evil circumstances. Arendt was nevertheless aware of subsequent contradictory information (as she writes in a parentheses in her second edition) not made available during the trial. In a subsequent article in *The Saturday Evening Post*, Gideon Hausner, the trial prosecutor, noted that Eichmann had been found by psychiatrists to be a "perverted, sadistic personality … a man obsessed with a dangerous and insatiable urge to kill, arising out of a desire for power" (Hausner, 1962, p. 20).

Eichmann's demeanor in Jerusalem certainly contributed to the confusion about the psychiatric state of his mind. He had the capacity to win people over. Stangneth's description (2015) contributes a significant insight:

> Everyone who dealt with the Eichmann in Israel said they were sure they had been an important attachment figure for him. Interrogator, prison director, doctor, psychologist, theologian, Deputy Attorney General—they all praised his willingness to cooperate, remarked on how happy he was to talk, and believed he was particularly grateful to them for their conversations. ... They all had the impression of the grateful prisoner.
>
> (p. 365)

The Eichmann she portrays here has, on the one hand, an interpersonal talent, but, on the other, a quality clinicians recognize in certain narcissistic or sociopathic personality disorders. Hausner's description of cross-examining Eichmann supports the clinical impression of a malevolent narcissist or outright psychopath:

> In fact, Eichmann looked like nothing much at all. The man facing me was the kind you might rub elbows with in the street any day and never notice him. He was nondescript, in his middle 50s, balding, lean, of dark complexion and of medium height. The first unusual thing one noticed was a twitch around his mouth which, when he lifted his lips, gave his face a strange, almost grotesque appearance. Only his narrow eyes behind the heavy eyeglasses disclosed his real personality. During the course of my cross-examination, when he was cornered on some particularly slippery ground, those eyes would light up with bottomless hatred. Once, when this happened, my assistant tugged at my robe and whispered, "Did you notice his eyes? They frightened me." But such moments were rare. Almost immediately afterward Eichmann was able to revert to his usual, gray, nondescript appearance. It was an appearance that, thanks to our system of justice, he was able to cultivate carefully in advance.
>
> (Hausner, 1962, p. 20)

In two weeks of cross-examination, Hausner was not able to extract any semblance of confession from Eichmann beyond "following orders."

Trivial details can also be illuminating. During Eichmann's incarceration, he ate everything that was served. On one occasion he inadvertently received four extra pieces of bread, which he dutifully made himself eat but then the next day requested he be given the usual ration. There was no external reason he could not have just left the extra bread over. The impression that ineluctably comes to mind is to someone with severe obsessive-compulsive disorder or even Asperger's, who spontaneously and reflexively submits to mindless order, self-created rules, and concrete obedience within a rigid frame. Alternatively, it could be supposed he was someone trying to convince others that he follows orders.

Although he tried to dissemble his way out of a death sentence, he did not admit to feeling guilty in any sense. When the court psychologist mentioned Pontius Pilate, Eichmann thanked him for the comparison. He exclaimed enthusiastically:

> That's exactly my position! When he washed his hands, Pilate was signifying that he didn't identify himself with that course of action. He was forced to do it. If I am entitled to compare myself with such a great historical figure, then his situation was the same as mine.
>
> (quoted by Stangneth, 2015, p. 223)

The juxtaposition of images of a powerless individual passively carrying out orders and a "great historical figure" confirms Eichmann's "conscience" as being involved with the idea of doing a great job, carrying out his responsibilities. He may even have believed that by being tried in Israel he was gaining a kind of absolution, in the sense advanced by Ernest Becker (1968), though making a further contribution to the Reich. For Becker, evil must be considered as part of social process—individual and social forces operating reciprocally. The monster may, on the one hand, draw energy from social process but then depends on the monster to fulfill its aims. Thus, evil has a ritual role in which society "must provide some form of sacred absolution, regardless of the particular historical disguise that this absolution may wear" (p. 115). Such a view is embedded in a peculiar line of reasoning Arendt abstracts from the trial transcripts. Eichmann, in a convoluted explanation of why he hadn't earlier returned voluntarily to Germany for trial, expresses his preference for being tried in an Israeli, rather than German court, because the latter still lacked "objectivity." He goes on to say that by being tried in Israel, he hoped to do his part in lifting the burden of guilt from future generations of German youth!

It is tempting to conclude that Eichmann's lack of guilt may have no meaning beyond his psychopathic character structure, but it is attribute able to not thinking he has done anything wrong. Evil acts, Neiman (2002) writes, "acquire significance in relation to the web of beliefs in which they occurred" (p. 256). For the Nazis, oppression was presented as a means of "ethnic salvation from fragmentation and decline" (Koonz, 2003, p. 71). Violence was justified by the necessity of main-taining order, the need to protect the state and the *Volk* with the direst measures, including terror. Paranoid conspiracy theories, particularly involving degenerate plots, fears of infection leading to the moral necessity of exterminating the bacillus of racial corruption fueled by cascades of rage as perpetrator was represented as victim. This confirmed the psychic wellsprings of this and many social movements and ideologies that wrap evil acts in the cloak of goodness, even hero-ism. It is the enemy who is always understood to be evil.

The earliest history of humanity is marked by an attempt to find order in the world through explanatory systems from which myths, religion, and finally science flowed. The psychotic person creates belief systems solely on the basis of projected wishes or fears without any concern for percep-tion or logic. These belief systems arise out of a kind of intention to create intelligibility, and the two kinds of systems may only be distin-guished by social consensus. Thus, a belief in the psychotic realm is clas-sified as a delusion when it is not shared. A dimension of the problem must be understanding evil as an attack on intelligibility. If we also under-stand evil as a function of intention, it is an intention, either primary or secondary to another aim, to undermine reality. In many mythic and reli-gious traditions, the antagonist of good—Satan, Anasi, Loki, the devil, the demon—is represented as a great deceiver. The magnitude of the suffering Eichmann caused potentially overwhelms the realization of that line of deceit. Evil is an attack on intelligibility itself, one that permits and then permeates the narrative of the Holocaust. The distortion of that narrative continues to this day in the form of Holocaust denial, which is the prov-ince of mostly anti-Semitic ideologies denying it happened while feeling satisfied it did. Belief systems become the instruments, alternately or simultaneously, of establishing and undermining intelligibility. Evil is then defined by its relationship to belief systems and reality, and by stopping people from being able to think.

The "web of beliefs," the molding of reality, begins with a Manichean authority. Rulers—from antiquity through the Enlightenment—claimed authority from God for the good of all. Heidegger insisted on the pursuit of greater purpose in life through a will to essence. This goal would be achieved by the discipline of a "relentless clarity" in which "old assumptions would be 'shattered'" and "thus the creation of a battle community that fused labor, power and knowledge" (Koonz, 2003, p. 53). The Nazi's mission, as per Heidegger, was to crush the existing web of beliefs. Heidegger's word "clarity" relies on the power and authority to establish the parameters of understanding the world. To quote an earlier and perhaps more straightforward philosopher, Lewis Carroll:

> "When I use a word," Humpty Dumpty said, in rather a scornful tone, "it means just what I choose it to mean—neither more nor less." "The question is," said Alice, "whether you can make words mean so many different things." "The question is," said Humpty Dumpty, "which is to be master—that's all."
>
> (Carroll, 1872/1934, p. 205)

And here, instead of "evil" contributing to intelligibility, it is the intention to mold reality by either creating a false reality, by arbitrarily declaring it to serve some end or undermining a true reality.

Freud proposed a complex system for tracing the evolution of beliefs from their origins in drives and it was his nephew, Edward Bernays (1928), who promoted "invisibly" shaping beliefs through what he called "propaganda." The founder of "public relations," Bernays inverted the idea of the unconscious by developing a new discipline, or more accurately an old one in modern form, "public relations," which could invisibly shape beliefs and thus—in his view—not only sell products but also serve democracy by spreading positive ideas. Where his uncle pioneered the study of the psychopathological consequences of false beliefs in individuals, Bernays failed to appreciate the power of malignant beliefs and the manipulation of reality. Josef Goebbels stands as Bernays's mirror image. His mastery of the dark art of propaganda made Nazi ideology emerge from purportedly objective sources using the appearance of truth to inculcate paradigms of belief in ordinary people on whose cooperation Nazi policies depended; this indoctrinated the German people so totally that "not mindless obedience but selective compliance characterized Germans' collaboration" (Koonz, 2003, p. 12).

The creation of false beliefs is enabled by successful strategies of deception. Thus, evil is able to invade reality by appealing to wishes. For example, Hitler was an astute reader of his audiences' desires; he promised to repair the humiliation of defeat with greatness, restore what had been stolen, and defend honor and dignity from degeneracy. Eichmann likewise facilitated the implementation of the "Final Solution" by manipulating the beliefs of his victims. Referring to his ability to enlist the cooperation of Jewish Councils, Stangneth (2015) writes:

> Like a mirror, he [Eichmann] reflected people's fears and expectations, whether they were fearing for their own lives or hoping he would confirm a theory of evil. Behind all the mirror images lay Eichmann's will to power and desire to control people's thoughts, disguised as diligence.
>
> (p. 367)

In America, a future president would attribute success to appealing to people's hopes and dreams (Trump & Schwartz, 1987).

Reality has been undermined throughout history by what today is famously described as "alternate facts." In the act of creating false equivalence between objective reporting and concocted reports, objectivity is drowned in a sea of explicit confabulation; the fabric of reality is the emperor's new clothes. The pervasiveness of this phenomenon descends through time. The scope of the Nazi accusation of *Lugenpresse* (lying press) reflected in today's "fake news" arguably goes back to the hieroglyphs of Mesopotamia and the Bible. Over the ages, the basics remain constant, the technology advances. Rumors of poisoned wells and "blood libels" spread by word of mouth led to slaughters; later, splashed on newspaper broadsheets, rumors incited riots and war. Just as Hitler was able to use a new technology, the radio, as a tool to spread lies, today's demagogues are able to use the Internet to direct disinformation to targeted populations, spreading virulent falsehoods. Outrageous claims can be made with absolutely no evidence, leading to horrific actions. Dylan Roof, who murdered eight in a Charleston church, got his "information" from Internet hate sites. The idea that telephone calls were "bugged" through the microwave might be labeled as a delusion in a psychiatric mental status examination rather than a plausible defense by a chief spokesperson and advisor to the president of the United States on a cable news network. Spreading terrible assertions from hateful imaginations, the term "viral" is unintentionally apt. The technique of creating a virtual echo chamber for delusions until they are reported by credible media—who are then credited as the source—has been perfected. Twitter is the latest instrument coopted for evil.

Arendt turns out to have been massively wrong and massively right. She failed to comprehend the extent of Eichmann's malevolence and deceit. Indeed, he had such confidence in his deception that he expressed surprise to his lawyers at his ultimate conviction by an Israeli court. One of the effects of trauma is something central to Arendt's conception of evil: a failure to use reason. "Thoughtlessness" was one of the effects of trauma for her, a failure to use reason. A more contemporary psychoanalytic conception of thoughtlessness might also include dissociation. Perhaps the trauma of her confrontation with destructiveness made her vulnerable to Eichmann's capacity to deceive: "banality" may have been a rhetorical attempt to respond to Nazism with contempt and defiance. Ultimately, she might have been better served giving her book the subtitle: "The Thoughtlessness of Evil." Contemporary thinking about trauma creates a symmetry here; if evil flows from "thoughtlessness," one of major effects of trauma on its victim is thoughtlessness or dissociation.

Arendt's own error is paradoxically an example of what she was right about. For her, evil could not be demonic because it was ultimately "shallow." She thought of it as the incapacity to think from another person's point of view. She wrote about evil as a failure to engage with oneself, to think. In the "banality of evil," it is possible to see the convergence of Neiman's (2002) Lisbon earthquake and Auschwitz, Arendt's metonymies for natural evil and human evil. Eichmann, as the agent of suffering, can be conceived as an act of nature, a defect in the biology of mind, a break in a gene, a neurotransmitter gone awry, a lesion in a neural structure, the same order of natural fault that produced the Lisbon earthquake. Arendt was deceived by surfaces. Her conclusion about Eichmann's "stupidity" was—at surface level—just wrong. It was wrong in the sense that he was anything but "stupid" in his cunning, or mundane in his intentions. Her conclusion about his thoughtlessness, his failure to use reason appropri-ately posits that the sine qua non of intelligence and thought requires going below the surface. Alas, even then the problem may not be resolved. (No one would ever accuse Heidegger of thoughtlessness.) Indeed, care-fully crafted ideologies are more likely to lead to genocide than simple criminal intent (Prince, 2016). For example, Solzhenitsyn (2007), like Arendt, singled out Iago and Macbeth as villains but—exactly oppositely to her—characterized them as "lambs" in comparison to ideological killers. He wrote:

> To do evil a human being must first of all believe that what he's doing is good … it is in the nature of the human being to seek a justification for his actions. Macbeth's self-justifications were feeble—and his con-science devoured him. Yes, even Iago was a little lamb too. The imagination and the spiritual strength of Shakespeare's evildoers stopped short at a dozen corpses. Because they had no *ideology*.
>
> (p. 77)

Before the Israeli court, Eichmann pled "Not guilty in the sense of the indictment" to 15 counts of crimes against humanity. Arendt asks, "In what sense then did he think he was guilty?" (Arendt, 1962, p. 19). She reports that no one during the trial ever asked him this question. It might be imagined that if he would have told the truth, his only sense of guilt was that he failed to exterminate every Jew—in the same sense that he felt a compulsion to exactly complete the task (that is, eat every slice of bread his jailers put on his plate). He might have had the cap-acity to reflect that his commitment to order and obedience was a vice not a virtue. He might also have admitted to not understanding that the essence of intelligibility is empathy. In the end, despite her character-ization of Eichmann's evil, Arendt did feel that his sentence to be hanged for his crimes was just.

A free concert was held in 1969 at the Altamont Speedway for which the Rolling Stones hired a motorcycle gang to maintain order. Some concertgoers were beaten and, as urban legend has it, one was stabbed to death during the performance of "Sympathy for the Devil." Actually, it was immediately after. The accuracy of the detail is as important for this article—which is concerned with actual not alterna-tive facts—as is the irony in the name of the gang, the Hell's Angels.

History shows that order must be maintained. Perhaps it is a function of evil toward off the greater evil of chaos, but great care must be taken at concerts and in history. One instrument is deception. Josef Goebbels (see Lisciotto, 2007) is purported to have said,

> If you tell a lie big enough and keep repeating, people will eventually come to believe it. The lie can be maintained only for such time as the state can shield the people from the political, economic and/or military consequences of the lie. It just becomes vitally important for the State to use all of its powers to repress dissent, for the truth is the mortal enemy of the lie, and thus by extension, the truth is the greatest enemy of the State.
> (http://www.holocaustresearchproject.org/holoprelude/goebbels.html)

In the Hebrew Bible, the Book of Job seeks to make suffering intelligible. The God of Job challenges the protagonist; the message is that the unintelligible woes visited on a man of virtue is beyond human ken and understood only by God. That view has bedeviled us ever since. Neiman (2002) writes, "any form of theodicy—including that God's ways are beyond understanding—involves some form of bad faith" (p. 114). Harari (2015) offers a rationale for susceptibility to "bad faith," what I have called deception:

> So, monotheism explains order, but is mystified by evil. Dualism explains evil, but is puzzled by order. There is one logical way of solving the riddle: to argue that there is a single omnipotent God who created the entire universe—and He's evil. But nobody in history has had the stomach for such belief.
>
> (p. 221)

Perhaps the best we can do is resist the temptation to deception and, acknowledging the message of *Job*, reconcile ourselves to it. As I tried to imply at the beginning of this article, evil is overwhelming, and nothing is certain, so perhaps *Job* too is an evasion. I think Kant offers an alternative: an inward solution, an internal feeling of the moral. On his tombstone he had inscribed: "Two things fill the mind with ever new and increasing admiration and awe, the more often and steadily we reflect upon them: the starry heavens above me and the moral law within me." But Arendt was far more modest in her goals: "to find my way around in reality without selling my soul ... [in] the way people in earlier times sold their souls to the devil" (cited by Neiman [2002], p. 300).

This article begins with questioning the propriety of its own conceit, i.e., sympathy for the devil. Both Kant and Arendt, by their inward turn, implicitly offer sympathy for the devil's condition of inner emptiness. Psychoanalysis is more explicit as it strives to remedy the void by its empathic engagement. It explores the functions of deception, pointedly self-deception, and thus is inevitably sympathetic in appreciation of that function. As it struggles with the legitimacy of points of view, objective reality—though extremely difficult to establish, buried as it is in the folds of distortion, construction, wish, and malevolence—is still there to be found in its hiding places (Prince, 2017). Deception testifies to the existence of concrete historical reality in the very act of assault on it. Psychoanalysis witnesses and memorializes that testimony. Deception is the instrument the devil uses to lead astray, but psychoanalytic empathy offers an inner and outer compass to find a way home.

Acknowledgments

Robert Prince, Ph.D. Sympathy for the Devil: Evil, Social Process, and Intelligibility. *Contemporary Psychoanalysis*, copyright © the William Alanson White Institute of Psychiatry, Psychoanalysis & Psychology and the William Alanson White Psychoanalytic Society, www.wawhite.org, reprinted by permission of Taylor & Francis Ltd, http://www.tandfonline.com on behalf of the William Alanson White Institute of Psychiatry, Psychoanalysis & Psychology and the William Alanson White Psychoanalytic Society.

Note

1 In German, the word *Volk* may mean *folk* (simple people), people in the ethnic sense, and *nation* (https://en.wikipedia.org/wiki/Volk_[German_word].

References

Armstrong, K. (2015). *Fields of blood: Religion and the history of violence.* New York, NY: Anchor.

Arendt, H. (1962). *Eichmann in Jerusalem: The banality of evil.* New York, NY: Penguin.

Becker, E.(1968). *The structure of evil.* New York, NY: The Free Press.

Bernays, E. (1928). *Propaganda.* Brooklyn, NY: Ig Publishing.

Browning, C.(1998). *Ordinary men: Reserve police battalion 101 and the final solution in Poland.* New York, NY: Harper.

Carroll, L. (1872/1934). *Through the looking-glass.* London, UK: Macmillan and Co. Limited.

Freud, S. (1930). Civilization and its discontents. *The standard edition of the complete psychological works of Sigmund Freud,* Volume XXI (1927–1931): The future of an illusion, civilization and its discontents, and other works, 57–146.

Friedlander, S. (1997). *Nazi Germany and the Jews, 1939–1945: The years of extermination.* New York, NY: Harper-Collins.

Harari, N. (2015). *Sapiens: A brief history of humankind.* New York, NY: Harper-Collins.

Hartman, G. (1996). *The longest shadow.* Bloomington, IN: Indiana University Press.

Hausner, G. (1962). "Eichmann and his trial," *Saturday Evening Post, 235*(39), 19–25.

Jagger, M., & Richards, K. (1968). *Sympathy for the devil.* (Recorded by the Rolling Stones.) On *Beggars Banquet* (record). London, UK: Decca.

Koonz, C. (2003). *The Nazi conscience.* Cambridge, MA: Belknap.

Lisciotto, C. (2007). Joseph Goebbels "The poison dwarf". Downloaded from Holocaust Education & Archive Research Team. http://www.holocaustresearchproject. org/holoprelude/goebbels.html.

Neiman, S. (2002). *Evil in modern thought.* Princeton, N.J.: Princeton University Press.

Prince, R. (2016). Predatory identity. In J. Mills & R. Naso (Eds.), *Humanizing evil: Psychoanalytic, philosophical and clinical perspectives*(108–128). London, UK: Routledge.

Prince, R. (2017). The stowaway: Reality, the Holocaust and the historical unconscious. In R. Frie (Ed.), *History flows through us: Germany, the Holocaust, and the importance of empathy* (91–107). London, UK: Routledge.

Solzhenitsyn, A. (2007). *The gulag archipelago abridged: An experiment in literary investigation.* New York, NY: Harper Perennial.

Stangneth, B. (2015). *Eichmann before Jerusalem: The unexamined life of a mass murderer.* New York, NY: Vintage.

Trump, D., & Schwartz, T. (1987). *The art of the deal.* New York, NY: Random House.

Chapter 9

Die Hitler in uns (The Hitler in us)

Evil and the psychoanalytic situation

Emily A. Kuriloff

The term "evil" is of ecclesiastical origin, initially attributed to anyone who defied the word of the Almighty. It was only in modern times that the word became generally associated with moral depravity. The church, then the state—but not the mental health profession—typically decreed which individual's acts and mien were so heinous as to render them not only beyond forgiveness but, worse, beyond understanding. Put differently, those designated as evil were now bereft of any human—not only a religious—connection. The interpersonal/relational psychoanalyst has been less interested, perhaps somewhat uncomfortable with, moral or any other sort of authority, preferring instead to forge a meeting rather than turning away of one mind from another. Witnessing, dialogue, repetition, and new experience are all central to this project. How, then, is the isolating mantle of "evil" relevant to psychoanalytic work? Do its implications defy our very sensibilities and goals?

Let us begin closer to home amidst the perhaps conflictual, or even split off, evil in the hearts, minds, and deeds of psychoanalysts in and out of the consulting room. Psychoanalytic theory and practice in Nazi Germany allows us a particular view of this dark journey, and it may prove a useful cautionary tale for our times, as well as for all times.

Perhaps we can begin by considering evil not as a fixed trait in isolation. If we modify the epithet with a verb—the possibility, that is, for evil—that is an action potential in the context of internal/private and external/interpersonal/cultural pressure, in some combination with history, fantasy and memory. In this view, the potential for evil becomes more or less universal.[1]

One need only consult the now classic psychological studies on aggression and authoritarianism conducted by Milgram (1963) and Zimbardo

(1971)—when a random sample of normal subjects "inflicted" great pain on others under certain conditions. As Christopher Browning (1992), the Holocaust scholar, puts it, such are the "inclinations and propensities common to human nature" *in context*. Browning studied the men in the Nazi killing squads, the *Einsatzgruppen*, who shot thousands to death simply because they were Jewish. He sought to find out how these "ordinary men—shaped by a culture that had its own particularities but was nonetheless within the mainstream of western, Christian, and enlightenment tradition—under specific circumstances willingly carried out the most extreme genocide in human history" (p. 223).

As I have noted previously (Kuriloff, 2014), the French psychoanalyst Madame Janine Chasseguet-Smirgel (1988) takes on some of these disturbing questions. In a book review in which she critiques a 1984 edited volume of essays by German analysts entitled *Les Années Brunes* [The Brown Years]: *Psychoanalysis under the Third Reich*, Chasseguet-Smirgel highlights each contributor's lack of awareness of his or her own murderousness in thought and indeed. She posits that without this recognition, it becomes impossible to resist one's own, or to pinpoint one's patients' identifications with the aggressors who were their fathers and forefathers.

She warns: "One would hope that all analysts would agree that we all have *Die Hitler in uns*, and that only by integrating this diabolical part of oneself is it possible to disentangle oneself from it" (p. 1061).

Yet, owning this potential is particularly threatening to our security and esteem. It may be denied or frankly dissociated from awareness. In fact, thinking and feeling one's way into such aspects of self feels unbearable, precisely because it raises the specter of shame and, worse, rejection—the threat of being expelled from the tent, isolated and endangered in the emotional and physical wilderness. It is "the moment when you are seeing yourself not as you wish, but as others see you ..." as Philip Bromberg (1998) explains. "This moment," he knows, "is perhaps the most common feature of everyday interpersonal trauma."

Evil as it emerges in oneself and in familiar proximity can thus be missed, particularly as it emerges in small, yet impactful, ways. Consider here the notion of "microaggression" (Pierce, 1970), or the casual, even subliminal degradation of "them"—those outside the circle, those not like "us"—unworthy of respect and understanding. Over time, "their"

distinction as inferior is less startling than assumed, if not openly acknowledged. Bit by bit, such evil becomes the norm, so that not only the perpetrator, but the victims may fail to become sufficiently alarmed.

Nor should we pass over the terrible choices people make in the heat
of a threatening moment in which they are themselves in danger. We
must keep in mind the danger to non-Jewish psychoanalysts in the
1930s should they have abandoned what became the "Third Reich."
Indeed, I have noted elsewhere (Kuriloff, 2014, p. 69) the eloquent
words of author and psychoanalyst Robert Wallerstein (1987), com-
menting upon that time, who asks his readers what they themselves
might have done if they, too, were:

> among that band, Aryan Germans, trained psychoanalysts, with life,
> family and career solidly in Germany … with Ernest Jones the IPA
> president advising that we not panic and flee, but stick together to main-
> tain the flame of psychoanalytic reason against the demonic and
> irrational forces threatening … how many [of us] would have dared to
> join the protests …?

And thus: How many of us would stay in Germany and begin to practice "Nazi psychoanalysis"? The British psychoanalyst John Rickman,
who traveled to Berlin after the war, in 1946, reported that many of the
German doctors he found there were, to varying degrees as he put it,
"deteriorated" (Brecht et al., 1993, as cited in Goggin & Goggin, 2001,
p. 135). Goggin and Goggin (2001) likewise advance a somewhat more
polemical group judgment in supposing that most of the analysts at
what became known as the Berlin Göring Institute (renamed after the
Field Marshal's cousin, the psychiatrist Mathias Göring), developed "a
propensity to make increasingly greater compromises with their professional standards the longer the regime lasted" (p. 135).

The Goggins' understanding of the psychoanalyst Dr. Carl Mueller-
Braunschweig's ultimately compromised behavior is illuminating. He
had been analysed by Karl Abraham[2] and later Hanns Sachs, two prominent Jewish clinicians of the highest rank during the days of the
prewar Berlin Institute. Mueller-Braunschweig was known by them and
their colleagues as a competent analyst, and a "decent" man. Goggin
and Goggin indicate that he was also viewed by peers as rather conventional and loyal, perhaps to a fault.

Tasked by Matthias H. Göring to lead the ideological campaign as a part of the ongoing program of "Aryanization" of both the Institute and psychoanalysis (R. Lockot, personal communication, 2010), Mueller-Braunschweig initially seemed more compliant than eager, and his appointment was acceptable to an unenthusiastic but realistic Sigmund Freud. Freud hoped that Mueller-Braunschweig's presence would protect the community from the obvious dangers. But both Freud and Mueller-Braunschweig also feared the influence of "neo-Freudians," concerned that their control was being wrested from them. According to Geoffrey Cocks (1985) this is why the more overtly anti-Nazi analyst, Harald Schultz-Hencke, was not particularly favored by Freud for a prominent role in the transition. Indeed, after the war and despite a record relatively unscathed by participation in fascism, Schultz-Hencke's theoretical orientation kept him outside the circle, as Lockot (personal communication, 2010) notes in her description of the reorganization of post-World War II psychoanalysis. (More about the uses and misuses of these theoretical wars later in this article.)

Early in his tenure, Mueller-Braunschweig visited the Viennese Psychoanalytic Institute after the Anschluss (Hitler's annexation of Austria to Nazi Germany) to discuss plans for its "Aryanization" with Anna Freud, who soon began to cry, prompting Mueller-Braunschweig to write her a comforting follow-up letter in which he expressed his hope that psychoanalysis in Vienna would maintain its independence from National Socialism (Lockot, personal communication, 2010). The letter was discovered by authorities who had been monitoring the activities of "Miss Freud." As a result, Mueller-Braunschweig was humiliated, not allowed to step foot in the Institute, and permitted to work only from his home office. Goggin and Goggin (Lockot, personal communication) view the public nature of this punishment—this humiliation—as contributing to what they characterize as his ever-increasing desire for approval from the Nazis. Whether or not their hypothesis is meaningful, evidence reveals that his anti-Semitic views deepened in the years ahead. Anna Antonovsky (1988), a Jewish Austrian émigré and psychoanalyst, notes how far he soon went: "Müller-Braunschweig's 1942 plan for the Göring Institute clearly lists the teaching of the theories of heredity and race and names among the lecturers Herbert Linden, the director of the euthanasia program for the untreatable mentally ill" (p. 228).

As for the milieu itself, Antonovsky characterizes the Göring Institute as anti-analytic, arguing that its goals ran counter to the emphasis on managing affects and actions via self-reflection and personal responsibility. Instead, she explains, the standard was a subordination of individual minds to the superordinate "whole":

> the entitlement to life was seen as conditional, linked to the individual's place in a hierarchy of race, heredity, and perhaps also gender; and behind all this lay a relinquishing of constraints on the unleashing of one's destructiveness against those perceived as strangers, deviants, or enemies.
>
> (Antonovsky, 1988, p. 228)

Finally, Antonovsky (1988) appends a critique of Mueller-Braunschweig's 1930 paper, *Psychoanalyse und Weltanschauung* (*Psychoanalysis and Worldview*), that she sees as a harbinger of things to come; she highlights a discussion in which he equates a "psychically hard-won acceptance and trust toward one close person with the mush of 'love of the whole,' without making the slightest attempt to consider what is involved in an individual's relating to 'the whole.'" (p. 228).

Official Nazi policy in fact demanded that physicians and psychiatrists no longer administer to a single patient, but instead to the corpus of the German society, the *Volksgemeinschaft*. That is, humans who did not fit within the standard were essentialized as threats—carriers of disease who would contaminate the larger organism. They required healing or, in its absence, killing. Although Cocks (1985) offers evidence that there were some Göring Institute analysts who attempted to save "deviant" homosexuals from a death sentence by automatically classifying them as "cured," Goggin and Goggin (2001) claim that the process by which "cure" was decided was particularly humiliating and sadistic: each patient was forced to perform heterosexual sex in front of a panel of the doctors.

Carl Jung, among the best known of the analysts associated with the National Socialist agenda was Swiss, rather than German. Nevertheless, he assumed the so-called racial identity of a northern European "Aryan," an identity that extended beyond national borders and, in his view, reached deep into the unconscious. Jung was comfortable reviving his theory, first published in 1918, that there was a difference between the Jewish and the German psyche, claiming that the psychologies of

Adler and Freud were particularly appropriate to the Jewish mind. In stressing such difference, he appealed to the all-too-familiar bias that Germans were rooted in the soil, unlike the Jews. It is not surprising that Jung became an early favorite of the Nazi psychiatrist Matthias Göring, who invited him to lecture at the new institute repeatedly.

In 1933, Jung took on the presidency of the General Medical Society for Psychotherapy. This was a professional body founded in 1927 with members from several countries, but primarily based in Germany, and more or less under Nazi control, by virtue of the German national group being the largest component (Samuels, 1992, quoted in Kuriloff, 2014, p. 91). By remaining in this post, he claimed he was preserving the international character of the body as well as providing an alternative organizational outlet for Jews. Nonetheless, Jung was also giving tacit support to the program of "Aryanizing" so-called Jewish psychoanalysis in Germany, and this was not simply a matter of titles, because he "often came to Berlin to give lectures and seminars, and one time he came to give an interview for German radio" (Goggin and Goggin, 2001, p. 71). Yet, even for the reader rightly troubled by this information, many of Jung's views on other matters, such as unconscious communication, remain difficult to dismiss, for they seem to anticipate, and enrich the postmodern relational turn. As Kenneth Eisold (2002) puts it, Jung's notions suggest an interactive matrix that is more affectively than logically driven, one in which the psychoanalyst is as much shaped by the responses of his patient as the other way round.

However, Jung's notion that primal fantasies and identifications and unconscious communication generally emerge unbidden from a deeper, nonindividual stratum help determine his understanding of a psyche shaped both by endemic myth *and* the rational restrictions of culture. Part of Jung's anti-Semitism rested on his belief that the "wandering Jew" does not have as much access to this intuitive and essentially collective realm of experience, for he or she "is badly at a loss for that quality in man which roots him to the earth and draws new strength from below ... the Jew has too little of this quality—where he has his own earth underfoot" (quoted in Samuels, 1992, p. 20). Bromberg (personal communication) suggests that the Swiss Protestant Jung considered Freud's attempts to intellectualize "from above"—to logically organize and concretize psychic life in terms of a unitary energic mass, implicitly a material possession distinct from its surround—typically Jewish. That Jung applied his otherwise useful critique of aspects of Freud's system in order to devalue him as a Jew—and particularly at the moment when the Jews were so very vulnerable—is indeed shocking and reprehensible.

Still, Jung's anti-Semitic orientation would not have distinguished him as particularly fanatical in mid-century Europe. Moreover, it would not necessarily render him a Nazi. Why, then, did he aid the new regime in the way that he did? Was Jung blinded to the perniciousness of the Nazis by his own feeling of vindication? His fame and Aryan credentials were, after all, sought after by them as a stamp of approval for their policies, at least at the beginning. Or, did he agree to present psychoanalysis as more German than Jewish out of fear: that is, in order to protect his theory and the careers of his followers? As Frosh (2009, p. 260) puts it:

> the anxiety felt by the psychotherapy profession in Germany in 1933 was understandably great, and was fueled by the general popular and political association of them with the Jewish discipline of Freudian psychoanalysis. If the whole profession was tainted with this Jewish stain, it could destroy them all.

It could be claimed that Jung's motives involved the hope that German psychoanalysis, under his particular "Jungian leadership, could offer … an umbrella under which threatened individuals might shelter" (Frosh, 2009, p. 262). Deirdre Bair, in her 2003 book, *Jung: A Biography*, attempts to exonerate him along these lines, citing letters Jung wrote to contacts "in England and the United States, often ordering them to 'help this Jew'" (pp. 459–460) in reference to some individual in danger. Cocks (1985) reports that when Jung accepted the presidency of the General Medical Society for Psychotherapy in 1933, he "claimed to be acting in the interests of the Jewish members of the international wing" because his plan was to allow the disenfranchised German Jewish doctors to join the international organization as individuals. When this plan was put into action, it became something of a model, for Ernest Jones followed suit some six months later in terms of the International Psychoanalytic Association. According to Jung's son, Jung also protected the Jewish analyst Gerhard Adler, and aided in his escape from Germany to Switzerland (Cocks, 1985, p. 134).

Bair adds that later, during the 1940s, Jung apparently had influence with the U.S. government. She reveals his connection to Allen Dulles, who entered Switzerland in November 1942, secretly working as the "advance man" for the U.S. Office of Strategic Services (OSS) in Switzerland. For some time, she explains, Jung became Dulles's advisor on a weekly, if not almost daily, basis. Bair (2003) quotes Dulles to the effect that Jung understood:

> the characteristics of the sinister leaders of Nazi Germany and fascist Italy. His judgment on these leaders and on their likely reactions to passing events was of real help to me in gauging the political situation. His deep antipathy to what Nazism and Fascism stood for was clearly evidenced in these conversations.
>
> (p. 493)

That many of us feel compelled to qualify both Jung's culturally normalized anti-Semitism, and, moreover, his Nazi ties, seems further indication of the difficulty in identifying evil in one's midst, particularly its insidious and slow rise in context. Our need to make excuses may also stem from the anxiety in knowing the "not me" aspect of ourselves, of those we esteem, and with whom we identify. The Göring Institute, where Jung did *not* practice, afforded some psychoanalysts a space to continue, and even popularize psychoanalytic concepts and methods. To one degree or another, however, too many became "handmaidens" (Goggin & Goggin, 2001, p. 209) to the principles of a nefarious regime. Such complicity thus becomes a cautionary tale that disposes of the conceit of the neutral and transcendent professional, possessed of a singular (and unassailable) analytic identity across culture and circumstance. As Bernd von Nitzchke (1991, as cited in Goggin & Goggin, 2001, p. 210) argues, such a positivist ideal may have only helped some of the German analysts who remained in the Reich to rationalize going along with, and even embracing, National Socialism (Kuriloff, 2014).

Even within the postwar psychoanalytic community, the topic of evil has been mired in thick theoretical debates. As I explicate in more detail elsewhere (Kuriloff, 2014), seminal psychoanalysts had themselves been *too immersed in* the egregious trauma they suffered in the *Shoah*, after which picking up the pieces of their shattered lives left little room to see, let alone to digest or address the dastardly conflagration at their door.

Consider also that even before the *Shoah*, Sigmund Freud's initial (1930/ 1961) introduction of the death drive—his introduction to the notion of endemic destructiveness—was more theoretical than not, and did not, in the main, appeal to phenomena that were clinically observable. Thus, analytic clinicians felt neither inspired nor compelled to embrace it. However, Freud's tone towards the notion shifted somewhat when he revisited it in 1930, during a time of mounting anti-Semitism and extremist, militaristic challenges to moderate government in Central Europe. As if anticipating what was soon to happen in his own city, he writes rather emphatically of the ubiquity of a destructive instinct directed outward, rather than towards the self:

> anyone who calls to mind the atrocities committed during the racial migrations or the invasions of the Huns, or by the people known as Mongols under Jenghiz Khan and Tamerlane, or at the capture of Jerusalem by the pious Crusaders, or even, indeed, the horrors of the recent World War—anyone who calls these things to mind will have to bow humbly before the truth of this view.
>
> (Freud, 1930/1961, p. 111)

Yet when the Nazis assumed power, the Viennese analysts did not, in fact, bow humbly. Consider the somewhat infamous *Freud–Klein controversies*, set against the backdrop of the London Blitz, where newly arrived Viennese refugees arrived amidst long-established, often native British colleagues. Both groups ignored the bombs outside, and within the Institute engaged in vicious internecine fighting, in nothing less than a parallel process that was barely acknowledged. This, despite the fact that the very content of their argument often concerned the origins and development of a primal destructiveness! The details of these vociferous disagreements lie beyond the scope of this article (see Kuriloff, 2014, for more). Suffice it to say that the fight resulted in Anna Freud's postwar abandonment of Britain as her theoretical home, whereas the famed British Psychoanalytic Society nearly fell apart. Anna went on to place her hopes in America, where—not coincidentally—Melanie Klein's ideas remained unpopular until the close of the 20th century. Instead the notion of an endemic destructiveness, beginning at birth, was widely criticized. Why such resistance, why such conflict regarding the place of evil in psychoanalytic theory and method? Once again,

Anna Freud fled Vienna after suffering interrogation by the Gestapo, after her home and office were sacked, as was the psychoanalytic Thec Verlag—the psychoanalytic publishing house. Klein had left Germany before Hitler came to power, and was separated from any personal Nazi attack by the English Channel.

Distances matter: They can mean life or death; they can mean insight or traumatic dissociation and/or avoidance.

Psychic distance matters as well, or, as Stern (2004) puts it, determines how and when the "eye can see itself." The degree to which one can "stand in the spaces" (Bromberg, 1998), between parts of experience that recall and evoke terror, humiliation, and disempowerment, while still feeling like oneself is thus variable for a host of reasons. The capacity, in other words, to both participate and to observe oneself, to sense the "chafing" or "snags" that make simply continuing in one reality impossible (Stern, 2004), can be hindered by the shame and fear of the loss of a real and fantasized "other." What, then, is left for us to do in the face of evil wishes and deeds?

Chasseguet-Smirgel (1987) turns what may seem an academic question to a more urgent, existential one by considering a postwar context. Consider her depiction of what happened in Eastern Europe within the decade after Hitler's demise:

> When the communists came to power in an Eastern European country, they asked the analysts to declare that psychoanalysis was a 'piece of capitalist putridity', after which they would be allowed to work and retain their party membership. Quite a number signed this declaration. The authorities then said: 'you see, they say so themselves', and decided to dissolve the society. The interesting thing is that apart from a few émigrés, no one remembers this story any longer.
>
> (p. 435; see also Kuriloff, 2014, for further elaboration on this comment)

More recently, we have become aware of American psychologists who participated in developing methods for the torture of prisoners at Guantanamo Bay. Psychoanalysts may note that these psychologists have not undergone an analytic process by which conflicted, hidden, or unformulated psychic experience is mentalized in order to manage parts of themselves more consciously. Still, they are, presumably, self-aware professionals. In all, we are left with a bevy of trained professionals who have behaved in destructive ways despite their training, sensibilities, and personal and professional insights.

What traction, then, does the individual psychoanalyst, the analytic dyad, or the analytic community possess to resist evil? What, after all, is the "cash value in Freud's mapping of the regressive pull of the group, the archaic fantasies and identifications, the anxiety of rejection?" Consider here Frosh's (2009) insight regarding the irony in both Mueller-Braunschweig's and Carl Jung's decision to remove the Freudian Jewish "taint" from psychoanalysis. As Frosh puts it, in doing so, these "Aryans":

> Jettisoned many of the elements of Freudian thought that might have protected them from conforming to Nazi demands ... Freud (1930) famously theorized the individual as always opposed to society, always discontented within it; on a personal level, and despite considerable ambivalence, he identified his own Jewishness as a major, even necessary, spur to achievement precisely because it set him outside the social norm. "To profess belief in this new theory", he wrote, called for "a certain degree of readiness to accept a situation of solitary opposition—a situation with which no one is more familiar than a Jew."
>
> (Frosh, 2009, p. 268, quoting from Freud, 1927, p. 222).

Freud was indeed a Jew, and like many Jews in Europe, he was also an immigrant. His family had resettled in Vienna from what was then a small town in the erstwhile nation of Czechoslovakia. Adam Philips (2002) describes all of psychoanalysis as "an immigrant science," conceived and practiced by those lacking in the familiar comforts of home. Let no analyst languish in comfort, particularly when evil insinuates itself into our midst, and into ourselves. Self-deception, pride, and inertia may result from many a psychic source, but are less acceptable for the uncomfortable outsider on the inside. As the German philosopher Arthur Schopenhauer (1871/2000, p. 200) put it, "Discovery is seeing what everybody else sees, but thinking what nobody else has thought" (p. 110).

Acknowledgments

Emily A. Kuriloff, Psy.D. *Die Hitler In Uns* (The Hitler in Us): Evil and The Psychoanalytic Situation. *Contemporary Psychoanalysis*, copyright © the William Alanson White Institute of Psychiatry, Psychoanalysis & Psychology and the William Alanson White Psychoanalytic Society, www. wawhite.org, reprinted by permission of Taylor & Francis Ltd, http://www. tandfonline.com on behalf of the William Alanson White Institute of Psychiatry, Psychoanalysis & Psychology and the William Alanson White Psychoanalytic Society.

Notes

1 The philosopher Immanuel Kant puts forth a much earlier (1785) noneccle-siastical notion of evil, based on his view of humans as radically free, with a propensity towards both good and evil, faced with a choice. Brandell (1979) and Makari (2008) have made note of Kant's influence on Freud's model of mind.
2 According to Regine Lockot, Mueller-Braunschweig had many conflicts with Abraham, and the analysis did not go well.

References

Antonovsky, A. M. (1988). Aryan analysts in Nazi Germany: Questions of adaptation, desymbotization, and betrayal. *Psychoanalysis & Contemporary and Thought, 11*, 213–231.
Bair, D. (2003). *Jung: A biography.* New York, NY: Little, Brown and Company.
Brandell, G. (1979). *Freud: A man of his century.* Atlantic Highlands, NJ: Humanities Press.
Bromberg, P. M. (1998). *Standing in the spaces: Essays on clinical process, trauma, and dissociation.* Hillsdale, NJ: Analytic Press.
Browning, C. (1992). *Ordinary men: Reserve police battalion 101 and the final solution in Poland.* New York, NY: HarperCollins.
Chasseguet-Smirgel, J. (1987). Time's white hair we ruffle: Reflections on the Hamburg Congress. *International Review of Psycho-Analysis, 14*(3), 433–444.
Chasseguet-Smirgel, J. (1988). Review of J-L. Evard (ed.): Les années brunes: Psychoanalysis under the Third Reich. *Journal of the American Psychoanalytic Association, 36*(3), 1059–1066. doi:10.1177/000306518803600410.
Cocks, G. (1985). *Psychotherapy in the Third Reich.* New York, NY: Oxford University Press.
Cocks, G. (1997). *Psychotherapy in the Third Reich: The Göring Institute* (2nd ed.). Oxford, England: Oxford University Press.

Eisold, K. (2002). Jung, Jungians and psychoanalysis. *Psychoanalytic Psychology, 19*(3), 501–524. doi:10.1037/0736-9735.19.3.501.

Freud, S. (1961). Civilization and its discontents. In J. Strachey (Ed.& Trans.), *The standard edition of the complete psychological works of Sigmund Freud* (Vol. 21, pp. 57–146). London, UK: Hogarth Press. (Original work published 1930).

Freud, S. (1961). The future of an illusion. In J. Stauchey (Ed. & Trans.), *The standard edition of the complete psychological works of Sigmund Freud* (Vol. 21, pp. 1–56). London, UK: Hogarth Press. (Original work published 1927).

Frosh, S. (2009). Foreignness is the quality which the Jews and one's own instincts have in common: Anti-Semitism, identity and the other. In L. Aron & L. Henik (Eds.), *Answering a question with a question. Contemporary psychoanalysis and Jewish thought* (pp. 345–369). New York, NY: Academic Studies Press.

Goggin, E., & Goggin, E. (2001). *Death of a Jewish science: Psychoanalysis in the Third Reich*. West Lafayette, IN: Purdue University Press.

Grosskurth, P. (1985). *Melanie Klein*. London, England: Hodder & Stoughton.

Kant, I. (1997). *The groundwork of the metaphysics of morals* (M. Gregor, Trans. & Ed.). New York, NY: Cambridge University Press. (Original work published 1785).

Kuriloff, E. A. (2014). *Contemporary psychoanalysis and the legacy of the Third Reich: History, memory, tradition*. New York, NY: Routledge.

Makari, G. (2008). *Revolution in mind: The creation of psychoanalysis*. New York, NY: Harper.

Milgram, S. (1963). Behavioral study of obedience. *Journal of Abnormal & Social Psychology, 67*, 371–378. doi:10.1037/h0040525.

Phillips, A. (2002). *Promises, promises*. New York, NY: Basic Books.

Pierce, C. M. (1970). Offensive mechanisms. In F. B. Barbour (Ed.), *The Black Seventies* (pp. 264–282). Boston, MA: Porter Sargent.

Samuels, A. (1992). National psychology, national socialism, and analytical psychology: Reflections on Jung and anti-Semitism part 1. *Journal of Analytical Psychology, 37*(1), 3–28.

Schopenhauer, A. (2000). *Parerga and paralipomena* (Vol. 2) (E. F. J. Payne, Trans.). Oxford, England: Oxford University Press. (Original work published 1871).

Stern, D. B. (2004). The eye sees itself. *Contemporary Psychoanalysis, 40*, 197–237. doi:10.1080/00107530.2004.10745828.

Wallerstein, R.S. (1987). The terms of the dialectic. In J. Chasseguet-Smirgel (Ed.), *Maintenance of the psychoanalytical identity and functioning in a world of flux* (Vol. 6, pp. 21–59). New York, NY: The International Psychoanalytical Association Monograph Series.

Zimbardo, P. G. (1971). The power and pathology of imprisonment. *Congressional Record*. (Serial No. 15, 1971-10-25). Hearings before Subcommittee No. 3, of the Committee on the Judiciary, House of Representatives, Ninety-Second Congress. Washington, DC: U.S. Government Printing Office.

Chapter 10

Dissociation and counterdissociation

Nuanced and binary perceptions of good and evil

Richard B. Gartner

Dissociative reactions to trauma are common. In this article, I argue that what I call counterdissociated reactions to countertrauma are also common. Analysts may react to patients' dissociative states by entering counterdissociative states of their own. These counterdissociative states may help or hinder the movement of the treatment. They may hinder by disallowing the therapist's otherwise clear view of what is occurring or did occur. Yet, they may also allow the treatment bond to be maintained by enabling the therapist to avoid being overwhelmed, whether by the horror of patients' reports of monstrous, unthinkable evil done to them, or by the patients' own reenactive fantasies or behaviors.

Traumatic and non-traumatic dissociation

The literature is, of course, replete with definitions, examples, and discussions of dissociation. As Howell and Itzkowitz (2016a) note, the concept of dissociation has roots in spirit possession, hypnosis, hysteria, and splitting. It is considered in one form or another in early work by Charcot (1887), (Breuer & Freud, 1893), Janet (1907), Ferenczi (1933/1988), Sullivan (1953), Rycroft (1962), and Kohut (1971), among others, as well as by more contemporary writers including Briere (1989, 1991, 1992), Kluft (1989), Bromberg (1991, 1993, 1994, 1996), Herman (1992), Putnam (1992), Davies and Frawley (1994), Pizer (1996), Gartner (1999), Howell (2005, 2011), Itzkowitz, Chefetz, Hainer, Hopenwasser, and Howell (2015), and Howell and Itzkowitz (2016b).

Dissociation involves an unconscious severing of connections between one set of mental contents and another. These sets include affects and knowledge of facts, sensation, and/or interpersonal patterns. The severing occurs before these affects or knowledge enter awareness. In dissociated states, "good and bad feelings about the same object can ... coexist without conflict, for there are no connections between them that would alert the individual to the incongruities involved" (Gartner, 1999, p. 134).

Broadly speaking, there are three kinds of dissociation:

Everyday dissociation is a nearly universal phenomenon. It would be hard to manage all of life's tasks without using some dissociation. We may, for example, drive past 10 exits on a highway while working on some personal problem, then look up, wondering how we got there, having dissociated the previous 20 minutes while we drove safely but without conscious thought about what we were automatically doing.

Adaptive dissociation in the moment of trauma can be a life-saving response (Briere, 1992; Bromberg, 1994; Gartner, 1999; Barlow & Freyd, 2010). For example, an individual in a burning building may be so flooded with horror that he[1] cannot think clearly enough to escape.

The ability to dissociate panic allows him to make a plan of action and follow through on it. Only when safely out of the building does his full terror enter consciousness. In similar fashion, a child being held down and sexually abused may instantly dissociate the experience, floating out of his body up to the ceiling, where he watches "another" child being abused. Later this child may "reenter" his body and only then feel shame, anger, humiliation, and/or pain.

On the other hand, if the child is repeatedly and/or brutally abused and assaulted in similar fashion, he may learn to *not* reenter his body much of the time, remaining instead in a state of chronic dissociation. Then dissociation develops into a habitual way of dealing with anxiety, becoming the *maladaptive* or *pathological dissociation* described throughout the clinical literature (e.g., Davies & Frawley, 1994; Gartner, 1999; Chefetz, 2015; Howell, 2005, 2011; Howell & Itzkowitz, 2016b).

Thus, for the individual sexually betrayed by a trusted parent, caretaker, or institution (cf. Smith & Freyd, 2014; Burmester, 2018), adaptive dissociation may help in getting through the immediacy of the traumatic moment. But when trauma is repetitive, severe, and/or concurrent with other significant trauma, dissociation can become maladaptive, developing into an individual's go-to defense against feelings of anxiety. Perceptions of the world then become warped, because dissociation leaves a person with only a partial understanding of what is happening around him. In turn, this may lead to black-and-white thinking, making subtlety and nuance an impossibility. In this fashion, submission and domination, pain and pleasure, good and evil, are all seen as absolutes, with little discernment of the many possible gradations between them or any possible flexibility in perception.

Countertrauma and counterdissociation

Elsewhere, I have (Gartner, 2014, 2017) described the ways severely traumatized and shattered patients may communicate their traumatized states—dissociated or not—to their analysts. Although this phenomenon is often called "vicarious traumatization" (cf. Pearlman & Saakvitne, 1995), I believe "countertrauma" better captures how these feelings, emerging from the two-person, co-constructed analytic dyad, represent "the full spectrum of contrapuntal internal reactions flowing between patient and analyst" (Gartner, 2017, p. 7).

I have thus defined countertrauma (Gartner, 2014, 2017) as the traumatic reactions an analyst or therapist has over time to hearing from patients about deeply traumatic experiences. This may induce in the analyst a countertraumatic response based partly on the material itself and partly on the patient's reactions to it, especially if the patient is dissociating his reactions. In the context of their co-constructed relationship and shared experience, this may evoke in the analyst contrapuntal countertraumatic feelings, based on both the analyst's own personal history and his history of listening to trauma.

Likewise, I now define counterdissociation as the dissociation a therapist may manifest when faced with the flow of severely dissociative and/or traumatic material. As with countertrauma, counterdissociation emerges from the two-person, co-constructed dyad of therapist and patient, with the emotional flow back and forth between them producing the counterdissociative reaction.

Dissociation and counterdissociation in the clinical moment

In this section, I trace how dissociated perceptions of sexual abuse are communicated to the analyst. Part of the analyst's countertraumatic and counterdissociated responses to these perceptions may include participating in distorted and dissociated assessments of perpetrators. In many cases, this creates an identification or over-identification with the abused part(s) of our patients.

Terry: dissociating and counterdissociating malevolent introjects

I have elsewhere (Gartner, 2015, 2018) described in detail Terry's abuse and its effect on our treatment relationship. A professional man in his early 50s when we first met, he spoke in flat tones when he talked about his sexually, verbally, physically, and emotionally abusive father: "I've always hated him. It started before I have memory—before I was two. Always in the bathroom, usually in the shower. It excited him so much to see my skin. He'd suck on it, lick it, moan over what he tasted and smelled. He loved it if I cut myself and he could suck the wound before bandaging it. Sometimes he would take peanut butter into the shower, spread it on his penis and have me lick it off."

"And I ..." Terry gulped, "I am ashamed to say that each time he approached me in the bathroom I was so hungry for his touch that I was glad. He always started by crooning and hugging, saying how much he loved me. And I'd forgot where it would lead. Or I thought maybe this time would be different, that he would just love me. But it never stayed like that".

Listening to Terry, at first my skin crawled as I pictured a father malevolent enough to treat his young son so dreadfully. Was it right to question Terry's view of his father when I shared it? If so, how could I ever help Terry let go of hating someone so seemingly evil, to allow a more nuanced vision of what surely had been a very troubled man? But as time went on and more and more details emerged, I began to uncomfortably share at least some of his perceptions of his father as coldblooded and immoral. Thoughts about his humanity crossed my mind less and less.

"I learned to always be dressed around him. The sight of my skin aroused him too much. Otherwise I only remember him touching me when beating me. It always boiled down to my not being the son he wanted. He really beat me for that, no matter what the specific provocation."

Terry's voice grew gravelly as he spat out his words. "I learned never to cry when he beat me. It would have pleased him too much."

Revisiting these early sessions many years later, Terry underscored how totally dissociated and removed he had been when first talking to me about his father. "I didn't want anyone in the room when I talked about my father. I was there alone and for those moments you did not exist. It was the only way I could talk about him. I was so unwell!"

Because Terry nearly always spoke in lifeless, detached tones about any emotionally laden material, I had not realized that he had dissociated my very existence when speaking of his father. In retrospect, however, I realize I felt drained by having to work continually to stay in contact with him.

I never totally lost my perception of Terry's father as a presumably traumatized, deeply dissociated man. I considered whether he had been in a dissociated state while murmuring about the taste of Terry's skin or beating Terry for being who he was. Yet with each new detail, my concurrent sense of Terry's father as evil gained credibility and dominance in my mind.

Terry sighed.

I thought all boys did these things with their fathers. I didn't know what to call it. I just knew how unhappy I was. Then I tried to kill myself when I was 11. That's when it stopped. For once, my mother—who spent most of her time in bed staring at the ceiling—got herself dressed and dragged me and my father to a child guidance clinic. My father was terrified. Somewhere he knew where my despair came from. I started therapy with a sweet older woman who sat behind her desk and talked to me. And once in a while I talked back. We met for at least a year. I never told her about my father's treatment of me—I wouldn't have known if it was relevant or what to say about it. But I talked. And although I have felt suicidal many times since then, I have never tried to kill myself. That lady must have been doing something right. I liked her, although I had no idea why. And my father never touched me again.

Terry mused,

> It never occurred to me I was being abused. Not till my 30s, when the
> therapist I was seeing at the time stopped me as I described what hap-
> pened and told me I had been sexually abused. I was shocked. But it
> made sense because I hate him so much.

Terry spoke about his hatred in the present tense even though his father
had been dead for years.

*I imagined living a life so isolated that I had no way of knowing that
not all boys were brutally violated at ages six, four, three, two ... It was
unbearable to me and I stepped back from my own disgust, instead con-
centrating on my fury at the vile man who was Terry's father. One effect of
my counterdissociation was that I dismissed his father's humanity, just as
Terry did. To the extent I counterdissociated, it was less painful to me than
considering the interplay between father and son as understandable in any
way from a human perspective. When I was angry with his father,
I thought he was a psychopath. When I had perspective, I wondered if he
had a dissociative identity disorder.*

Terry had ways of getting revenge beyond not crying when beaten.
A series of events occurred in which Terry defeated his father's efforts
to relate to him. For example, on Terry's wedding day, his father said
to him, "So, I guess everything turned out all right after all," as if they
had ever had a conversation in which they talked through the turbulent
events of Terry's childhood. Terry turned to him. "I said nothing.
I knew how to stare him down by then. He shriveled before my eyes."

Terry's revenge culminated in the period before his father's death:

> I knew he had cancer and he was terrified. He denied he was sick,
> refused to go to a doctor, just got weaker and more frightened until
> near the end. And he'd call me and ask me to come see him, told me
> how proud he was of me, said he knew I'd get things in order, make
> sure his health improved. But as far as I was concerned, he was evil,
> with no redeeming qualities. So, it never even occurred to me to fly
> out there to see him or to make sure he went to a doctor, or, later, to
> arrange for a second opinion and accompany him to it. I was implac-
> able. I refused to see him. I never said that, I just never went. And in
> the end, my sister called and said I'd better come soon if I was going

to come, and later my father called and said he was looking forward to seeing me tomorrow. I could have already been there. I certainly knew how grave things were. But I said I'd see him tomorrow, knowing I wouldn't go till the day after that, when I was pretty sure he would be dead. And so he died before I got there.

Terry's tone was truculent, angry, and almost inhuman.

I felt a heaviness in my stomach as I considered Terry's relentless hatred. How could I reconcile this heartlessness with the wounded child/ man that by now I had known for years? In order to maintain my analytic bond I had to counterdissociate at least some of my patient's cold-bloodedness.

The violence in Terry's soul was encapsulated in fantasies he withheld from me for several years, fantasies that became almost overwhelming when he saw men on the street or in public restrooms, especially if they were wearing shorts or otherwise showing skin. "I see a man's knees when he is wearing shorts, or I see his feet in open sandals, or his torso if his shirt is unbuttoned or, God forbid, he is bare chested. To me he is naked, revolting, and dangerous. In a nanosecond I have raped him in my mind, cut him up, eaten his flesh."

Inwardly I gasped from the horror I felt as I first heard these fanta-sies of rape and cannibalization. Did I have another Jeffrey Dahmer in my office?[2] Did I need to worry about him acting on these bizarre, frightening impulses? Would I have to notify authorities about him and ruin the trust we had finally begun to establish? Upon my inquiring, though, it became clear he had never come close to acting on his urges; nor, in my judgment, did it seem likely he would do so in the future. Comforting myself with this assessment and the knowledge that Terry's sadism had always stayed fully contained in his fantasy life, I protectively counterdissociated the intensity of his nearly hallucino-genic visions, neither forgetting them nor letting them overwhelm me as they had in those moments after he first described them.

I have recounted (Gartner, 2015, 2018) the extent of Terry's paternal sexual abuse and the long transferential struggle we engaged in over the course of his analysis as he furiously attacked me, perceiving me as a likely abuser. Yet eventually he said he loved me and brought me Father's Day cards each year thereafter.

After 10 years of psychoanalysis Terry looked back on his life-long hatred of his "evil" father and reluctantly recognized that his father, too, had had an enormously difficult childhood. He acknowledged something he had always "known" and yet not synthesized into his view of his father: His father had been horrifically abused sexually, physically, and emotionally by his own father and three older half-brothers, and then went on to abuse his own full younger brother. By recognizing his father's childhood traumas, Terry humanized his father, something that all his life he had been loath to do. He took a more nuanced view of his father, although he could not forgive him, conscious that his father's history did not earn him a pass on having abused Terry so appallingly. But Terry no longer saw him simply as a malicious, inhuman, evil monster.

And as Terry allowed his father's humanity into the room, so did I. We each let go of our respective dissociation and counterdissociation, and it became possible to reconsider who his father was—a man, who, like Terry, had been viciously abused, but who, unlike Terry, had revisited this evil upon his son.

When Terry talked again about how he had dealt with his father's death, he was subdued, sad, almost defeated.

> He was as hungry for affection as I was. He did terrible things but he just wanted to be loved. He wanted his son to be a good father to him. He wanted an athletic All-American son to teach him how to be a man. I wasn't that son, and he never let me forget it, even when he was ravenous for me. I sleepwalked through most of my childhood. It made it difficult for me to benefit from anything in my life. What my father thought of me was paramount, as if him thinking better of me would have made a difference by then ... So sad, so sad.

Returning to thoughts of how he behaved as his father was dying, Terry wondered, "If I could talk to my younger self, what could I say? 'You'll feel better 20 years from now if you treat him better now? You'll feel more like a human being if you treat him like one?'"

In my work with Terry, my counterdissociation (counterintuitively) helped protect our therapeutic relationship. For example, I never for a moment forgot Terry's furious attacks on me, which devoured much of our time and energy in the early stages of treatment. Yet, to maintain a safe space in my office for both of us, I needed to dissociate his attempts to keep me at bay so I could find the frightened boy Terry remained in late middle age.

Likewise, my counterdissociation allowed me to continue to strengthen my bond with Terry rather than let it get fractured by the cannibalistic fantasies that so alarmed me when he first told me about them. Once I concluded Terry was in no danger of acting on his impulses, I was able to put them away in a corner of my mind and not let them distract me from the desperate needs this man brought to his analysis. And when our relationship deepened and strengthened, I was able to allow those cannibalistic fantasies back into my consciousness, knowing that, although they signified an important aspect of Terry, they certainly did not represent who he was as a man.

Duncan: dissociating and counterdissociating positive introjects

I have previously (Gartner, 2014, 2017) described Duncan's treatment in detail, as well as my personal countertraumatic reactions to his unfolding accounts of appalling abuse, sex trafficking, and sexual torture. To summarize, as a boy, Duncan (now in his 60s) had lived the remnants of a middle-class suburban existence. He attended private school sporadically and somehow convinced his negligent, self-involved parents that he spent so many nights at his coach's house because of late evening or early morning practices.

Duncan saw the coach who abused him as a good man who looked out for him, loved him, and would never let him come to harm. In his memory, their "relationship" remained the best in Duncan's life. These feelings remained strong even as we explored the life his coach led him to—one of prostitution, sexual exploitation, and even the filming of sickening forced sex and brutalization.

Duncan had gone through his life from adolescence—he was involved with his coach from ages 12 to 18—until his 60s, with a fixed idea that this coach, whom he called Papa, had nothing to do with the multiple sexual traumas Duncan suffered. "He was always good to me. He took me to museums and bought me clothes. We went to shows and the beach. He was so sweet with me!"

Having groomed[3]Duncan sufficiently, Papa became his "lover," then his pimp. He brought Duncan to stay with "friends of his" who would have sex with Duncan that ranged from conventional to brutally sadistic. Eventually, Papa would dress Duncan as a girl and bring him to parties where he was auctioned off and raped by the highest bidder. Still later, Papa introduced Duncan to the man who offered him a "modeling career," sending him to "photographers" who intimidated him with physical and sexual violence, literally strong-arming him into appearing in hardcore sado-masochistic bondage pornography. In spite of all of this, Duncan continued in his dissociated states to maintain the fiction that Papa knew nothing about this and that he, Duncan, had sole responsibility for his travails even though he was no more than 12 when all this began.

It was obvious to me that Papa was a hardened pedophile who trafficked in young boys, a pimp who kept his boys in line. Duncan maintained dissociated images that differentiated Loving Papa from Pimp Papa, and by far the overwhelmingly dominant image was of Loving Papa. The more he insisted that Papa was his caring and kind "adoptive father," the more my counterdissociation made me screen out any possible positives in Duncan's relationship with his abusing coach and to see Papa as an evil presence in Duncan's life. Every time Duncan mentioned how wonderful Papa was to him, I inwardly protested that the "wonder" was that Duncan ever survived his treatment at the hands of this man.

At one point, Duncan was abducted for three days, blindfolded, and repeatedly raped by mobsters who were apparently getting revenge on Papa for running his teenage prostitution ring on their territory without paying them off. Yet Duncan could still not bring himself to say there was anything wrong with Papa having sent him to johns four or more times a week, often two or more times in a night. He did not let himself consider how much money Papa was making from prostituting Duncan and the other teenage boys in his stable while the boys themselves received only occasional pocket change. Duncan even claimed that johns were always nice to him, having dissociated that they were often not as benevolent as he imagined. But he eventually conceded that some of them forced rough sex on him, leaving him bleeding and in need of medical care both for STDs and anal tears and fissures.

It was difficult for me to take in that—on one level—Papa offered Duncan a level of caretaking to which the other boys in his stable had no access. And, crucial to Duncan, Papa showed him the interest Duncan was starved for from a mentoring adult. He asked about Duncan's interior life, joked with him, made tender love to him. To my eyes this hardly made him the loving daddy/lover Duncan described so glowingly. But was it my job to get Duncan to associate these nurturing activities with the evil this man was doing?

At my suggestion Duncan wrote Papa a letter—never intended to be sent—in which he begged for an explanation of all that had transpired. In this letter, Duncan told Papa how much he meant to him and how he had continued to love him all his life, even through decades of marriage and fatherhood. Starting from the position that there must have been an innocent explanation for Papa's actions, Duncan's tone shifted as he began to add up how much money Papa must have made from sending Duncan to johns and from the parties where Duncan was auctioned off to the highest bidder. Writing the letter brought his divergent thoughts and perceptions too close to one another to allow his dissociation to remain entirely intact. I did my best to inquire neutrally about the disparities in these dual images, but it was clear to Duncan that I saw Papa from a very different perspective than he did. Aspects of his idealization began to crumble. For example, he finally acknowledged that Papa "probably" knew what would happen after he introduced Duncan to the man who, after enticing him to become a model, forced him to make hardcore, brutal pornographic films in which he was forced at gunpoint to rape younger children.

Yet Duncan saw himself as the depraved one. "If anything, I was the one who was bad. I was a dirty, shitty kid who hurt the children in those movies and deserved everything I got during the rapes and tortures and abduction. I just wanted drugs and sex. I was nothing."

How should I deal with a man who had so completely dissociated the evil that had been done to him? I counterdissociated my own impulses to shake him out of his idealized fantasy. Making clear my sympathy for his difficult position, I tried to inquire in more and more detail about the flashbacks that returned him to such horrendous circumstances of assault and abuse.

Eventually, and with immense difficulty, Duncan conceded—at least for moments at a time—that Papa must have known about, and perhaps even engineered, all the many sexual, physical, and psychological traumas Duncan had suffered. "But I cannot use the word abuser about him. I cannot call him an abuser! I still love him," he said defiantly. "Yet I know he was mixed up in all of that—the torture and the filming and the parties." He then illustrated the level of his dissociation regarding Papa: "I cannot keep the two versions of him in my head at the same time. First, I am on one track, then the other, never both at the same time for more than a second."

At this point in the treatment, Duncan, who has progressed in many ways, cannot combine his dissociated images of Papa into a whole man, or even keep them in consciousness simultaneously. And I, too, have difficulty merging my own multiple perceptions of Papa. His evil gets by far most of the airtime in my inner musings about him. But every once in a while, I suddenly see how he took a lonely, bright boy whose same-sex leanings were already in evidence, and made him feel valued, loved, and cherished. In retrospect, my more nuanced perceptions of Papa occurred in concert with Duncan's increasing acceptance of the extent of Papa's role in his tragically catastrophic series of traumas.

In Duncan's case, therefore, my counterdissociation played a different role than it did with Terry. Duncan's dissociation of what I considered Papa's evil was nearly absolute. In his eyes, Papa was the best thing that ever happened to him. Contrapuntal to his extreme dissociative idealization of Papa, my counterdissociation involved an inner derision of Papa's supposed positive qualities. At times I felt I was nearly bludgeoning Duncan with my counterview that Papa was malevolent, calculating, devious, wicked, and greedy. Not that I used those words, but this was my view of Papa, and no doubt this came through to Duncan often enough. We struggled in our sessions to the point that I began to question what I was trying to achieve by opening Duncan's eyes to the evil that had been done to him. I had to remind myself that his deep depression, his alcohol and drug abuse, his self-cutting, his terror of being near his grandchildren (or any children), his difficulty maintaining relationships of any sort, his phobias about transportation, phones, and touch, all had their roots in the fact that he dissociated Papa's evil, taking it into himself and making it his own.

In his mind, Duncan had become the abuser, the evil spirit, the madman who sat in his dungeon, as he called the dark corner of his cellar where he spent most of his free time. In order to rescue him from a downwardly spiraling self-perception that might eventually kill him, it was vital that I break into his dissociation of Papa's evil. The more I succeeded, the more Duncan was able to make room in his psyche for discernment of his own kindness, moral decency, and even humor. Accomplishing this required endless sessions in which we went back and forth about who had been good and who evil during his liaison with Papa. We started with diametrically opposed views of the positive or negative characteristics of both Papa and Duncan. But every time I introduced nuance into our dialogue, Duncan moved slightly toward a more balanced view of himself as well as of Papa. By breaking through my counterdissociation, I helped him break through his dissociation.

Adaptive and maladaptive counterdissociation

Like dissociation, counterdissociation can be both adaptive and maladaptive. It can be maladaptive if it serves to detach the analyst from crucial aspects of what is going on in the room. But it can be valuable to the analyst who eventually discerns it in himself.

Counterdissociation can be especially adaptive in teaching the analyst about dissociated aspects of his patient's experience. In a kind of enactment, the patient's disowned and dissociated knowledge and affects are communicated to the analyst. In turn, the analyst, once he understands what is going on, can use his own experience to help the patient connect the dots in his semi-denied understanding of his history and current experience.

Thus, counterdissociation can (counterintuitively) help protect and develop the therapeutic relationship. However, like dissociation itself, counterdissociation contributes to binary thinking and can rob both victim and perpetrator of their humanity. My counterdissociation in Terry's case led me to demonize his father for a period of time and to join with Terry in not admitting his father had human qualities. It was quite different with Duncan. His extreme idealization through dissociation found its counterpart in my counterdissociated inner disparagement of Papa's supposed positive qualities.

In each case, breaking through both dissociation and counterdissociation led us to a more nuanced view of who these abusers might actually have been.

Collective dissociation and counterdissociation

A well-known public example of counterdissociation on a societal level occurred in relation to Jerry Sandusky, the center of scandals that erupted in 2011 about his abuse of adolescent boys at Pennsylvania State University. Most of those who knew him before his indictment appear to have perceived him as a genuinely good guy with a big heart, a pillar of his community. He was, of course, skilled at conveying this impression. Those who thus idealized him ignored any signs that things were awry, even though there were behavioral hints that all was not well. But those who only heard about him *after* the young men's revelations often vilified him and saw him as the incarnation of evil. Neither position took in the subtleties of human experience, behavior, and moral character.[4]

Dissociating (and counterdissociating) people into binaries robs them of their humanity. Furthermore, making victimizers "not human" allows us to avoid considering that human beings can and do act as they did. Thus, black-and-white thinking leads to a myopic vision of the perpetrator and prevents analysts, and indeed all of society, from understanding that perpetrators of violence, abuse, and assault are undeniably human beings. Both dissociation and counterdissociation may thus stop us from understanding that terrible acts are in the realm of what humans can do, and consequently prevent us from discovering what leads human beings to commit what we consider unthinkable acts.

Acknowledgments

Richard B. Gartner, Ph.D. Dissociation and Counterdissociation: Nuanced and Binary Perceptions of Good and Evil. *Contemporary Psychoanalysis*, copyright © the William Alanson White Institute of Psychiatry, Psychoanalysis & Psychology and the William Alanson White Psychoanalytic Society, www.wawhite.org, reprinted by permission of Taylor & Francis Ltd, http://www.tandfonline.com on behalf of the William Alanson White Institute of Psychiatry, Psychoanalysis & Psychology and the William Alanson White Psychoanalytic Society.

Notes

1 For ease of expression, and because I am writing about male patients in this article and I am myself male, I will use the masculine pronoun throughout when referring to victims, patients, and analysts. What I say applies equally to female patients, analysts, and victims.
2 Jeffrey Dahmer was a serial killer and sex offender who committed rape, murder, and dismemberment of 17 men and boys between 1978 and 1991. Many of his later murders involved necrophilia and cannibalism (Wikipedia entry, n.d.).
3 "Grooming" refers to nonviolent behaviors designed to gain the trust of a potential child victim, leading slowly to increasingly seductive and sexualized behaviors and demands (Lanning, 2001; Clemente & Hakes, 2018).
4 See Burmester (2018) for a fuller analysis of the dissociation surrounding the Sandusky case.

References

Barlow, M. R., & Freyd, J. J.(2010). Adaptive dissociation: Information processing and response to betrayal. In P. F. Dell & J. A. O'Neil (Eds.), *Dissociation and the dissociative disorders: DSM-V and beyond* (pp. 93–105). New York, NY: Routledge.

Breuer, J., & Freud, S. (1893–1895). *Studies on hysteria. Standard Edition, 2*, 1–306. London, UK: Hogarth Press, 1962.

Briere, J. (1989). *Therapy for adults molested as children: Beyond survival.* New York, NY: Springer Press.

Briere, J. (1991). *Treating victims of child sexual abuse.* San Francisco, CA: Jossey-Bass.

Briere, J. (1992). *Child abuse trauma: Theory and treatment of the lasting effects.* Newbury Park, CA: Sage.

Bromberg, P. M. (1991). On knowing one's patient inside out: The aesthetics of unconscious communication. *Psychoanalytic Dialogues, 1*, 399–422. doi: 10.1080/10481889109538911.

Bromberg, P. M. (1993). Shadow and substance: A relational perspective on clinical process. *Psychoanalytic Psychology, 10*, 147–168. doi:10.1037/h0079464.

Bromberg, P. M. (1994). "Speak! That I may see you": Some reflections on dissociation, reality, and psychoanalytic listening. *Psychoanalytic Dialogues, 4*, 517–547. doi:10.1080/10481889409539037.

Bromberg, P. M. (1996). Standing in the spaces: The multiplicity of self and the psychoanalytic relationship. *Contemporary Psychoanalysis, 32*, 509–535. doi:10.1080/00107530.1996.10746334.

Burmester, W. (2018). Interpersonal and institutional dissociation in the sexual abuse of boys. In R. B. Gartner (Ed.), *Understanding the sexual betrayal of boys and men: The Trauma of Sexual Abuse* (pp. 204–246). New York, NY: Routledge.

Charcot, J. M. (1887). *Lessons on the illnesses of the nervous system held at the Salpêtrière* (Vol. 3). Paris, FR: Progrès médicalen A. Delahaye and E. Lecrosnie.

Chefetz, R. (2015). *Intensive psychotherapy for persistent dissociative processes: The fear of feeling real.* New York, NY: W. W. Norton.

Clemente, J., & Hakes, F. (2018). Profiling real-life child sex offenders. In R. B. Gartner (Ed.), *Healing sexually betrayed men and boys: Treatment for sexual abuse, assault, and trauma* (pp. 263–281). New York, NY: Routledge.

Davies, J. M., & Frawley, M. G. (1994). *Treating the adult survivor of childhood sexual abuse: A psychoanalytic perspective.* New York, NY: Basic Books.

Ferenczi, S. (1933/1988). Confusion of tongues between adults and the child. *Contemporary Psychoanalysis, 24,* 196–206. doi:10.1080/00107530.1988.10746234.

Gartner, R. B. (1999). *Betrayed as boys: Psychodynamic treatment of sexually abused men.* New York, NY: Guilford.

Gartner, R. B. (2014). Trauma, countertrauma, resilience and counterresilience. *Contemporary Psychoanalysis, 50,* 609–626. doi:10.1080/00107530.2014.94 5069.

Gartner, R. B. (2015). Altered (self) states: A meditation on "Exploring dissociation and dissociative identity disorder." *Psychoanalytic Perspectives, 12*(1), 84–86.

Gartner, R. B. (2017). Trauma and countertrauma, resilience and counterresilience. In R. B. Gartner (Ed.), *Trauma and countertrauma, resilience and counterresilience: Insights from psychoanalysts and trauma experts* (pp. 13–26). New York, NY: Routledge.

Gartner, R. B. (2018). Treating sexually abused and assaulted boys and men. In R. B. Gartner (Ed.), *Healing sexually betrayed men and boys: Treatment for sexual abuse, assault, and trauma* (pp. 7–39). New York, NY: Routledge.

Herman, J. L.(1992). *Trauma and recovery.* New York, NY: Basic Books.

Howell, E. F. (2005). *The dissociative mind.* New York, NY: Routledge.

Howell, E. F. (2011). *Understanding and treating dissociative identity disorder: A relational approach.* New York, NY: Routledge.

Howell, E., & Itzkowitz, S. (2016a). From trauma-analysis to psycho-analysis and back. In E. Howell& S. Itzkowitz (Eds.), *The dissociative mind in psychoanalysis: Understanding and working with trauma* (pp. 20–32). New York, NY: Routledge.

Howell, E., & Itzkowitz, S. (2016b). *The dissociative mind in psychoanalysis: Understanding and working with trauma.* New York, NY: Routledge.

Itzkowitz, S., Chefetz, R. A., Hainer, M., Hopenwasser, K., & Howell, E. F. (2015). Exploring dissociation and dissociative identity disorder: A roundtable discussion. *Psychoanalytic Perspectives, 12*(1), 39–79. doi:10.1080/ 1551806X.2015.979467.

Janet, P. (1907). *The major symptoms of hysteria.* New York, NY: Macmillan.

Kluft, R. (1989). Playing for time: Temporizing techniques in the treatment of multiple personality disorder. *American Journal of Clinical Hypnosis, 32,* 90–98. doi:10.1080/00029157.1989.10402806.

Kohut, H. (1971). *The analysis of the self.* New York, NY: Analytic Universities Press.

Lanning, K. (2001). *Child molesters: A behavioral analysis for professionals investigating the sexual exploitation of children* (4th Ed.). Alexandria, VA: National Center for Missing & Exploited Children, U.S. Department of Justice.

Pearlman, L. A., & Saakvitne, K. (1995). *Trauma and the therapist: Counter-transference and vicarious traumatization in psychotherapy with incest survivors.* New York, NY: W. W. Norton.

Pizer, S. (1996). The distributed self: Introduction to symposium on "The multiplicity of self and analytic technique." *Contemporary Psychoanalysis, 32,* 499–507. doi:10.1080/00107530.1996.10746333.

Putnam, F. (1992). Dissociative phenomena. *Review of Psychiatry, 10,* 145–160.

Rycroft, C. (1962). *Beyond the reality principle.* In *Imagination and reality* (pp. 102–113). London, UK: Maresfield Library, 1968.

Smith, C. P., & Freyd, J. J.(2014). Institutional betrayal. *American Psychologist, 69*(6), 575–587. doi:10.1037/a0037564.

Sullivan, H. S.(1953). *The interpersonal theory of psychiatry.* New York, NY: W. W. Norton

Wikipedia entry. (n.d.). Jeffrey Dahmer. Retrieved from https://en.wikipedia.org/wiki/Jeffrey_Dahmer.

Chapter 11

Dancing with the Devil

A personal essay on my encounters with sexual abuse in the Catholic Church

Mary Gail Frawley-O'Dea

> That this ravaging of souls has been administered by priests entrusted with a sacred covenant to protect and enliven souls is despicable. That bishops and other clerical leaders have covered up and lied about the sexual crimes committed by priests in their charge is as bad, or worse it is evil itself.
>
> (Frawley-O'Dea, 2002, p. 28)

Background

The polarities of religiously mediated horror and awe, terror and transcendence, were personified for me growing up Catholic in a city in which you were identified more by your parish affiliation than by your street address (I was a Sacred Heart kid). Horror was the Devil, the once-good fallen angel, who was always at the ready to rip you from a state of grace into a doomed state of mortal sin (at least until Saturday when the sacrament of Confession could clean the soul slate for the time being). The Devil was real, the Prince of Evil, the concierge of Hotel Hell, a place you could end up if you stole, gossiped jealously and dishonestly about your friend, or had impure thoughts well before you knew what impure thoughts even were. Luckily, awe was available by contemplating and allying with the Divine.

Until early adulthood my faith was my soul center. The Mass entranced me as a positive aesthetic experience (Bollas, 1987) and entry way to the transcendent. Partly as an antidote to my family dynamics, which were laced with their own measure of horror, the Church offered consistency, hope, and goodness. I was perhaps the only kid in Lowell throwing a temper tantrum in order to be *allowed* to attend an all-girls Catholic High School, the Academy of Notre Dame run by the Sisters of Notre Dame de Namur. The school represented a garden of intellectual stimulation, kindness (no sadistic nuns wielding paddles there), safety, and devotion to social justice. Later, as a student at St. Mary's College, then the sister-college to the all-male University of Notre Dame, an intellectual and spiritual banquet was served by a faculty and administration for whom social justice activism, I thought, was a primary and pristine value. My two Notre Dames were awesome intellectual and spiritual providers.

The Catholic Church was central to my spiritual development and to my formation of a social conscience. I was baptized, made my first communion, was confirmed, and married the first time in the Church. In high school, I went to Mass daily during Lent, went to chapel every morning, and was active in Catholic community service organizations. Much of what I still like best about myself was formed in association with the Church.

Since those girlhood days, however, my religious and spiritual identity has changed due to life circumstances and, in large measure, also to my exposure to evil in my work as a psychoanalytic trauma therapist. In addition, in my work with trauma survivors, I found that the horror of what we trauma therapists bear witness to volleys with an awe that words are insufficient to capture, casting trauma work as dance in which the partner is sometimes the Devil and, at other times, the Divine. My engagement with the Catholic sexual abuse scandal and its victims only intensified both sides of that coin and has made difficult any involvement with institutionalized religion.

Encounters with Evil and Transcendence in the Roman Catholic Sexual Abuse Scandal

Author Andrew Delbanco (1995) refers in his book on evil to Milton's Devil.

> He [Satan] invades his prey, as Milton tells it, by a rape ... "in at his Mouth the Devil Enter'd." Milton's description is uncanny in its evocation of sexual abuse. Uncanniness is scary, but Delbanco comforts us. He tells us that this "night time burrowing into [human] bodies" represents Satan's power, but it is borrowed power and limited. Christianity, he says, reassure us that, ultimately, the devil

will be defeated, "driven out of his playground world" by God and goodness. But, what happens when you are *young, still visit playgrounds, and the devil is a priest?*

(Frawley-O'Dea, 2007b, pp. 8–9).

In the early 2000s, I was trying to move away from my total immersion in trauma work. I needed a break, I thought, from the countertrauma of focusing so exclusively on abuse. Right before Easter, however, a fellow New York analyst, Therese Ragen, Ph.D., contacted me about writing an Op-Ed for *The New York Times* together about the sexual abuse scandal in the Catholic Church, which was beginning to get some heavy press coverage. I was ambivalent, but we wrote it. It did not get published, and I figured I was off the hook. Therese had other plans. One of her childhood pals happened to be the administrator of the secretariat of the United States Conference of Catholic Bishops (USCCB) that was planning a focus on sexual abuse at the organization's upcoming June 2002 meeting in Dallas. She contacted her friend, wondering if I might speak at the conference. He contacted me and assured me there was probably no role for me in Dallas, but why didn't I send along my curriculum vitae for future opportunities? Which I did. Several weeks later, he called to invite me to speak to 330 Catholic bishops at the conference about the aftermath for the victim of sexual abuse. He came to New York, took me to lunch, and explained that I would be in front of the bishops, but really speaking to a larger audience as the conference would be televised; I could say anything I wanted, he said. Well, okay. For me as a seeker of social justice, this was a chance to give back to the leaders of a Church that had formed me spiritually.

Although I had drifted away from Catholicism by 2002, it still held a place in my spiritual core and heart. Or, as my husband once said, "You can take the girl out of the Catholic Church, but you can't take the Catholic Church out of the girl," and there was a lingering, latent yearning to "go home." I am sure there was an inchoate fantasy that I could earn my way back to the Church by bringing my knowledge and gifts to the bishops and helping them fix this terrible and tragic abuse crisis. It was the fantasy of a child hoping to bring healing to her narcissistic and abusive parents. But, under the sway of this notion, when my USCCB contact asked how much I would like to be paid, I said, "Nothing. It is a gift. Just pay my expenses." Oy vey.

It was a pretty short deadline to get the paper written so I headed off to Barnes & Noble one Saturday to avoid distractions at home. As I walked through the mall to get there, my feet began to hurt. By the time I was ready to go home, my hands hurt, there were painful red dots around the base of my fingers, and my throat kind of ached. At home, I called a doctor friend who decided I was suffering from Coxsackie disease, a hand-foot-and-mouth infection usually seen in children and probably brought home by my preschooler. Hmmm, that's weird I thought as I hung up the phone. Then it hit me: "Oh, good Lord, I have 'cock-suckie' disease! What have I gotten myself into?" Within an hour of the "interpretation," the symptoms were gone and I was much more consciously anxious and conflicted about my impending Dallas debut.

My husband and three-year-old daughter accompanied me to Dallas. Dennis, more comfortably confirmed as a former Catholic than I, was skeptical about the good-heartedness of my hosts and decided I might need a loved one to unload on. We lunched the day we arrived in the atrium restaurant of Dallas's five-star Fairmont Hotel and watched as dozens of ecclesiastical royalty arrived sporting their pectoral crosses, elegant rings, and French cuffs. At one point, I got up and noticed a bishop sitting alone behind me. I introduced myself and my mission, saying that I would be talking to the bishops the next day about the consequences to the victim of sexual abuse. "And who are you?" I asked cheerfully. A deep and somber voice responded, "My name is Gabriel Montalvo. I am the papal nuncio" (essentially the Vatican's ambassador to the United States). Now well on my way to the land of high anxiety, I even more cheerfully (read hysterically) said, "Oh, wow. That's so cool. You live on Embassy Row and get to go to all those parties. See you tomorrow!" I could almost feel the wool of my old Catholic school uniform as I scurried away. He may have had his own countertraumatic reaction after what had to have been a highly unusual interaction bereft of the reverence in which he was characteristically held, even by his brother bishops.

The next morning, my talk was preceded by poignant stories told by three survivors, then by Scott Appleby, a noted professor of history at Notre Dame, and Margaret O'Brien Steinfels, a well-known Catholic and editor of *Commonwealth*, a leading magazine for lay Catholics. At the coffee hour just before I spoke, I witnessed a bishop walk over to

Cardinal Bernard Law—then spending a good deal of time being deposed by various lawyers about his role in Boston's ground zero sexual abuse debacle—take his hand, and say, "I just wanted you to know how proud I am of what you are doing in Boston." I was speechless; a petite religious sister standing next to me grabbed my hand and said she'd like to take her shoe off and throw it at both of them. I was beginning to sense my audience might not be as appreciative and welcoming to what I was about to say as I had hoped.

Clad in a deep pink suit, pearls, and pearl earrings, all consciously designed to be disarming and very Catholic ladylike circa 1958, I launched into my tour of the psychological house of horrors through which clergy sexual abuse survivors struggle to make their way, sometimes never finding the exit door. My husband reported that a bolt of electricity went through the room when I announced,

> *Make no mistake about it. The violation of a child or adolescent by a priest IS incest.* It is a sexual and relational transgression perpetrated by THE father of the child's extended family; a man whom the child is taught from birth to trust above everyone else in his life, to trust second only to God. Priest abuse IS incest.
>
> (Frawley-O'Dea, 2002)

After the talk, some bishops thanked me with tears in their eyes; others entirely avoided eye contact and did not acknowledge my presence. When, soon after Dallas, I concluded that the meeting was mostly an exercise in public relations and not many hearts or minds had been changed, I decided I wanted to know more about how the Church got to this point. Since then, I have been involved with the sexual abuse crisis in the Catholic Church as speaker to the Conference of Major Superiors of Men, two groups of New York Jesuits, and a handful of other Catholic organizations and associations, as a writer (Frawley-O'Dea, 2002, 2004a, 2004b, 2005, 2006, 2007a, 2007b, 2008, 2010a, 2010b, 2011a, 2011b, 2012, 2013, 2014a, 2014b, 2014c, 2015, 2016a, 2016b, 2016c, 2016d; Frawley-O'Dea & Goldner, 2007), media commentator in 2006, 2007, and 2013, expert witness, and even played myself in an Oscar-nominated documentary film (Berg, 2006).

During this time, I have come to know the basest evil enacted by Catholic priests fueled by the vilest covering-up of that evil orchestrated by other priests, bishops, cardinals, and popes. I have been traumatized by the secreted moral and sexual filth of my once beloved Church and I have been shocked bone-deep by the passivity, even collusion with abuse and cover-up, of too many of the laity. Surprisingly, however, I also have found transcendence and a deepening of my spirituality as regressive ties to my personal old-time religion have been loosened and mourned.

The Devil

Rev. Mark Roberts admitted to whipping his male victims and pouring hot candle wax on them while they stood with their arms outstretched as if they were on a cross.
(Johnson, 2003, in Frawley-O'Dea, 2007b, p. 44)

Archbishop Tarcisio Bertone, a Vatican official, did not think bishops should report sexual abuse to civil authorities. Clergymen should not have to fear legal consequences when they confided in their bishops and society "must also respect the professional secrecy of priests."
(Dunklin & Egerton, 2002, quoted in Frawley-O'Dea, 2007b, p. 165)

We didn't protect the children. They were our brothers who did these things. We heard the rumors. We heard the suspicions. Only two or three of us spoke up at great risk to ourselves. What is it that made us, the Boston presbyterate so supine, so passive, so inert, so passive, so unwilling to react, to take risks, and to speak out?
(Gibson, 2003, p. 212, quoted in Frawley-O'Dea, 2007b, p. 183)

When Phil Saviano and other alleged victims of Fr. David Holley filed a lawsuit, Saviano received a fax from a parishioner saying, "You fucking pussies ought to let go of the past and the blow jobs you all enjoyed".
(France, 2004, p. 332, quoted in Frawley-O'Dea, 2007b, p. 189)

From the perpetrating priests to their brother clergy, from bishops, cardinals, and popes to the people in the pews, a great many members of the worldwide community of Catholics were, to greater or lesser extent, complicit in the sexual abuse of hundreds of thousands of children and adolescents around the globe.

In the United States, about 5% of the priesthood abused over 5,200 young people between 1950 and 2004 (John Jay College of Criminal Justice, 2004; United States Conference of Catholic Bishops, 2006). These numbers are based on self-reports from various dioceses and religious congregations and are therefore undoubtedly low. In addition, we can safely assume that many victims never came forward to report the abuse. Abusing priests were routinely shifted by bishops from parish to parish when reports were made to superiors about sexual abuse and the new parish was rarely informed about the priest's alleged or substantiated prior behavior. When individuals or families reported abuse to diocesan officials, they usually were given false assurances that "Father" would be removed from contact with children and prevailed upon not to "bring scandal to the Church" by going to civil authorities. Most complied, adhering to the adage that Catholics are expected to "pray, pay, and obey." The further back in time one goes, it is also clear that, not infrequently, civil authorities colluded with Church officials to keep sexual abuse secrets.

When a priest's sexual violations were made public, parishioners almost always sided with the priest, lobbing cruel remarks at the victims and their families or excluding them from parish life. Fr. Mark Lehman of Phoenix was convicted of molesting parish girls and sentenced to 10 years in prison. The victims' mothers received death threats, had their tires slashed, and were aggressively confronted in court by fellow parishioners there to support Lehman. When Patty Hanson, one of the mothers, met another parishioner on the street after the trial, that woman called Hanson a "blasphemous bitch"; a number of parishioners threw Lehman a party before he left for prison (Kennedy, 2002, pp. 112–123).

None of this is so unusual in the world of sexual abuse. As reports of sexual abuse of the young have emerged from other religions (Hirvonen, 2016; Neustein, 2009) prep schools (Abelson, 2016; Bidgood, 2017; Harris, 2017; Kamil, 2012; Moynihan, 2016), scouting (Felch & Christensen, 2012), and other organizations, it is clear that institutional betrayal trauma, including sexual abuse, is usually kept under wraps with officials, alumni, and even parents supporting the perpetrator and the institution at the expense of survivors and their families. What distinguishes the Catholic scandal is that, unlike other institutions, the Catholic Church has long held itself to be the one, true church of Jesus Christ. Its teachings are considered within the group to be not just one take on truth, but the ultimate truth, especially in matters of morality. For many, as it was for me once, the Church served as a pillar of belief in shared goodness as well as the possibility of being cleansed of sin. It was the route to the Divine.

Catholics believe that, at the moment of ordination, an ontological change occurs to the priest through which he becomes an "alter Christus" (other Christ). They also believe that every priest is ordained by bishops who are direct successors of the Apostles. Priests, therefore, are—or at least were—tinged with hues of divinity: God-ish mediators of divine grace and gatekeepers to the sacraments to which every Catholic craves access. Children, at least in the not so distant past, were raised to believe that the priest was the *Über*-father of their family and community, a man to be trusted above all else and second (maybe) only to God. If a priest took an interest in little Johnny, many parents would be thrilled, never suspecting an overnight with Father at a mountain cabin would include their son's molestation or rape. And Johnny would never tell, because who would believe him and, anyway, how do you tell on God? The mind-fucking and spiritual devastation inflicted on victims was at least as damaging long term as the bodily violence and penetration.

During my 15 years of involvement with the Catholic scandal, I have been engulfed at times by the "smoke of Satan" (*America*, 2004) that the USCCB's National Review Board concluded was let into the Church by the "grievously sinful" (*America*, 2004), sexually abusive acts of priests and the cover-up executed regularly by bishops. That smoke gets into your marrow and leaves some long-lasting alterations.

Rage

> Whoever welcomes one such child in my name welcomes me. If any of you put a stumbling block before one of these little ones *who believe in me, it would be better for you if a great millstone were fastened around your neck and you were drowned in the depths of the sea.*
>
> (Matthew 18:5–6, New Revised Standard Version; emphasis added)

In general, we trauma therapists become somewhat like cops; we become intimately acquainted with a palette of evil that is truly unimaginable for most people. There is no violation, no sadistic act, no vicious infliction of interpersonal mayhem that, if told to me, I would find unbelievable. I can still find and appreciate the beauty, kindness, and generosity of life, but that is edged with a cynical assumption that a potentially horrifying underbelly lurks not too far away.

It has always been difficult for me, therefore, to listen to people who, shielded from the evil I confront regularly in my work, express platitudes or make statements born of ignorance about betrayal traumas like domestic violence, sexual abuse/assault, physical abuse, psychological abuse, etc. Declarations about those things not happening in our neighborhood/zip-code/school/church/socioeconomic strata enrage me. Excuses made for alleged perpetrators, like Jerry Sandusky, also enrage me, as do suggestions about how the victim may have been "asking for it," is probably making it up, or should have told someone right away.

Given how vital the Church was to my spiritual development, however, it has been especially infuriating to have wandered around behind the altar for 15 years to find that the emperors have no clothes on—sometimes literally. I felt that I had been duped, tricked by ecclesiastical P. T. Barnums introduced to me in infancy. The rage ebbs and flows, but today is often my default reaction to many things Catholic.

It also has been enraging to confront the yawning chasm of hypocrisy between what the Church says it is and the degree to which priestly sexual abuse has been enabled by centuries of bishops, cardinals, popes, and people in the pews. The late priest and novelist, Rev. Andrew Greeley, asked:

> Bishops may express verbal apologies. They are certainly sorry that they have attracted unfavorable media attention. However, they do not seem to have any sense of the suffering of victims nor any real guilt that they were personally responsible for this suffering. … How can one be guilty of so many objective mortal sins and not break down in pain? Why don't they rush off to monasteries to expiate?
>
> (Greeley, 2003, quoted in Frawley-O'Dea, 2007b, p. 157)

At least one bishop did go off to a monastery, but most have not. Nor has any bishop been seen heading for the beach with a millstone tied around his neck. Most have projected blame and guilt on to a media trying to destroy the Church, dissident Catholics trying to destroy the Church, Jews, or the sexual revolution of the 1960s (Frawley-O'Dea, 2007b), all of which is also enraging. Things have begun to improve some under Pope Francis; he has appointed bishops and cardinals who appear to have true pastoral hearts, but his papal commission on sexual abuse has gone nowhere fast and its most eloquent survivor member stepped down because of the lack of any tangible accomplishments.

Psychosomatic symptoms

> Then Jesus summoned his twelve and gave them authority over unclean spirits, to cast them out, and to cure every disease and every sickness.
>
> (Matthew 10:1, New Revised Standard Version)

In general, I do not tend to somatize. The "cock-suckie" episode described above surprised me. Since then, however, especially after a two-day expert witness evaluation of a survivor in litigation with the Church, I experience painful gastrointestinal distress that lasts for hours. I have understood it as an evacuation of the load of often gruesome narratives of abuse and the sickening sequelae of sexual violation and relational betrayal reported by the survivor with whom I have spent so much concentrated time. It is literally too much to metabolize and so I am taken over internally by devilish cramping, heartburn, and expulsions of the excrement of evil. The spiritual irony is that exposure to the Catholic hierarchy's "unclean spirits," for me and for many survivors of priestly abuse, induces physically expressed soul sickness rather than eliciting healing from ostensible direct successors of the Twelve.

Loss of comfort in organized religion

> Woe to you, scribes and Pharisees, hypocrites! For you are like whitewashed tombs, which on the outside look beautiful, but inside they are full of bones of the dead and all kinds of filth.
>
> (Matthew 23:27, New Revised Standard Version)

Like the Mike Rezendes character in *Spotlight* (McCarthy et al., 2015), the Oscar-winning movie about the *Boston Globe*'s investigative reporting on sexual abuse in the Archdiocese of Boston, I always thought that

I could go back to the Church at some point. Short of that, maybe there was another denomination that could become a church home, so I tried the Episcopalians, Methodists, Presbyterians, and Lutherans at different times. They all offered something and I admire aspects of each, but like Richard B. Gartner's (2004) patient Julian stated, "I am a Catholic. And I have nowhere I can go to be one" (p. 95).

The Divine

Trauma can kill its victims or render their lives an endless litany of suffering. At the same time, my patients have shown me that courage and determination, the willingness to trust someone again, and the tools that trauma studies and psychoanalysis have given me, can pull triumph and a good-enough life out of the ashes of tragic loss, humiliation, and human-inflicted harm. I am struck again and again by the gritty determination of so many survivors of the unspeakable to thrive, not just survive, and by their willingness to remember and relive hellish experiences of abuse and neglect in order to claim lives they could not imagine prior to treatment. They inspire me and regularly instill awe and belief in the transcendent. Not every patient triumphs, but enough do to sustain my belief that the human spirit is often magnificent and can flourish despite having been subjected to once unspeakable evil.

It is difficult to convey fully the transcendent experiences I have been gifted through this work because much of it is ineffable. Even more so than countertrauma, counter transcendence is wordless, embedded in positive aesthetic experiences akin to those derived through encounters with religion, spirituality, art, poetry, music, or nature, and are held in reverence and deemed sacred by the individual (Frawley-O'Dea, 2014a). According to Bollas (1987), aesthetic moments are timeless and wordless, experienced more as "a spell which holds itself and other in symmetry and solitude" (p. 30); they are often followed by a "sense of profound gratitude" (p. 31). My engagement with the Catholic sexual abuse crisis has offered experiences countervailing to those listed above.

Fellowship

I have met a number of "friends of God and prophets" (Johnson, 2003, p. 307) who have gifted my soul with fellowship and offered moments of positive aesthetic experience that I carry with me as talismans of wonder. Theologian Elizabeth Johnson (2003) says that these folks

> enter into a mutual relationship with God, freely, with trust and affection; caring passionately about what God cares about. [Being a prophet] … is to raise your voice in criticism against injustice [it is] being without honor in your own country and among your own people.
>
> (p. 307)

Reporters, victims, advocates, some clergy, fellow commentators, and clinicians have shared humor, support, and good will that has lifted me up and reminded me of the goodness and resilience of the human soul.

An unexpected avocation

I may have almost as many books on my shelves that address theology/ spirituality/feminist theology/prayer practices from many traditions as I do psychoanalytic works. The study of religion and spirituality has become an enlivening avocation that I may never have pursued were it not for my involvement in the sexual abuse scandal in the Catholic Church. My reading and reflection are foyers to the transcendent and have become important parts of my life.

A deepening spirituality

Before 2002, I had not thought deeply about God or even prayed much for many years. But at the same time that my faith in religious institutions became brittle, my belief in the ongoing work of Creation and in the immanence of the Divine became deeper, more profound, more challenging, in part because of my activity in the Catholic sexual abuse crisis. Now I am free to choose what moves my spirit without the constraints of a particular dogma or doctrine and I seek the transcendent, as Bollas (1987) suggests, through the positive aesthetic experiences I find in art, music, poetry, and, especially, nature. I have learned that I can always honor and savor the spiritually enlivening and challenging strands of my Catholic heritage, especially the emphasis on social justice, while embracing traditions from other faiths and cultures that feed my soul.

Making a difference

My engagement with the sexual abuse crisis has allowed me to make a difference in ways that have moved me greatly. After the talk in Dallas, I received a number of appreciative emails and cards from survivors who had heard the speech. One 70-something survivor wrote that, until he heard me speak, he did not think anyone could understand his experience. He did not know how much time he had left, but he was going to begin therapy so whatever was left could be better than what had gone before. Likewise, I have received letters or emails from survivors I have evaluated as an expert witness who felt understood during our time together and have since entered therapy. I also have been able to write often for the public, frequently in *National Catholic Reporter*, and have therefore reached a wider audience, I hope raising consciousness about sexual abuse and its consequences. It is ironic that it was my Catholic formation that taught me that making a difference was a responsibility to embrace and to live out and the Church's scandal provided a way to do it.

As I was struggling to figure out how to end this article, I took a break by going to Facebook. One of my favorite Jesuits had posted a new article by one of his younger brethren entitled "Is Evil for Real?" (Gottschall, 2017). The author does not define evil, so I will refer to Jeffrey Burton Russell (1977), a medievalist who wrote four volumes on evil and its personification in Devil figures variously named throughout history. Russell's definition is simple: "the essence of evil is abuse of a sentient being, a being that can feel pain. Evil is never abstract. It must always be understood in terms of the suffering of the individual" (1977, p. 17). He says that it is our moral obligation to see evil when and where it occurs, speak it, lift it up to be recognized by others rather than turning a blind eye.

The young Jesuit discusses the reality of evil and the tendency we have to call it something else, in part because once we acknowledge that evil is accessible to all of us, we must look at our own history with it. He says, "This is an uncomfortable reality, yet if I am willing to call out the evil actions of others, I need to be able to admit my own" (1977, p. 7). Russell likewise advises us to look squarely at our own capacity to enact evil, and indeed to reflect honestly on the instances in which we have committed evil, lest we project it onto others. He insists that recognizing, understanding, and integrating evil is the only way for it to be tamed rather than disowned and acted out unconsciously.

Perhaps another blessing of the work with survivors of diabolic acts and amidst the evil of the Catholic abuse crisis is the opportunity to know my own capacity for evil and my own list of evil acts; to look them squarely in the face without flinching or losing all hope of goodness and redemption. Gottschall (2017) states, "Guilt accompanies this admission [of evil], but guilt is not a feeling to be wallowed in; it is a motivation to seek forgiveness, reconciliation, and healing."

As trauma therapists, we know that many sexual abuse perpetrators and those who enable them, in and out of the Catholic Church, rarely admit their evil-doing or even experience guilt, leaving it for the survivor to shed guilt, shame, and blame with which she or he has projectively identified and that should be owned by another. It is a lengthy and hard-fought part of the clinical journey. Because we are human and because of the work we do as trauma therapists, it is inevitable that we too will hurt our patients, colleagues, and family members. It may be "evil" with a small "e," as opposed to capital "E" evil, or in Catholic terms, venial sin versus soul-blackening mortal sin, but it still hurts another sentient being. At that point, we, unlike so many of the evil-doers to whom our patients have been exposed, can indeed seek forgiveness, reconcile a ruptured relationship, and foster healing. We expiate our own evil acts by reaching inward to access the residue of our transcendent experiences, reclaiming the capacity for compassion, humility, and love.

Horror and awe, terror and transcendence, the Devil and the Divine. They are the goblins and the graces that visit me through the work that I do. All are welcome.

Acknowledgments

Mary Gail Frawley-O'Dea, PhD. Dancing With The Devil: A Personal Essay On My Encounters with Sexual Abuse in the Catholic Church. *Contemporary Psychoanalysis*, copyright © the William Alanson White Institute of Psychiatry, Psychoanalysis & Psychology and the William Alanson White Psychoanalytic Society, www.wawhite.org, reprinted by permission of Taylor & Francis Ltd, http://www.tandfonline.com on behalf of the

William Alanson White Institute of Psychiatry, Psychoanalysis & Psychology and the William Alanson White Psychoanalytic Society.

References

Abelson, J. (2016). Phillips Exeter still reeling from sexual abuse claims. *The Boston Globe*. Retrieved from http://www.highbeam.com/doc/1P2-40335786.html? refid=easy_hf.

America Magazine. (2004, March 15). Sign of the times: Sexual abuse brought "smoke of Satan." Retrieved from https://www.americamagazine. org/issue/477/news/signs-times.

Bidgood, J. (2017, May 22). St. Paul's School acknowledges decades of sexual misconduct. *The New York Times*. Retrieved from https://www.nytimes. com/2017/05/22/us/st-pauls-school-acknowledges-decades-of-sexual-misco nduct.html/.

Berg, A. J. (Writer & Director). (2006). *Deliver us from evil* [Motion Picture]. United States: Lionsgate.

Bollas, C. (1987). *The shadow of the object: Psychoanalysis of the un thought known*. London, UK: Free Association Books.

Delbanco, A. (1995). *The death of Satan: How Americans have lost the sense of evil*. New York, NY: Farrar, Straus and Giroux.

Dunklin, R., & Egerton, B. (2002). Vatican panelists names examined: Two have advised bishops not to report abusers; Some fear a stacked deck. *The Dallas Morning News*. Retrieved from www.dallasnews.com.

Felch, J., & Christensen, K. (2012, September 19). Release of scout's files reveals decades of abuse. *The Los Angeles Times*. Retrieved from http://www.latimes.com/local/la-me-scouts-oregon-20121019-story.html.

France, D. (2004). *Our father: The secret life of the Catholic Church in an age of scandal*. New York, NY: Broadway Books.

Frawley-O'Dea, M. G. (2002, June 13). *The experience of the victim of sexual abuse*. United States Conference of Catholic Bishops Spring Meeting. Retrieved from www.usccb.org/issues-and-action/child-andyouthprotection/archives.cfm. C-Span (2002, June 13). Catholic Bishops Conference, Day 1, Part 2, 1.13.04–1.49.50. Retrieved from https://www.cspan.org/video/?170525-2/cath olic-bishops-conference-565-day-1-part-2.

Frawley-O'Dea, M. G. (2004a). Psychosocial anatomy of the Catholic sexual abuse scandal. *Studies in Gender & Sexuality*, 5(2),121–138. https://doi.org/10.1080/15240650509349244

Frawley-O'Dea, M. G. (2004b). The history and consequences of the sexual abuse crisis in the Catholic Church. *Studies in Gender & Sexuality*, 5(1), 11–30. https://doi.org/10.1080/15240650509349238.

Frawley-O'Dea, M. G. (2005, December 7). Homosexual priests scapegoated in sexual abuse scandal. *National Catholic Reporter*.

Frawley-O'Dea, M. G. (2006, December 28). Church officials play the blame game. *National Catholic Reporter.*

Frawley-O'Dea, M. G. (2007a, March 11). A dangerous closet. *Boston Globe Magazine.* Retrieved from http://www.boston.com/news/globe/magazine/art icles/2007/03/11/a_dangerous_closet/.

Frawley-O'Dea, M. G. (2007b). *Perversion of power: Sexual abuse in the Catholic Church.* Nashville, TN: Vanderbilt University Press.

Frawley-O'Dea, M. G. (2008, May 16). Papal visit a 'both/and' moment in sexual abuse crisis. *National Catholic Reporter.*

Frawley-O'Dea, M. G. (2010a, July 28). A proposal for dealing with priest perpetrators. *National Catholic Reporter.* Retrieved from http://ncronline. org/blogs/examining-crisis/proposal-dealing-priest-perpetrators.

Frawley-O'Dea, M. G. (2010b, May 2). The gift of shame. *National Catholic Reporter.* Retrieved from https://www.ncronline. 2016aorg/blogs/examining-crisis/gift-shame.

Frawley-O'Dea, M. G. (2011a, July 21). The John Jay study: What it is and what it isn't. *National Catholic Reporter.* Retrieved from https://www.ncronline. org/blogs/examining-crisis/john-jay-studywhat-itand-what-it-isnt.

Frawley-O'Dea, M. G. (2011b, March 25). Where is Catholicism's Tahir Square? *National Catholic Reporter.* Retrieved from https://www.ncronline. org/blogs/examining-crisis/where-catholicisms-tahrirsquare.

Frawley-O'Dea, M. G. (2012, May 7). Hierarchy's inability to mourn thwarts healing in the church. *National Catholic Reporter.* Retrieved from https:// www.ncronline.org/news/accountability/hierarchys-inability-mournthwarts-healing-church.

Frawley-O'Dea, M. G. (2013, April 23). Hard work awaits Pope and survivors. *National Catholic Reporter.* Retrieved from https://www.ncronline.org/news/ accountability/hard-work-awaits-popeand-abuse-survivors.

Frawley-O'Dea, M. G. (2014a). God images in clinical work with sexual abuse survivors. In D. F. Walker & J. D. Alten (Eds.), *Spiritually oriented psychotherapy for trauma* (pp. 169–188). Washington, DC: American Psychological Association.

Frawley-O'Dea, M. G. (2014b, May 30). SNAP is wrong to discourage victims from meeting the Pope. *National Catholic Reporter.* Retrieved from https:// www.ncronline/org/news/accountability/snap-wrongdiscouragevictims-meeting-pope.

Frawley-O'Dea, M. G. (2014c, April 30). Will Francis tend to those most impoverished by the Church? *National Catholic Reporter.* Retrieved from https:// www.ncronline.org/news/accountability/will-francis-tend-thosemost-impoverished-church.

Frawley-O'Dea, M. G. (2015, September 9). Pope sends painful mixed messages to abuse victims. *National Catholic Reporter.* Retrieved from https://www. ncronline.org/news/accountability/pope-sendspainfully-mixedsignals-abuse.

Frawley-O'Dea, M. G. (2016a). Suicide and the search for justice after sexual abuse. *America: The Jesuit Review.* Retrieved from https://www.america maga zine.org/issue/suicide-sexual-abuse-ans-search-justice.

Frawley-O'Dea, M. G. (2016b, June 6). Trauma can bring about growth. *National Catholic Reporter.* Retrieved from http://www.ncronline.org/news/ accountability/trauma-can-bring-about-growth.

Frawley-O'Dea, M. G. (2016c, May 23). There is hope for survivors to heal. *National Catholic Reporter.* Retrieved from https://www.ncronline.org/news/ accountability/there-hope-survivors-heal.

Frawley-O'Dea, M. G. (2016d, May 9). Child abuse and neglect take their toll. *National Catholic Reporter.* Retrieved from https://www.ncronline.org/news/ accountability/childhood-abuse-and-neglect-take-their-toll.

Frawley-O'Dea, M. G., & Goldner, V. Eds. (2007). *Predatory priests, silenced victims: Sexual abuse and the Catholic Church.* Hillsdale, NJ: Analytic Press.

Gartner, R. B. (2004). Predatory priests, sexually abusing fathers. *Studies in Gender & Sexuality, 5,* 31–56. doi:10.1080/15240650509349239.

Gibson, D. (2003). *The coming Catholic Church: How the faithful are shaping a new American Catholicism.* San Francisco, CA: Harper San Francisco.

Gottschall, B. (2017, July 3). Is evil for real? *The Jesuit Post.* Retrieved from https://thejesuitpost.org/2017/07/is-evil-for-real/.

Greeley, A. (2003, August 3). Are bishops sorry at all? *Chicago Sun-Times.* Retrieved from www.suntimes.com.

Harris, E. A. (2017, April 13). Sexual abuse at Choate went on for decades, school acknowledges. *New York Times.* Retrieved from https://www.nytimes. com/2017/04/13/nyregion/sexual-abuse-choate.

Hirvonen, H. (2016, February 25). Jehovah's Witnesses' sex abuse scandal is a lot like Catholic Church's. *Reveal: The Center for Investigative Reporting.* Retrieved from https://www.revealnews/org/blog/jehovahs-witnesses-sex-abusescandal-is-a-lot-like-catholic-churchs/.

John Jay College of Criminal Justice. (2004, February). *The nature and scope of the problem of sexual abuse of minors by Catholic priests and deacons in the United States 1950–2002.* Presented at the meeting of the United States Conference of Catholic Bishops, Washington, D.C.

Johnson, E. A. (2003). *Truly our sister: A theology of Mary in the communion of saints.* New York, NY: Continuum.

Kamil, A. (2012, June 6). Prep school predators: The Horace Mann School's secret history of sexual abuse. *The New York Times Magazine.* Retrieved from http://www.nytimes.com/2012/06/10/magazine/the-horacemann-schools-secret -history-of-sexual-abuse/html.

Kennedy, E. (2002). *The unhealed wound: The Church, the priesthood, and the question of sexuality.* New York, NY: St. Martin's Press.

McCarthy, T. (Director), Bederman, M., Dorros, B., King, J., Lawson, P., Marchand, X., Omidyar, P., Ortenberg, T., Singer, J., Skoll, J. (Executive Producers), Faust, B. P., Golin, S., Rocklin, N., Sugar, M., Producers,

Churchill, K., von Lintel, Y. (Co-producers), & Mizner, D., (Associate Producer). (2015). *Spotlight* [Motion Picture]. United States: Open RoadOpen.

Moynihan, C. (2016, August 8). Teacher out at Fordham Prep after school says '84 sexual abuse claim is credible. *New York Times*. Retrieved from http://www.nytimes.com/2016/08/09/nyregion/teacher-out-at-fordhamprep-after-school-says-84-sexual-abuse-claim-is-credible.html.

Neustein, A. (2009). *Tempest in the temple: Jewish communities and child sex scandals*. Waltham, MA: Brandeis University Press.

Russell, J. B. (1977). *The devil: Perceptions of evil from antiquity to primitive Christianity*. Ithaca, NY: Cornell University Press.

United States Conference of Catholic Bishops and the Office of Child and Youth Protection, National Review Board. (2006). *Report on the Implementation of the Charter for the Protection of Children and Young People*. Washington, DC: United States Conference of Catholic Bishops.

Chapter 12

The developmental roots of psychopathy

An attachment perspective

Adriano Schimmenti

Introduction

Psychopathy is a personality disorder comprising a constellation of interpersonal, affective, and behavioral characteristics. It entails features such as deceptiveness, egocentricity, grandiosity, impulsivity, irresponsibility, lack of empathy, and lack of remorse, together with violations of legal norms and social expectations (Hare & Neumann, 2008). Contemporary research on the origins of psychopathy is mainly focused on neurobiological vulnerabilities that may predispose to the disorder (Glenn & Raine, 2014). Perhaps because of an early conceptualization of psychopathy as a constitutional disorder (Bisch, 1925; Cleckley, 1941), the role of environmental and relational factors in the development of psychopathic personalities has received limited attention until recent years. This dominant view of psychopathy as a constitutional disorder independent from environmental factors is summarized in the words of Harvey Cleckley, the author of the seminal *The Mask of Sanity* (1976), who stated: "During all my years of experience with hundreds of psychopaths (...) no type of parent or parental influence, overt or subtle, has been regularly demonstrable" (p. 412). However, following a renewed interest in the dynamics and consequences of childhood adversities (Bowlby, 1980; Finkelhor, 1979), an increasing number of studies have been published in the last three decades that examine the childhood of psychopaths.

Historically, it is in the very first edition of the *Diagnostic and Statistical Manual of Mental Disorders* (DSM; American Psychiatric Association, 1952) that an environmental origin of psychopathy was postulated: the Sociopathic Personality Disturbance (the official nomenclature of psychopathy at the time of the first DSM) already included the subcategory of "dyssocial reaction", which classified those individuals who showed disregard for the common social norms and came in conflict with such norms as a result of growing up in abnormal moral environments. Actually, the locution "secondary psychopathy" (Karpman, 1948) is still in use to distinguish the psychopathic variants resulting from exposure to disturbing and often traumatizing environments from other psychopathic variants whose origins are likely to be found in neurobiological and genetic vulnerabilities, usually defined in term of primary or constitutional psychopathy. However, even though such distinction between primary and secondary psychopathy might maintain some diagnostic and clinical meaning in the evaluation of specific psychopathic traits, the current knowledge on the epigenetics of human development indicates that a more comprehensive perspective, based on the interaction between genetic and environmental factors, should be preferred for a better understanding of psychopathy and its etiology (Schimmenti, Di Carlo, Passanisi, & Caretti, 2015). In this context, childhood trauma and related attachment disturbances may interact with inborn genetic vulnerabilities, which account for about 50% of variance in psychopathic traits (Blonigen, Carlson, Krueger, & Patrick, 2003; Tuvblad, Bezdjian, Raine, & Baker, 2014), and may foster alterations in the development of brain regions that have been associated with psychopathic behaviors. These alterations involve, among other brain structures, the orbitofrontal cortex, which has a central role in the cognitive processes of decision making (Koenigs, 2012), and the limbic system, especially the amygdala, which is particularly implicated in emotional learning and emotional responses (Carré, Hyde, Neumann, Viding, & Hariri, 2013).

Thus, research on the childhood experiences of psychopaths may be critical for better understanding how psychopathy can develop in some individuals. Clearly, this research might have enormous implication for both prevention and treatment of psychopathic behaviors.

The relationship between child maltreatment and psychopathy

Early research in psychopathy clearly suggested a positive relationship between relational adversities in childhood and the development of psychopathic traits. For example, Partridge (1928) reported that 12 psychopathic adolescents from a reform school were all rejected by their parents during childhood. Similarly, Field (1940) found that 92% of children with psychopathic traits who were hospitalized in a psychiatric institute had been rejected by their mothers in early childhood. Haller (1942) found that the majority of 52 paroled individuals with psychopathy in a mental hospital had either been neglected or rejected as children. Silverman (1943) examined 75 criminal psychopaths and found that almost two-thirds of them were exposed to rejection, psychological abuse, sexual abuse, separation from parents, and/or loss of parents before the age of 15. Bowlby (1944), in his famous study on 44 juvenile thieves at the London Child Guidance Clinic, identified a subgroup of 14 psychopaths; almost all of them had suffered from early separation from caregivers and had spent most of their early childhood in hospitals or residential homes. McCord and McCord (1956) observed that most of the psychopathic boys under their treatment were exposed to parental neglect, psychological abuse, rejection, inconsistent discipline, and parental conflict during their entire childhood. Also, Robins (1966) found that children who had experienced abuse and absent or inconsistent discipline during childhood were more likely to show prominent psychopathic traits after 30 years.

All these early studies call attention to the attachment relationships of psychopathic individuals, supporting the view that many psychopaths lacked positive experiences with their caregivers during childhood. This is in line with Karpman's original theory (1941, 1948) that "secondary" psychopathy might result from childhood exposure to parental rejection and abuse that fostered extreme feelings of hostility and hatred in the child. Contemporary research with valid and reliable measures, such as the Psychopathy Checklist (PCL; Hare, 1980) and its derivative measures, such as the Psychopathy Checklist-Revised (PCL-R; Hare, 1991, 2003), the Psychopathy Checklist: Youth Version (Forth, Kosson, & Hare, 2003) and the Psychopathy Checklist: Screening Version (Hart, Cox, & Hare, 1995) seem to support these early findings.

For example, De Vita, Forth, and Hare (1990) examined the family background of 107 adult male offenders, and they found that paternal rejection and lack of parental supervision were related to the offenders' psychopathy scores. Weiler and Widom (1996) compared the PCL-R scores of 629 individuals with documented experiences of abuse and neglect in childhood with a matched control group, and found that those who were abused and/or neglected scored significantly higher on psychopathy than controls. Koivisto and Haapasalo (1996) examined a sample of 52 offenders, and found that those who had experienced parental absence, physical abuse, or neglect in childhood had higher psychopathy scores than the offenders without such experience.

In 1999, Marshall and Cooke published one of the most relevant studies on the relationship between attachment trauma and psychopathy. They administered the PCL-R and the Childhood Experience of Care and Abuse (CECA; Bifulco, Brown, & Harris, 1994), which is considered a highly valid and reliable measure for the retrospective assessment of child abuse and neglect (Schimmenti & Bifulco, 2015), to a sample of 105 convicted adult male offenders (50 psychopaths and 55 non-psychopaths). They found that the psychopaths in their sample had been exposed to more severe experiences of neglect, inconsistent discipline and supervision, psychological abuse, and antipathy (i.e. rejection) than non-psychopaths. They further examined the impact of different experiences of child neglect and abuse on specific psychopathic traits and concluded that their results "suggest a specificity of effect with familial experiences being more closely linked with the personality features of the disorder and the societal influences being more closely associated with the behavioral features of the disorder" (p. 220).

Odgers and colleagues (2005) examined the relationship between psychopathy scores and child victimization in 125 females from 13 to 19 years of age who were incarcerated in a correctional facility. The majority of these teens reported victimization by their primary maternal figure, with 88% of them reporting that they had experienced psychological abuse, 53% indicating that they had been physically abused, and 36% reporting that they had witnessed domestic violence.

In 2006, Farrington and colleagues published the results of the Cambridge Study in Delinquent Development, a 40-year prospective longitudinal study on the development of antisocial behavior, which is considered one of the most comprehensive studies examining the influence of family-related factors on psychopathic traits. They measured many individual, family, and social risk factors in 411 boys aged 8 to 10; at age 48, psychopathy was measured in 304 of these participants. A number of negative attachment experiences were related with high levels of psychopathy, including lack of supervision, harsh discipline, physical neglect, disrupted family, uninvolved fathers, depressed mothers, and convicted parents. These relationships were stronger with the factor of psychopathy concerning social deviance (including the erratic lifestyle and the antisocial features of psychopathy).

Krischer and Sevecke (2008) examined self-reported experiences of childhood victimization in a sample of 185 detained adolescents and in a control group of 98 adolescent students, and found that the detained adolescents were more traumatized than the students in the control group. Also, they found significant associations between psychopathy scores and physical and emotional abuse among boys in the detainee group, but not among girls, for whom nonparental living arrangements such as living in foster care were more linked with psychopathy scores.

Weizmann-Henelius and colleagues (2010) examined the forensic psychiatrists' reports concerning the childhood psychosocial background characteristics of 565 homicide offenders (102 women and 463 men), and found that violence in the family, institutional or foster placement, parental divorce, parental criminality, and parental alcohol abuse were associated with higher levels of psychopathy in both women and men; furthermore, sexual abuse was specifically associated with psychopathy scores among females, whereas physical abuse was specifically associated with psychopathy scores among males in their study.

Graham and colleagues (2012) examined specific types of child maltreatment (emotional abuse, physical abuse, sexual abuse, and neglect) and psychopathy scores in a sample of 223 male convicted sexual offenders who were evaluated for civil commitment, and found that psychopathy was positively associated with childhood experiences of neglect; they also found that being exposed to multiple types of child maltreatment was related to increased psychopathy scores in their sample. Borja and Ostrosky (2013) examined psychopathy scores and self-reported childhood trauma in a sample of 194 male inmates: they found that participants with low psychopathy scores were less exposed to physical abuse than participants with medium or high psychopathy scores, and that participants with high psychopathy reported higher experiences of emotional abuse and sexual abuse than participants with low levels of psychopathy. Craparo and colleagues (2013) examined child abuse and neglect in a small sample of 22 Italian inmates convicted for violent offenses, and found that 87.5% of the eight inmates who displayed high levels of psychopathy in this group reported an attachment trauma before age 10 (emotional neglect and/or physical, sexual, or emotional abuse).

Kolla and colleagues (2013) examined childhood trauma and psychopathy scores in 10 violent offenders with antisocial personality and psychopathy, 15 violent offenders with antisocial personality but without psychopathy, and 15 nonoffenders, and found that levels of physical abuse in childhood and total trauma scores differentiated the three groups, with those suffering from both psychopathy and antisocial personality showing the highest level of victimization during childhood. Giovagnoli and colleagues (2013) examined CECA scores and psychopathy scores in 30 forensic psychiatric inpatients: they found that lack of supervision, neglect, antipathy, and discord in the family were predictive of psychopathy.

Schraft and colleagues (2013) found weak but positive and significant associations between self-reported childhood trauma scores and psychopathy scores in a sample of 147 adolescents in a detention center. In particular, they found that the interpersonal facet of psychopathy was associated with emotional abuse; the affective facet of psychopathy was associated with emotional neglect; the lifestyle facet of psychopathy was associated with sexual abuse, physical neglect, emotional neglect, and emotional abuse; and the antisocial facet of psychopathy was associated with physical abuse.

Schimmenti and colleagues (2014) found that seven out of 10 participants who obtained the highest scores in the validation study of the PCL-R in Italy were exposed to multiple and severe attachment trauma during their childhood, including physical, psychological, and sexual abuse; neglect; parents with psychiatric disorders; witnessing violence; and/or living in residential care or foster homes since young childhood. In a subsequent study, Schimmenti and colleagues (2015) examined the relationship between psychopathy scores and exposure to child maltreatment in a group of 78 male violent offenders, and found that almost two-thirds of the sample experienced either emotional, physical, or sexual abuse in childhood, with 17% experiencing all three types of abuse. Emotional abuse showed a predictive relationship with overall levels of psychopathy and with its two factors (interpersonal-affective and social deviance) in this study.

Dargis and colleagues (2016) further observed in a sample of 183 male criminal offenders that the severity of self-reported child maltreatment was positively linked to psychopathy scores. The associations were significant for physical abuse, physical neglect, emotional abuse, and emotional neglect, but not for sexual abuse.

Forouzan and Nicholls (2015) reported the findings from a case-controlled prospective design on 82 young adult women previously placed in youth centers, and found that those who were diagnosed as psychopaths were more likely to be placed in foster care during childhood. Among the many variables investigated in this study at different times, having suffered from incest in early adolescence and exposure to physical and verbal abuse in late adolescence were able to differentiate psychopaths from non-psychopaths. Among the family variables, there were many significant differences between psychopathic and non-psychopathic young women. The psychopaths were more likely to have a conflictual and aggressive mother in late adolescence, and especially a very problematic relationship with the father figures during their entire life (i.e., a higher likelihood of having an absent father in early childhood; an aggressive, psychologically, physically, and emotionally abusing father in late childhood; a conflictual and sexually abusing father in early adolescence; an emotionally and physically abusing father in their late adolescence).

Ometto and colleagues (2016) assessed psychopathy in 66 adolescents who were maltreated during childhood and 41 adolescents who were not exposed to abuse or neglect: the maltreated adolescents scored higher than the other adolescents in all psychopathy scores. In their study, emotional neglect was linked to the interpersonal facet of psychopathy; physical neglect was linked to the affective, lifestyle, and antisocial facets of psychopathy; and physical abuse was linked to the lifestyle and antisocial facets of psychopathy. Also, Sevecke and colleagues (2016) examined a sample of 341 adolescent detainees, and found that self-reported physical abuse positively predicted psychopathy scores in their sample.

This brief overview of research findings clearly indicates that the childhood of psychopaths is often characterized by experiences of severe abuse and neglect that warp individual development along the trajectory of atypical and maladaptive behaviors. Within the framework of attachment theory, these findings also indicate that many psychopathic individuals have failed to internalize their parents as a secure base and source of safety (Bowlby, 1988).

In fact, many psychopaths have learned on both a conscious and an unconscious level (frequently via abuse, neglect, loss, and inconsistent discipline), that the world is dangerous, and they cannot trust anyone. Consequently, survivors of childhood maltreatment develop internal representations (or working models) of a world that is rejecting, critical, abusive, and violent. Living in a ruthless, inhumane, and compassionless world where what and whom one holds dear and essential for survival is fleeting and dubious, some of them learn to take what they need or desire from others and from society, without guilt or remorse. These considerations are in line with Bowlby's seminal description of the "affectionless character". In his study on 44 juvenile thieves, Bowlby (1944) believed that these individuals may suffer from a "massive inhibition of object-love combined with excessive and relatively uninhibited libidinal and aggressive impulses" (p. 67). Indeed, attachment theory helps us elucidate the developmental roots of some psychopathic personalities (Schimmenti et al., 2014).

Attachment and psychopathy: exploring the linking mechanisms

Attachment is a biologically-based motivational system that initially regulates the proximity of the child to his or her caregivers, so that the child can be protected from danger and threats and can safely explore the environment (Bowlby, 1969/82). The interactions with caregivers will constitute the basis for the development of internal working models of attachment (IWMs) in the child. The IWMs are affective and cognitive schemata including representations of self, representations of the other, and representations of the relationship between self and the other. These representations will lead the child in future behaviors and relationships (Bowlby, 1973). As adults, those who have secure IWMs tend to enjoy close and intimate relationships, to display feelings of trust and openness toward others and social interactions, and to adequately regulate their emotions (Schimmenti et al., 2014). Those showing insecure attachment styles are at increased risk for psychopathology. People with an anxious attachment tend to have a high desire for company, intimacy, and closeness, but they worry that others will not reciprocate their feelings; they may also display under-regulation of affects, and may be prone to develop internalizing disorders, such as anxiety disorders (Schimmenti & Bifulco, 2015). On the contrary, those with an avoidant attachment style tend to be emotionally detached from others and are usually dismissive in close relationships; they are often unwilling or unable to share feelings with others, are emotionally over-regulated, and may be prone to develop psychosomatic symptoms and externalizing disorders (Schimmenti & Caretti, 2018). Individuals who were exposed to relational trauma during childhood may also show disorganized attachment; that is, they could present unresolved trauma and/or loss, and sometimes also an inconsistent pattern of responses to attachment-related stimuli where the conflicting characteristics of anxious and avoidant attachment styles are both present (Schimmenti et al., 2014).

Not surprisingly, a recent meta-analysis on the relationship between psychopathic traits and attachment styles (van der Zouwen, Hoeve, Hendriks, Asscher, & Stams, 2018), comprising 12 studies and a total of 1,876 participants, showed that psychopathy was positively related to insecure and disorganized attachment, with an overall effect size of the association significantly deviated from zero (where zero corresponds to a lack of associations) of .18, and with stronger associations observed in clinical, forensic, and prison samples. Therefore, it is critical to explore how the attachment failures in childhood may contribute to the development of psychopathic traits.

It is possible to postulate that the internal processing of attachment trauma may lead some vulnerable children to develop severe psychopathic traits. In fact, the mind of the child has limited cognitive and emotional resources to elaborate the experiences of loss, neglect, and abuse in attachment relationships; thus it can only use the already available strategies that could allow the child to psychologically survive such experiences.

Among these, a possible way to survive child maltreatment is to identify with the aggressor (Ferenczi, 1932/1988, 1933/1949). In the identification with the aggressor, the abused child internalizes the psychological characteristics of the attachment figure who perpetrates the abuse. Howell (2014) has clearly described this process: "As a result of being overwhelmed, the child becomes hypnotically transfixed to the aggressor's wishes and behavior, automatically identifying procedurally and by mimicry" (p. 50). This "traumatic identification with the perpetrator's self" (Schimmenti, 2017) initially allows the child to perceive some sense of control toward the abuser, but can ultimately lead to the development of a sadistically controlling and potentially violent personality. In fact, the child's representations of the self will be modeled on the omnipotent perpetrator who enacts the traumatizing behaviors, and the representations of other people will take shape accordingly as simple instruments to be used, without remorse or guilt, for satisfying one's own needs; consequently, a representation of the relationships between self and others that is based on exploitation, deception, and mistreatment will emerge in the child's IWMs. This perspective is consistent with research showing that psychopathy is linked with a strong devaluation of attachment bonds (Schimmenti et al., 2014) and that antisocial personalities may tend to display derogating states of mind regarding attachment (Allen, Hauser, & Borman-Spurrell, 1996).

Furthermore, toddlers who display disorganized attachment because they have been exposed to a frightening and/or frightened caregiver may also develop controlling-punitive strategies in the preschool years (Lyons-Ruth & Jacobvitz, 2008) to resolve the internal conflict between the desire to approach and flee from the parent. This "fright without solution" (Main & Hesse, 1990) in relating with a parent who is at the same time the source and the solution of the infant's alarm is an extremely disorganizing experience for the child, and thus controlling behaviors may surface in the child that allow him or her to banish from consciousness the overwhelming fear of the attachment figure. Disorganized children may develop controlling-caregiving strategies in which they become compulsive caretakers of their own caregivers, in a significant process of role reversal (Bowlby, 1988); however, disorganized children may also develop controlling-punitive strategies, engaging the caregiver in a power struggle of dominance by using authoritarian behaviors such as verbal threats, harsh commands, and sometimes even physical aggression (Liotti, 2011). Literature findings show that controlling-punitive strategies are linked with increased risk of externalizing disorders in children (Bureau, Ann Easlerbrooks, & Lyons-Ruth, 2009; O'Connor, Collins, & Supplee, 2012). Therefore, research on controlling-punitive strategies might shed some light on the positive associations between psychopathic behaviors and unclassifiable states of mind regarding attachment in adulthood (Frodi, Dernevik, Sepa, Philipson,

& Bragesjö, 2001; Schimmenti et al., 2014): it is possible that psychopaths who had been abused and neglected during childhood may continue to have disorganized attachment representations (revealing that the highly conflicting features of anxious and avoidant attachment are both present in their IWMs) but they may also continue to display controlling and aggressive behaviors when relating with others and in society.

Itzkowitz (2018) has aptly summarized most of these considerations on the role of the identification with the aggressor and the controlling-punitive strategies in psychopathy, when he stated that "the need for attachment, because it creates feelings of danger and disorganization in the young child, is primarily what is dissociated in psychopathy" (p. 51). In other words, some psychopaths have implicitly learned in their childhood that the only way to survive attachment trauma was essentially to totally silence their attachment needs and to switch off their feelings, and to start attacking the world before the world would attack and destroy them.

Conclusions

From an attachment-based perspective, it is exactly the need to survive and adapt to a hostile and depriving relational environment that leads some children to devalue the positive role of attachment bonding and human relatedness in well-being and personal growth. The devaluation of attachment bonds allows these children to defensively exclude from awareness (Bowlby, 1980) the overwhelming memories related to attachment trauma and the consequent flood of emotional dysregulation, but it might also start the developmental sequelae that ultimately lead to the surfacing of severe psychopathic traits in vulnerable individuals. For this reason, appropriate preventative measures and intervention programs that are also informed by attachment theory should be widely promoted, especially with at-risk families, in order to avoid the painful roots of psychopathy spreading into and subverting our society.

References

Allen, J. P., Hauser, S. T., & Borman-Spurrell, E. (1996). Attachment theory as a framework for understanding sequelae of severe adolescent psychopathology: an 11-year follow-up study. *Journal of Consulting and Clinical Psychology, 64*(2), 254–263.

American Psychiatric Association (1952). *Mental disorders: Diagnostic and statistical manual*. Washington, DC: Author.

Bifulco, A., Brown, G. W., & Harris, T. O. (1994). Childhood Experience of Care and Abuse (CECA): A retrospective interview measure. *Journal of Child Psychology and Psychiatry, 35*(8), 1419–1435.

Bisch, L. E. (1925). Constitutional psychopathic states and the psychoses. In L. E. Bisch (Ed.), *Clinical psychology* (pp. 100–109). Baltimore, MD: Williams & Wilkins.

Blonigen, D. M., Carlson, S. R., Krueger, R. F., & Patrick, C. J. (2003). A twin study of self-reported psychopathic personality traits. *Personality and Individual Differences, 35*(1), 179–197.

Borja, K., & Ostrosky, F. (2013). Early traumatic events in psychopaths. *Journal of Forensic Sciences, 58*(4), 927–931.

Bowlby, J. (1944). Forty-four juvenile thieves: Their characters and home-life. *The International Journal of Psycho-Analysis, 25*, 19–53.

Bowlby, J. (1969/82). *Attachment and loss, Vol. 1: Attachment*. London, UK: Hogarth Press.

Bowlby, J. (1973). *Attachment and loss, Vol. 2: Separation – anxiety and anger*. London: Hogarth Press.

Bowlby, J. (1980). *Attachment and loss (Vol. 3): Loss – sadness and depression*. London: Hogarth Press.

Bowlby, J. (1988). *A secure base: Clinical applications of attachment theory*. London: Routledge.

Bureau, J. F., Ann Easlerbrooks, M., & Lyons-Ruth, K. (2009). Attachment disorganization and controlling behavior in middle childhood: Maternal and child precursors and correlates. *Attachment & Human Development, 11*(3), 265–284.

Carré, J. M., Hyde, L. W., Neumann, C. S., Viding, E., & Hariri, A. R. (2013). The neural signatures of distinct psychopathic traits. *Social Neuroscience, 8* (2), 122–135.

Cleckley, H. (1941). *The mask of sanity: An attempt to reinterpret the so-called psychopathic personality*. Oxford: Mosby.

Cleckley, H. (1976). *The mask of sanity* (5th ed.). St. Louis, MO: Mosby.

Craparo, G., Schimmenti, A., & Caretti, V. (2013). Traumatic experiences in childhood and psychopathy: A study on a sample of violent offenders from Italy. *European Journal of Psychotraumatology, 4*, 21471.

Dargis, M., Newman, J., & Koenigs, M. (2016). Clarifying the link between childhood abuse history and psychopathic traits in adult criminal offenders. *Personality Disorders: Theory, Research, and Treatment, 7*(3), 221–228.

De Vita, E., Forth, A. E., & Hare, R. D. (1990). Family background of male criminal psychopaths [Paper presented at the meeting of the Canadian Psychological Association, Ottawa]. *Canadian Psychology, 31*, 346.

Farrington, D. P., Coid, J. W., Harnett, L., Jolliffe, D., Soteriou, N., Turner, R., & West, D. J. (2006). *Criminal careers up to age 50 and life success up to age*

48: New findings from the Cambridge study in delinquent development. London: Home Office.

Ferenczi, S. (1932/1988). *The clinical diary of Sándor Ferenczi*. Cambridge, MA: Harvard University Press.

Ferenczi, S. (1933/1949). Confusion of the tongues between the adults and the child (The language of tenderness and of passion). *International Journal of Psycho-Analysis, 30*, 225–230.

Field, M. (1940). Maternal attitudes found in 25 cases of children with primary behavior disorder. *American Journal of Orthopsychiatry, 10*(2), 293–311.

Finkelhor, D. (1979). What's wrong with sex between adults and children? Ethics and the problem of sexual abuse. *American Journal of Orthopsychiatry, 49*(4), 692–697.

Forouzan, E., & Nicholls, T. L. (2015). Childhood and adolescent characteristics of women with high versus low psychopathy scores: Examining developmental precursors to the malignant personality disorder. *Journal of Criminal Justice, 43*(4), 307–320.

Forth, A. E., Kosson, D., & Hare, R. D. (2003). *The Hare Psychopathy Checklist: Youth version*. Toronto: Multi-Health Systems.

Frodi, A., Dernevik, M., Sepa, A., Philipson, J., & Bragesjö, M. (2001). Current attachment representations of incarcerated offenders varying in degree of psychopathy. *Attachment & Human Development, 3*(3), 269–283.

Giovagnoli, O., Ducro, C., Pham, T. H., & Woitchik, P. (2013). Impact of familial adversities during childhood on the onset of psychopathic personality. *Annales Medico Psychologiques, 171*(7), 509–511.

Glenn, A. L., & Raine, A. (2014). *Psychopathy: An introduction to biological findings and their implications*. New York, NY: University Press.

Graham, N., Kimonis, E. R., Wasserman, A. L., & Kline, S. M. (2012). Associations among childhood abuse and psychopathy facets in male sexual offenders. *Personality Disorders: Theory, Research, and Treatment, 3*(1), 66–75.

Haller, B. L. (1942). Some factors related to the adjustment of psychopaths on parole from a state hospital. *Smith College Studies in Social Work, 13*, 193–194.

Hare, R. D. (1980). A research scale for the assessment of psychopathy in criminal populations. *Personality and Individual Differences, 1*(2), 111–119.

Hare, R. D. (1991). *The Hare Psychopathy Checklist-Revised manual*. Toronto: Multi-Health Systems.

Hare, R. D. (2003). *The Hare Psychopathy Checklist-Revised* (PCL-R) (Second edition technical manual). Toronto: Multi-Health Systems.

Hare, R. D., & Neumann, C. S. (2008). Psychopathy as a clinical and empirical construct. *Annual Review of Clinical Psychology, 4*, 217–246.

Hart, S. D., Cox, D. N., & Hare, R. D. (1995). *Manual for the Hare Psychopathy Checklist-Revised: Screening Version (PCL:SV)*. Toronto: Multi-Health Systems.

Howell, E. F. (2014). Ferenczi's concept of identification with the aggressor: Understanding dissociative structure with interacting victim and abuser self-states. *American Journal of Psychoanalysis, 74*(1), 48–59.

Itzkowitz, S. (2018). Psychopathy and human evil: An overview. *Contemporary Psychoanalysis, 54*(1), 40–63.

Karpman, B. (1941). On the need of separating psychopathy into two distinct clinical types: The symptomatic and the idiopathic. *Journal of Criminal Psychopathology, 3*, 112–137.

Karpman, B. (1948). The myth of the psychopathic personality. *American Journal of Psychiatry, 104*(9), 523–534.

Koenigs, M. (2012). The role of prefrontal cortex in psychopathy. *Reviews in the Neurosciences, 23*(3), 253–262.

Koivisto, H., & Haapasalo, J. (1996). Childhood maltreatment and adulthood psychopathy in light of file-based assessments among mental state examinees. *Studies on Crime & Crime Prevention, 5*(1), 91–104.

Kolla, N. J., Malcolm, C., Attard, S., Arenovich, T., Blackwood, N., & Hodgins, S. (2013). Childhood maltreatment and aggressive behaviour in violent offenders with psychopathy. *Canadian Journal of Psychiatry, 58*(8), 487–494.

Krischer, M. K., & Sevecke, K. (2008). Early traumatization and psychopathy in female and male juvenile offenders. *International Journal of Law and Psychiatry, 31*(3), 253–262.

Liotti, G. (2011). Attachment disorganization and the controlling strategies: An illustration of the contributions of attachment theory to developmental psychopathology and to psychotherapy integration. *Journal of Psychotherapy Integration, 21*(3), 232–252.

Lyons-Ruth, K., & Jacobvitz, D. (2008). Attachment disorganization: Genetic factors, parenting contexts, and developmental transformation from infancy to adulthood. In J. Cassidy, & P. R. Shaver (Eds.), *Handbook of attachment theory, research, and clinical applications* .(2nd ed.), pp. 666–697). New York, NY: Guilford Publications.

Main, M., & Hesse, E. (1990). Parents' unresolved traumatic experiences are related to infant disorganized attachment status: Is frightened and/or frightening parental behavior the linking mechanism? In M. T. Greenberg, D. Cicchetti, & E. M. Cummings (Eds.), *Attachment in the preschool years: Theory, research, and intervention* (pp. 161–182). Chicago, IL: University of Chicago Press.

Marshall, L. A., & Cooke, D. J. (1999). The childhood experiences of psychopaths: A retrospective study of familial and societal factors. *Journal of Personality Disorders, 13*(3), 211–225.

McCord, W. M., & McCord, J. (1956). *Psychopathy and delinquency.* New York, NY: W. B. Saunders Company.

O'Connor, E. E., Collins, B. A., & Supplee, L. (2012). Behavior problems in late childhood: The roles of early maternal attachment and teacher–child relationship trajectories. *Attachment & Human Development, 14*(3), 265–288.

Odgers, C. L., Reppucci, N. D., & Moretti, M. M. (2005). Nipping psychopathy in the bud: An examination of the convergent, predictive, and theoretical utility of the PCL-YV among adolescent girls. *Behavioral Sciences & the Law, 23* (6), 743–763.

Ometto, M., de Oliveira, P. A., Milioni, A. L., Dos Santos, B., Scivoletto, S., Busatto, G. F., ... & Cunha, P. J. (2016). Social skills and psychopathic traits in maltreated adolescents. *European Child & Adolescent Psychiatry, 25*(4), 397–405.

Partridge, G. E. (1928). A study of fifty cases of psychopathic personality. *American Journal of Psychiatry, 84*(6), 593–973.

Robins, L. N. (1966). *Deviant children grown up: A sociological and psychiatric study of sociopathic personality.* Oxford: Williams & Wilkins.

Schimmenti, A. (2017). Traumatic identification. *Attachment, 11*(2), 154–171.

Schimmenti, A., & Bifulco, A. (2015). Linking lack of care in childhood to anxiety disorders in emerging adulthood: The role of attachment styles. *Child and Adolescent Mental Health, 20*(1), 41–48.

Schimmenti, A., & Caretti, V. (2018). Attachment, trauma, and alexithymia. In O. Luminet, R. M. Bagby, & G. J. Taylor (Eds.), *Alexithymia: advances in research, theory, and clinical practice* (pp. 127–141). Cambridge: Cambridge University Press.

Schimmenti, A., Di Carlo, G., Passanisi, A., & Caretti, V. (2015). Abuse in childhood and psychopathic traits in a sample of violent offenders. *Psychological Trauma: Theory, Research, Practice, and Policy, 7*(4), 340–347.

Schimmenti, A., Passanisi, A., Pace, U., Manzella, S., Di Carlo, G., & Caretti, V. (2014). The relationship between attachment and psychopathy: A study with a sample of violent offenders. *Current Psychology, 33*(3), 256–270.

Schraft, C. V., Kosson, D. S., & McBride, C. K. (2013). Exposure to violence within home and community environments and psychopathic tendencies in detained adolescents. *Criminal Justice and Behavior, 40*(9), 1027–1043.

Sevecke, K., Franke, S., Kosson, D., & Krischer, M. (2016). Emotional dysregulation and trauma predicting psychopathy dimensions in female and male juvenile offenders. *Child and Adolescent Psychiatry and Mental Health, 10* (1), 43.

Silverman, D. (1943). Clinical and electroencephalographic studies on criminal psychopaths. *Archives of Neurology and Psychiatry, 50*(1), 18–33.

Tuvblad, C., Bezdjian, S., Raine, A., & Baker, L. A. (2014). The heritability of psychopathic personality in 14- to 15-year-old twins: A multirater, multimeasure approach. *Psychological Assessment, 26*(3), 704–716.

van der Zouwen, M., Hoeve, M., Hendriks, A. M., Asscher, J. J., & Stams, G. J. J. (2018). The association between attachment and psychopathic traits. *Aggression and Violent Behavior, 43*, 45–55.

Weiler, B. L., & Widom, C. S. (1996). Psychopathy and violent behavior in abused and neglected young adults. *Criminal Behaviour and Mental Health, 6* (3), 253–271.

Weizmann-Henelius, G., Grönroos, M., Putkonen, H., Eronen, M., Lindberg, N., & Häkkänen-Nyholm, H. (2010). Psychopathy and gender differences in childhood psychosocial characteristics in homicide offenders: A nationwide register-based study. *Journal of Forensic Psychiatry & Psychology*, *21*(6), 801–814.

Chapter 13

The murder of Laius

Neville Symington

Introduction

The story of Oedipus is a myth. A myth functions as a dream in the social group. It also has this function for the individual within the group. Laius then represents an inner psychic reality. This is a detective story but a bit different from the usual format. We know there has been a murder; we do not know who the murdered person is; we want to know why the murder is hushed up.

Setting the scene

When the people of Thebes saw the royal carriage ride past carrying along their king and queen, Oedipus and Jocasta, all looked well. How fortunate it was that Oedipus, this knightly prince from Corinth, had sallied forth into Jocasta's bedchamber and so made up for the untimely death of Laius. All looked well in Thebes that day.

The challenge of assumptions

Of course, we know better than those innocents in Thebes. Yet, do we? What was so awful about Oedipus bound in wedlock to his mother? Oh, incest, you say. We all know there is a taboo against that. We all know that is wrong. All societies have condemned it. This is factually not true because there are exceptions—for instance, in the royal house of Hawaii before it was colonized by white Americans. But the question is "Why is incest wrong?" Or "Is it wrong?" Is it perhaps a taboo particular to primitive society that we should have long since abandoned in this scientific age? In this age of liberal values? Let us address ourselves to the first question of why there has been such a far-reaching taboo on incest. Then, let's see if that answer suggests lines of approach to the other question.

Why is it a crime for the boy growing into a young man to slay his father and sleep with his mother? Why is it that parricide has always been considered the worst of murders? Once you get past the expostulations "Oh well, it's obvious" and so on, it begins to be more difficult to define satisfactorily why the deed of Oedipus is such a heinous crime. The killing of Laius is an intricate part of the sin of Oedipus. In fact, I think it safe to say that it is because Oedipus can only sleep with Jocasta by first getting rid of Laius that sleeping with his mother becomes a crime. We must remember that Laius represents an inner psychic reality, that he is an intrapsychic person.

Imagine an alternative scene at Thebes. Laius' and Jocasta's long-lost son, Oedipus, arrives in the town and is revealed for who he is. So what happens? Teiresias is called and he removes forever the curse of the oracle at Delphi. Oedipus settles down to his princely tasks as heir apparent. He has a long wait before Laius dies and he comes into possession of sovereign power. He has to undergo a long apprenticeship. He has to find his own woman and pass along the painful pathway into adulthood.

By killing his father and jumping into bed with his mother he bypasses all this. He grabs his father's power yet remains a child because he has not done what he needs to do to become an adult. Although it looks otherwise, he is, in sorry fact, a child still with his mummy. The father who is needed to come and say "Now, now, Oedipus, it is time you left Mummy" is not there; he is absent. What is absent then? What is the inner reality that is absent, the inner reality that has been murdered?

Symbolic referent

We are concerned to get hold of the psychic reality to which this myth points. So what is absent intrapsychically? What has Oedipus not done in order for him to be an adult? There is no doubt that in any crime, however heinous, the key to the evil is to look not at the dramatic events that have been committed, but rather to consider and scrutinize what has not been done. Paradoxically it is not easy to see what is not done. The slaying of Laius is easy to see, the sleeping with Jocasta is identifiable. The crowds can shout and scream about these. You cannot scream about a vacuum, an absence, about what is not done. Yet I am sure that it is in the vacuum, in the absence, that we must look for the source of human disaster. In another context, I have referred to this as the principle of omission. So we have to look at what Oedipus did not do.

What we know is that he remained a baby with Mummy, although to the people of Thebes he looked a fully grown man. He had slain the Sphinx, so he looked doubly adult. Surely the slaying of the Sphinx was a rite of passage, an initiation into adulthood that no one could gainsay. I once knew a man who performed the most valiant deeds as a pilot in the Second World War, deeds for which he was justly decorated. His physical courage was an undoubted fact, but emotionally he was a puny child, a fact of which his wife and family were painfully aware. And so with Oedipus, he had slain the Sphinx and liberated Thebes from its terrors and yet he was wanting in the essence of manhood. He was still a baby with Mummy. It looked as if he was having intercourse with an adult woman, yet he was but a baby with Mummy. He looked like an adult and yet was a baby. We must conclude from this that adulthood is not conferred by acts of gallantry that draw the applause of the crowd, not by the fact of marriage, not by the physical ability to have intercourse, not by fathering children, not even by holding the post of king. Positions of high status do not confer adulthood. So of what does adulthood consist? What is its essence?

A conclusion forces itself upon us: that adulthood is not conferred by any external act—however valiant, however magnificent in its effects—but only by an internal act. Although the internal act has external repercussions, it is the internal act that confers adulthood. In the case of Oedipus, the external repercussion would have been to sever the bond with his mother, acknowledge his childhood, and take that enormous step of creating a wife. I use the word "creating" deliberately, because he will not find a wife of his pleasing. These, then, are the external repercussions. Had the story been different, Oedipus would have accepted himself as the child of Laius and Jocasta and would have set about the business of becoming a man.

As Freud [1939] has pointed out, the two royal families—that of Corinth and that of Thebes—are one and the same parents but divided in the myth. The murderous desires and the loving ones—the desires to protect the parents—are expressed in the myth by turning the one set of parents into two. Otto Rank (1914) in his book, *The Myth of the Birth of the Hero*, shows how heroes are frequently born mythologically of one set of parents but then reared by another. Often the hero is born of aristocratic parents, but is then brought up by humble parents or even sometimes by animals—for instance, Romulus. With Oedipus, the myth is similar except that both families are aristocratic. Freud suggests that this is to indicate more clearly that they are identical. I think the difference could be to indicate that Oedipus is not a hero but an anti-hero. Rather than being the father of a glorious dynasty he begets disaster in his progeny.

Had Oedipus taken the heroic path and set about the business of becoming a man, then one of the external repercussions of this would have been his taking a bride to wed. In the due passage of time, his father would have died and Oedipus, with his lawful bride, could have been seen driving through the streets of Thebes with his wife at his side to the acclaim of the populace. It would look the same as the Oedipus we know riding forth in the carriage with Jocasta but how different in reality it would be. That terrible catalogue of disaster would have been spared. There would be no suicide of Jocasta, no violent blinding of Oedipus, and none of that pitiful tale that continues in ever-increasing melancholy in Oedipus at Colonus and ends with its woeful waste of Antigone and her sister and the final annihilation of Oedipus, that ultimate in evil's potential within the human scene. This was finally followed in Antigone by that final insult to the human person: the refusal of burial. All this catalogue of disaster is put into action by Oedipus. Yet we have to come back to our question. What is the dreaded action that Oedipus has perpetrated?

I must remind you again that we must look to what Oedipus has not done. What is the internal action that Oedipus has not performed? To answer this, I want to draw your attention to the fateful voice of the Delphic oracle: "This child will kill his father and marry his mother." Oedipus is condemned to live out the trajectory of that fateful voice. It is an inescapable fate to which he consents. "You have no choice," it says, "but to live out this appalling destiny." What Oedipus did not do was to break the bonds of that appalling sentence. He did not cry from the depths of his soul against so vile a tyranny, against a savagery that robbed him of the very core that makes us human: the kernel of humanness that philosophers from the dawn of civilization have tried inexorably to describe, the transcendent seed in the hearts of human beings. You must know that I am talking of that deepest of human mysteries: I mean, of course, freedom. And freedom means choice. Instead he delivered himself up to fate. This masochistic submission, this killing of his own soul, was the murder. This was the inner Laius.

I have seen this malign force that had so inexorable a grip upon our Oedipus. I have seen it in myself; I have seen it in friends; I have seen it in patients. It is something worse by far than the more sensational manifestations of human depravity. You might say you cannot get worse than parricide combined with incest and yet I state confidently that these are the epiphenomena of a malignancy that is far worse. In fact, the killing of the father is the pseudo-attempt to break free: the delusional belief that Oedipus can set himself free from this malign force by killing the symbol of power rather than transforming the power itself. It is what the father symbolizes that requires transformation. To kill the father himself is the maddest madness, yet it is a madness that I believe I have witnessed on certain appalling occasions.

There is an action required of Oedipus if he is to break free of this strangling power. It is not an act of gallantry that will be recorded in the annals of the great, but a small quiet action whose enormous repercussions will travel down the avenues of history, although it will go unnoticed. It is not an action that will have any attraction for those who want fame, no lure for those who long for power. It is an act of faith in the potential of the child, the potential of the seed, to grow. This is followed by an inner resolution to be faithful to that initial pact with truth. All of this is within. There is no clapping audience to an action of this kind. There are no badges, no medals, for such an action. It is, however, the action, which bit by bit—inch by inch, with undoubted forwardness —drives back the power of that malign force that had so strangling a grip upon the soul of Oedipus.

The malignant power that this would-be action of Oedipus drives back takes the mind into its control. What we are witness to in the Oedipus myth is a mind in the grip of a malign negation. I believe that Oedipus was schizophrenic, and my evidence for this is that the negative fatefulness that ruled his soul is one of the most tell-tale signs of the schizophrenic condition. Behind the oracle's infernal words "The child will kill his father and sleep with his mother" is the implied taunt: "And that's all you're good for"; "You haven't got it in you to grow and come into possession of your own inheritance: to come into possession of your own powers." Another way of saying what I have just said is that the child—the child for whom a whole world of freedom and possibility expands in front of it— this child has been crushed, brutally murdered. The murder of Laius symbolizes the murder of the infant Oedipus. The infant is wounded in the foot, and it is when the wheel of Laius' carriage goes over the adult Oedipus' foot that he goes into a rage and assassinates his father, thereby symbolizing the hurt child who slays Laius. The murder is undertaken as a way of trying to murder the malign child but, with the act, is also a murder of the sane child. The negative malign power is born of the assassination of a wounded child.

It is a terrible thing to have such a malign power within. The human psyche can only flee from it. There are rare cases where an individual turns and stares it in the face and declares war upon it. This is the exception. In most cases, we flee it. What we see in the Oedipus myth is the mind in violent flight with its deceitful substitutes on external display. As I said at the beginning, "It all looks alright." This is the fraudulent mother, Jocasta, who Blomfield (1992) refers to. Jocasta is a person, an agent-person, in the self—a person so hated, so intolerable that it is instanced outside. The suicide of Jocasta is another false attempt just as the murder of Laius is. This psychotic negativism generates a deceitful array of solutions. At that famous junction of the three roads, the voice says, "If you kill him you will at last be free." And then when Jocasta's offer beckons, the voice says, "When you sleep with her you will be freed forever of the bonds of childhood and you will be forever a big man." When he slays the Sphinx, the voice whispers, "And now you can have supreme and kingly power."

When Oedipus murders Laius he believes that he will be freed. He is deceived into thinking that an external act will deliver him. An act is needed, but it is an internal act. There *is* something he must slay, but it is a mental power within, not King Laius riding out on his chariot. He had reason enough to hate Laius but slaying him did not free him of the inner childhood wound. He does need intercourse with his mother, but not sexual intercourse. He needs an internal intercourse where the child Oedipus can give motherhood to his mother and receive the nurture his child needs, the nurture he needs in order to grow. He needs to exercise power, great power, but an internal power. He is deceived at every point. It looks like the genuine article, but it is so disastrously false, so cunningly fake. It is so fake that the human spirit cannot ultimately bear it; it must be undone. I believe this is the reason why Oedipus has to expose the truth. The appalling deeds that unfurl at the end of Sophocles' play are the external manifestations of this inner evil. Although the external events are appalling, the inner malign power within is worse.

The climax of the corruption sets in with the murder of Laius. What is it that is murdered within? It is this potency, this capacity, to take that small great step: that act of belief in the child's capacity to grow followed by resolution to follow that path, come what may. At those crossroads Oedipus murdered his one hope, the one true possession he had, the seed of possibility. He had opted for a false root.

Reasons for negativism generating catastrophe

I am making the connection that the submission of Oedipus to the fateful voice of the Delphic oracle was what generated the awful events of which we are all familiar. I have suggested that the inner malign power that gripped the heart of Oedipus is worse than the catastrophic events that follow. Oedipus has to free himself from the terrible inner curse. Tiresias warns Oedipus not to continue with his appalling inquiry, but he cannot heed the warning. He has to do it. He can stand the bonds no longer. You might ask, but why does the inquiry have to lead to such a violent finale? We have to look back further and ask: "Why does Oedipus fulfill all that was pronounced by the oracle?" Why does he do it so violently?

We have to ask here what has generated this cruel voice in the heart of Oedipus? I believe the myth is right in suggesting that it is a state of mind implanted in infancy. It is a sour refusal, a bitter hatred of life itself that takes a grip within the child's mind at the very start of things. The voice says, "You will kill your father and marry your mother" and with a poisoned mind the child says, "OK, I will."

You may wish to tell me that such a sour intent, such poisonous bitterness, is not common among the ordinary thoroughfares of human decency: "Oh yes, in Thebes perhaps but not in our civilized twenty-first-century world, not surely in our comfortable developed world that we all know so well." Yet I believe such complacency is a risky path to take. In the psychoanalytic world, we are frequently confronted by appalling events. These events bear all the marks of violence, catastrophe, and psychic murder that the Oedipus legend foreshadowed.

I do believe that in an analysis we need to reach this level where the malign power lies if we can. If Oedipus were on our couch we would have great difficulty in keeping him long enough in analysis to reach his sour intent before he went out and slew Laius. The desire for magic is so strong, so violent, that we all fear the transformation of this malign mentality. We all hate the terrible ordeal of looking within. After all, it is a mentality that has been my trusty guardian all these years of my life, from my earliest infancy. Oedipus believes that by becoming king he can magically banish that inner curse. If I become an analyst and share the bedchamber with my own analyst, then I shall banish that inner curse. I shall become a big man, a mature woman. What!? Do you think I who have slain the Sphinx cannot banish so fearful an inner voice? It is so tempting to be deceived that—like Oedipus—we do not even see the inner Sphinx, the inner monster. When I am adorned with the grandiose robes of kingship I do not see. In fact, it is a condition of "turning a blind eye" (see Steiner, 1985) that I must be in kingly robes in order to act the blind man. So I believe I am king, yet, despite all appearances to the contrary, I remain a tiny baby with Mummy.

This negative fatefulness is not apparent on the surface. It is so terrible that Oedipus does not bear to look inside and see it. An analysis is a terrible threat to this dark inner blight. An analysis is an offer of hope, an offer of life; but it is a great threat to one in such a hell as Oedipus. It requires a total reversal, giving up his magical violence and unthinking thrust for power, which is most essentially the murder of the infant self, the emotional core of the personality. It is the core out of which I initiate, the core out of which I create responsiveness in my human environment, the one of creation, the one of freedom. It is this that is killed. It is because it is killed that Oedipus has no source out of which he can, with confidence, journey along that path from infancy to adulthood, from the seed to the fully grown tree. He leaps hastily into the shoes of Laius. But if he is in the shoes of Laius, then where is his own person? The source of personhood is in the crying infant. Herein also lies the source of freedom, and this has been murdered. What we meet is just an absence. The individual lives in the shoes of others, in their phrases, in their language, in their ideas. Taken to its fullest, there is then no person. A murder has been done. Like most murders, desperate measures are used to hide it. It is the guilt of discovery that leads Oedipus to blind himself and Jocasta to kill herself rather than start all over again from the beginning. Such disasters have many manifest-ations but they always find their source in a vile inner murder and a hidden malignity.

Conclusion

We are the people of Thebes. We see patients riding in their chariots every day for their analysis. It all looks fine. All the external signs are there; the credentials look impeccable. Are you sure though you are not looking at Oedipus? Has Laius been slain?

Acknowledgments

Neville Symington, Ph.D. The Murder of Laius. *Contemporary Psycho-analysis*, copyright © the William Alanson White Institute of Psychiatry, Psychoanalysis & Psychology and the William Alanson White Psychoana-lytic Society, www.wawhite.org, reprinted by permission of Taylor & Fran-cis Ltd, http://www.tandfonline.com on behalf of the William Alanson White Institute of Psychiatry, Psychoanalysis & Psychology and the William Alanson White Psychoanalytic Society.

References

Blomfield, O. H. D. (1992). *Fantasy and shock in Phocis*. Paper presented at the Australian Psychoanalytic Association Conference, Melbourne, Australia.

Freud, S. (1939). Moses and monotheism. In J. Strachey (Ed. and Trans.), *The standard edition of the complete psychological works of Sigmund Freud*, Vol. 23 (pp. 1–138). London, UK: Hogarth Press.

Rank, O. (1914). *The myth of the birth of the hero* (G. C. Richter & E. J. Lieberman, Trans.). Baltimore, MD: Johns Hopkins Press. (Original work published 1909).

Steiner, J. (1985). Turning a blind eye: The cover-up for Oedipus. *International Review of Psycho-Analysis*, *12*, 161–172.

Chapter 14

Psychopaths and the neurobiology of evil

Nathalie Y. Gauthier, Tabitha Methot-Jones, Angela Book and J. Reid Meloy

Introduction

Psychopathy has been traditionally defined as a personality syndrome characterized by shallow affect, a callous disregard for the well-being or rights of others, a lack of remorse, predatory manipulation of others, and a propensity towards antisocial behavior (Cleckley, 1976; Hare, 1993, 1996, 2003; Hare & Neumann, 2008). Classical case studies in psychopathy research sought to understand why psychopathic individuals were so clearly lacking a "conscience" (see Cleckley, 1976; McCord & McCord, 1964, etc.). One of the most intriguing features about psychopathic individuals is that they are not mentally ill, they do not suffer from delusions or intellectual impairment, and yet their cold-blooded nature tends to leave devastation in their wake. The question most often asked is why? What is it about how these individuals are "wired" that facilitates such cruelty? Cleckley (1976) described psychopaths as being incapable of feeling empathy for others, and that they were thus egocentric and unable to form any meaningful relationships with others. He suspected that there was a biological basis for this emotional deficit, and the resultant coldness and cruelty that psychopaths often exhibit. Glenn and Raine (2014) argue that the biological bases of psychopathy are best understood in "layers". The first layer is genetic, which, in combination with environment, forms the "ultimate" foundation in predicting psychopathic personality. Each of the other layers can be considered "proximate" factors that are closer in time to the behavioral presentation of the psychopathic individual. Some proximate layers are direct, such as the brain structures and function, while others are indirect, such as development and life experiences, and these can help explain how the characteristic features are manifested in different behavioral presentations in psychopathic individuals. Psychopathic personality traits have moderate to high heritability, and despite the uncertainty of how these traits will determine behavioral outcomes, what is clear is that there is a biological basis to psychopathy (Glenn & Raine, 2014; Larsson, Andershed, & Lichtenstein, 2006).

This review will thus explore some of the neurobiological findings related to some of the "hallmark" features of psychopathy, and the functional implications that may help explain the so-called "moral insanity" that has fascinated clinicians (Henderson, 1947; Hervé, 2007). This review will be organized by some of the answers to the question of "why", thought to be the underlying core functional differences exhibited in these individuals (such as a shallow affect, lack of empathy, lack of remorse, lack of responsivity to feedback, attenuated attention, and a propensity towards proactive aggression), as well as by the associated structures and neurobiological research findings that are most consistently found to help explain these differences. We start by the fundamental processing differences most common across all psychopathic individuals, as these results are most consistent across samples and subtypes. These also start with the more basic or "primitive" brain structures. As we move through more complex functions (and more variability in the neurobiological findings and also in the sample subtypes), we also are moving up to more complex and more recently developed and "evolved" brain structures associated with these features. As such, the findings related to these areas are also more nuanced.

This chapter will review the clinical presentation of psychopathy and will also consider how the same genetic and neurobiological mechanisms may present themselves in psychopaths who evade prison. To date, the majority of the research has examined clinical and criminal psychopaths and their underlying mechanisms, as they are more easily observed in these populations, and psychopathy is an important predictor of criminal and violent reoffending (Hare & Neumann, 2008; Hare, Neumann, & Mokros, 2018). However, Cleckley's (1976) seminal work emphasized that psychopaths were not typically aggressive or criminal, and instead could use their lack of empathy, fear, and remorse to become financially successful lawyers and doctors. More recently, research has been increasingly focused on investigating what has been deemed "successful" psychopathy, from those who remain out of prison to those who even use their psychopathic traits and lack of conscience to take advantage of others and gain positions of power in the corporate world (Babiak, 2007; Babiak & Hare, 2006; Babiak, Neumann, & Hare, 2010; Benning, Venables, & Hall, 2018; Lilienfeld, Watts, & Smith, 2015), and in politics (Lilienfeld et al., 2012). It is important to note that despite the personal prosperity that these psychopaths may achieve, this immorality comes at a great cost to society, both financially and in the personal detriment of others around them (Babiak et al., 2010; Mathieu & Babiak, 2016; Mathieu et al., 2012; Mathieu, Neumann, Hare, & Babiak, 2014). The latter portion of this chapter will address some of the neurobiological findings that differentiate between the predatory psychopaths that end up in prison and those who may end up on Wall Street.

Shallow affect

Lack of fear

Since its earliest research, psychopathy has been referred to as a "disease of the affect" (Hervé, 2007). One of the most distinguishing features of psychopathic individuals is their deficiency in emotional responding, especially a lack of fear. The early experimental research of psychopathy demonstrated that these individuals exhibited diminished physiological reaction (lower heart rate, less sweating) in the anticipation of pain compared to non-psychopaths (e.g. Hare, 1965; Lykken, 1957). Abnormal physiological responses to threat have been demonstrated in many experiments (e.g. Birbaumer et al., 2005; Flor et al., 2002; Lopez, Poy, Patrick, & Molto, 2013; Patrick, Cuthbert, & Lang, 1994; Rothemond et al., 2012), including a diminished startle response (Benning, Patrick, & Iacono, 2005; Glenn & Raine, 2014; Lilienfeld, Watts, Smith, & Latzman, 2018; Patrick, 1994, 2018; Patrick, Bradley, & Lang, 1993), which is attributed to a reflex of the brain stem after the amygdala sends threat cues present in non-psychopaths, but absent in psychopaths (Patrick, 2018).

It makes sense, therefore, that the neurobiological findings that are most frequently reported in psychopathy research are abnormalities within the limbic system (particularly the amygdala) and connected regions (such as the anterior cingulate cortex) as these areas are responsible for automatically processing threat cues and mobilizing reflexive "fight or flight" responses (Blair, Meffert, Hwang, & White, 2018; Patrick, 2018). This threat-detecting system takes sensory input from the outside world through the thalamus and activates the amygdala, which allows for faster unconscious defensive reactions to threat (Patrick, 2018).

Structural as well as functional abnormalities in the amygdala have been repeatedly found in psychopaths; specifically, in studies which have investigated what appears to be a psychopathic lack of fear (Blair et al., 2018; Glenn & Raine, 2014; Hiatt, Schmitt, & Newman, 2004; Larson et al., 2013; Yang & Raine, 2018; Yang et al., 2010; Yang et al., 2009). Research measuring cortical activity (which indicates regions of the brain that are being recruited during that time) has demonstrated that psychopaths show abnormal activation in the amygdala when processing personal cues of threat compared to non-psychopaths (see Blair et al., 2018; Larson et al., 2013; Yang & Raine, 2018 for a review). For example, using neuroimaging while completing visual tasks, psychopaths show decreased activation in the amygdala, and when they are presented with visual cues that appear to signal an impending shock (Larson et al., 2013; Yang & Raine, 2018). This can help explain why psychopaths show less brain activation during punishment conditioning than non-psychopaths (Birbaumer et al., 2005; Kiehl et al., 2001; Larson et al., 2013; Patrick, 2018; Yang & Raine, 2018).

Research has argued that the lack of fear response in psychopaths is not simply a matter of reduced amygdala function, but an interplay of other brain regions, which argues that they process emotional information differently than non-psychopaths (Baskin-Sommers et al., 2015a; Baskin-Sommers, Curtin, & Newman, 2015b; Glenn & Raine, 2014; Patrick, 2018; Yang & Raine, 2018). For example, some research has found that psychopaths compensate for diminished limbic activation for emotional information by recruiting other cortical regions to cognitively, rather than emotionally, process such information (e.g. Patrick, 2018; Yang & Raine, 2018). The implication is that psychopaths process emotional or threat-based information in the same way as they process neutral information (e.g. Deeley et al., 2006; Kiehl, Hare, McDonald, & Brink, 1999; Kiehl et al., 2001). More recently, research has argued that the deficient fear response in psychopaths (as demonstrated in the activation of limbic system as well as behavioral and physiological reaction) is actually a function of their attentional focus (Baskin-Sommers et al., 2015a; Baskin-Sommers, Curtin, & Newman,

2011; Baskin-Sommers et al., 2015b; Larson et al., 2013; Wilson, Juodis, & Porter, 2011). This line of research has demonstrated that psychopaths have greater activation in areas of the lateral prefrontal cortex (involved in selective attention and blocking out irrelevant peripheral information) compared to non-psychopaths, and lower limbic activation when processing threat cues, but only when those cues are secondary; for example, when they are focusing on a goal. Researchers also find that if psychopaths are explicitly trained to focus specifically on the threat cues, rather than the threat being a passive condition of punishment, the activation in the lateral prefrontal cortex is reduced, and the differences in amygdala activation between psychopaths and non-psychopaths becomes insignificant (e.g. Anderson et al., 2017). What is not clear, however, is if the inhibitive effects of selective attention are more dominant in psychopaths, "silencing" the threat-signaling activation of the amygdala, or if their amygdala, which overrides cognitive processes during threat in most non-psychopaths, is deficient and thus unable to prioritize attention to threat information (Larson et al., 2013). It has been hypothesized that psychopaths' lack of fear and decreased amygdala activation due to attentional focus causes them to fail to integrate peripheral information that would lead to learning empathy, remorse, and contextual cues informing potential consequences of their actions (Baskin-Sommers et al., 2015a; Baskin-Sommers et al., 2011, 2015b; Larson et al., 2013).

Lack of empathy

Understanding the neurobiology underlying the behavioral lack of fear demonstrated by psychopaths is integral, given that many conceptualizations of psychopathy center on a lack of affective fear, and that this is the foundation of understanding the coldness and lack of empathy and remorse exhibited by these individuals. If psychopaths are unable to personally experience negative emotions such as fear, then there is little hope for them to understand the negative emotions of others, as these same emotional systems are responsible for affective empathy (Blair, 2017).

Hare argued that the deficiency in affective empathy for others allows psychopathic individuals to manipulate and harm others, as the negative emotions typically displayed by others in reaction to such behavior do not serve as a deterrent (Blair, 2005; Hare, 2006; Hare &

Neumann, 2009). Psychopaths have demonstrated abnormal processing within the amygdala as well as other limbic and cortical areas, such as the anterior cingulate cortex and the anterior insula, which have been implicated in the recognition and understanding of fearful and other emotional facial expressions of others (e.g. Adolphs et al., 2005; Bernhardt & Singer, 2012; Blair, 2005; 2008a; Birbaumer et al., 2005; Dawel, O'Kearney, McKone, & Palermo, 2012; Deeley et al., 2006; Glenn & Raine, 2014; Kiehl, 2006; Kiehl et al., 2001; Patrick, 2018; Sethi et al., 2018; Yang & Raine, 2018). For example, when viewing photos of emotional facial expressions, a sample of psychopathic offenders showed reduced activation in the fusiform cortex when viewing negative emotional faces compared to neutral and happy faces (Deeley et al., 2006). The authors argue that this relates to their lack of empathy or regard for the pain and suffering of others, and is particularly of interest because in healthy controls, negative emotional faces showed increased activation relative to neutral and happy faces in the fusiform cortex, as this region is also modulated by feedback from the amygdala (Deeley et al., 2006). While brain imaging research implicates that psychopaths demonstrate a diminished response to the emotional cues sent from others, behavioral evidence suggests that they are still able to accurately recognize and identify the emotions of others (e.g. Blair, 2005, 2008a; Blair et al., 2018; Decety, Chen, Harenski, & Kiehl, 2013; Drayton, Santos, & Baskin-Sommers, 2018), suggesting that while they lack affective empathy, their cognitive empathy, or theory of mind, is intact. Cognitive empathy is related to cortical areas such as the dorsolateral prefrontal cortex, and the mid cingulate cortex, rather than the amygdala and insula areas (Decety et al., 2013; Eres, Decety, Louis, & Molenberghs, 2015). Other research finds that differences in the ability to recognize and understand the emotions of others without the burden of being emotionally affected by them allows psychopaths to exploit and manipulate others (e.g. Book et al., 2015; Book, Quinsey, & Langford, 2007; Hare, 2006; Patrick, 2018).

Lack of conscience or remorse

Emotional processing is also responsible for moral understanding (Blair, 2017). Research has demonstrated that because of their abnormal emotional response, psychopaths process moral violations in the same way that they process simple violations of conventional norms (such as social context-appropriate clothing; Aharoni, Sinnott-Armstrong, & Kiehl, 2014; Blair, 2017; Kiehl et al., 1999). It has been argued that psychopaths fail to value the valence or magnitude of these transgressions and instead make decisions in a "utilitarian" fashion (Blair, 2017; Gao & Tang, 2013). This lack of moral reasoning can be understood through the psychopath's shallow emotions and lack of affective empathy, as moral understanding depends on emotional responding, such as fear (Blair, 1995, 2017). In individuals with normal emotional responses and affective empathy, the negative emotions of others are empathetically experienced and serve as aversive conditioning (Blair, 2017; Decety, 2015; Decety & Cowell, 2017; Decety & Howard, 2013). In time, the aversive effect of experiencing the emotions of pain or fear of others (empathetically) becomes internalized as a system of moral values, and violating these values becomes experienced as remorse (Decety, 2015; Decety & Howard, 2013). Direct aversive conditioning is also responsible for moral reasoning, as in non-psychopaths the fear of punishment becomes associated with moral transgressions (Blair, 2017). In psychopathic individuals, the lack of fear undermines this learning, and results in a lack of conscience (Cleckley, 1976; Hare, 1993; Lykken, 1957, 1995).

Neuroimaging research supports this claim, as psychopaths have shown decreased activation in the amygdala, ventromedial prefrontal cortex, and dorsal anterior cingulate in response to punishment during moral learning tasks (Blair, 2017). The anterior cingulate, which serves as a connection between the amygdala and prefrontal cortex, helps with processing emotional information, and is also implicated with the perceived feelings of guilt (Blair, 2017; Korponay et al., 2017). The prefrontal cortex is also involved with moral and social decision-making, as well as learning from punishment (Anderson et al., 1999). Anderson and colleagues (1999) demonstrated that injury to these areas during early development yields impaired moral knowledge and understanding of social rules.

Predatory behavior

While a failure to feel fear or anticipate punishment can explain why psychopaths have a deficient conscience, it fails to explain why psychopaths have a propensity for harming others (Sonne & Gash, 2018; Yang & Raine, 2018). A large body of research has found that in addition to emotional and empathic deficits, psychopaths also demonstrate abnormally high sensitivity to reward (e.g. Blair et al., 2018; Hare, 2001; Koenigs, 2017; Patrick, 2018).

Some research shows that it is not necessarily a deficiency in responding to the negative emotions of others, but rather that they may enjoy the suffering of others (Decety et al., 2013; Glenn & Raine, 2009; Hosker-Field, Gauthier, & Book, 2016; James et al., 2014; Levenston, Patrick, Bradley, & Lang, 2000; Woodworth & Porter, 2002). Neuroimaging provides some explanation for this. For example, when imagining others in pain, some research has found that psychopaths exhibit neural activation in the ventral striatum, which is a brain region associated with reward (Decety et al., 2013).

Behavioral research also demonstrates that psychopaths primarily harm others for instrumental purposes (i.e. personal gain) rather than out of reactive aggression (Blair, 2017, 2018; Hare, 2001; Woodworth & Porter, 2002). As research has demonstrated an association between over-active reward brain systems in psychopaths, coupled with a lack of negative emotions regarding engaging in morally reprehensible behavior, this can facilitate the drive to get what they want as fast as they want, destroying anything that stands in their way.

Successful vs. unsuccessful psychopaths

While the core personality features and affective deficits of psychopathy do promote their propensity towards immoral behavior and taking advantage of others, this does not necessarily need to be violent or criminal. Many conceptualizations of psychopathy argue that violence and criminality should not be considered part of the defining features (Cleckley, 1976; Cooke, Michie, Hart, & Clark, 2004; Gao & Raine, 2010). Recently, research has been investigating more covert ways that psychopaths may still behave immorally while "successful" in the professional sense. For example, corporate psychopathy is still characterized by manipulation, deceitfulness, and exploitativeness (Babiak & Hare, 2006; Mathieu et al., 2014). Intimidation and lies serve to help the corporate psychopaths climb over others to get to the top, often gaining them positions of power (Babiak et al., 2010). While avoiding overtly violent behavior to get them arrested, they are still acting in predatory ways, often through psychological abuse and causing damage to those that work with them (Babiak & Hare, 2006; Mathieu et al., 2014). Corporate psychopaths are also associated with white-collar crimes (Lingnau, Fuchs, & Dehne-Niemann, 2017). How is it that the same underlying syndrome yields such different presentations of behavior?

Research has indicated that differences in executive function (and associated frontal lobes) could help explain the variability in maladaptive behavior in psychopathy (e.g. Morgan & Lilienfeld, 2000; Zeier, Baskin-Sommers, Hiatt Racer, & Newman, 2012). This evidence emerged when patients with frontal lobe damage began demonstrating aggressive behavior and callous disregard for others after their injury (Lantrip, Towns, Roth, & Giancola, 2016). More specifically, the ventromedial prefrontal cortex (PFC) as well as the connected pathways in regulating limbic and dorsal cognitive regions are associated with controlling impulsive behavior and reactive aggression. Injury to these regions (i.e., VMPFC) in previously healthy adults results in antisocial behavior, despite leaving intact moral knowledge and understanding of social norms (Bechara, Tranel, Damasio, & Damasio, 1996).

While both successful and unsuccessful psychopaths demonstrate fearlessness, lack of empathy, manipulation of others, and the ability to monitor and control behavior, successful psychopaths show greater ability to problem-solve and learn from errors (Lantrip et al., 2016). However, unsuccessful psychopaths demonstrate poorer executive function, and greater impulsivity and aggression (Lantrip et al., 2016). Neurobiological research also provides support for the functional distinction between these success subtypes. Incarcerated (unsuccessful) psychopaths also show reductions in prefrontal cortex volume, as well as in the medial frontal and orbitofrontal cortex, compared to successful psychopaths. The structural as well as functional differences seen between these groups can explain how successful psychopaths may benefit from their lack of fear or empathy but use these traits in conjunction with intact impulse control and consideration of contextual cues, to their advantage.

Conclusion and final considerations

Neurobiological research has helped uncover some of the underlying mechanisms that explain the core personality and emotional deficits that make psychopaths prone to immoral behavior or parasitic treatment of others (Fowles, 2003; Sonne & Gash, 2018; Veit et al., 2013; Yang & Raine, 2018). However, it is important to avoid taking a perspective of biological determinism, especially as no specific gene or brain region can "cause" evil behavior. While there is existing evidence of which "hallmark" features of psychopathy, there is still considerable variability in these findings across samples (incarcerated violent offenders, executive employees, community members) and across what measures and tasks are being used (e.g. Korponay et al., 2017; Morgan & Lilienfeld, 2000; Wilson et al., 2011). It is important to consider the role of environment and experience and how these can shape how the brain develops and results in different subgroups of psychopathy (Fowles, 2003; Glenn & Raine, 2014; Waldman, Rhee, LoParo, & Park, 2018). The argument has been made that the study of psychopathy as a unitary construct, rather than syndrome, has undermined efforts to identify mechanisms or brain abnormalities that could be underlying psychopathy (Glenn & Raine, 2014; Lantrip et al., 2016; Lilienfeld, 2015). A dimensional conceptualization, more in keeping with Cleckley's seminal conceptualization of psychopathy, would define it as a constellation of traits (e.g. Hervé, 2007; Lilienfeld, 2015; Patrick & Bernat, 2009; Patrick, Fowles, & Krueger, 2009). The study of psychopathy as a unitary construct in clinical samples using the PCL-R (Hare, 2003) has been associated with an overemphasis on antisociality as a core characteristic of psychopathy (Zeier et al., 2012). Further confounding this issue is a tendency to group psychopathic inmates together with individuals with Antisocial Personality Disorder in meta-analytic investigations (Morgan & Lilienfeld, 2000), which ignores idiosyncratic differences between these two groups. Specifically, this approach particularly ignores the emotional deficits, which are defining aspects of psychopathy, but not necessarily of Antisocial Personality Disorder (Gao & Raine, 2010; Glenn & Raine, 2014; Hare, 1993, 1996; Kosson, Lorenz, & Newman, 2006). Though it is true that psychopathic individuals are more likely to engage in antisocial behavior, it has been argued that antisocial behavior should not be considered a defining aspect of psychopathy (Glenn & Raine, 2014). Indeed, Cleckley's (1976) conceptualization of psychopathy was based on non-criminal clinical case studies, directly in contrast to the focus of the study of psychopathy today (Poythress & Skeem, 2006). The current focus on employing incarcerated samples may have resulted in psychopathy being confounded with antisociality, such that the psychopaths represented in these samples are inherently antisocial subgroups of psychopaths (e.g. Lilienfeld et al., 2015). Furthermore, examining psychopathy as a unitary construct ignores differences in the variability of psychopathic characteristics across psychopaths (as in the meta-analysis by Morgan & Lilienfeld, 2000; Polaschek & Daly, 2013). The result is that we may miss important differences in etiological pathways and targeted treatment options (Baskin-Sommers et al., 2015a; Baskin-Sommers et al., 2015b; Glenn & Raine, 2014; Lilienfeld, 2015; Polaschek & Daly, 2013). Finally, it is essential to consider the function of brain regions in conjunction with behavior, as differences in activity do not necessarily imply a functional deficit, especially if performance on these tasks is not being measured.

References

Adolphs, R., Gosselin, F., Buchanan, T.W., Tranel, D., Schyns, P., & Damasio, A.R. (2005). A mechanism for impaired fear recognition after amygdala damage. *Nature*, *433*(7021), 68–72.

Aharoni, E., Sinnott-Armstrong, W., & Kiehl, K.A. (2014). What's wrong? Moral understanding in psychopathic offenders. *Journal of Research in Personality*, *53*, 175–181.

Anderson, N.E., Steele, V.R., Maurer, J.M., Rao, V., Koenigs, M.K., Decety, J., Kosson, D.S., Calhoun, V.D., & Kiehl, K.A. (2017). Differential emotional processing and attention in psychopathy with functional neuroimaging. *Cognitive and Affective Behavioral Neroscience*, *17*, 491–515. doi: 10.3758/s13415-016-0493-5.

Anderson, S.W., Bechara, A., Damasio, H., Tranel, D., & Damasio, A.R. (1999). Impairment of social and moral behavior related to early damage in human prefrontal cortex. *Nature Neuroscience*, *2*, 1031–1037.

Babiak, P. (2007). From darkness into the light: Psychopathy in industrial and organizational psychology. In H. Hervé & J.C. Yuille (Eds.), *The psychopath: Theory, research, and practice* (pp. 411–428). Mahwah, NJ: Lawrence Erlbaum Associates.

Babiak, P., & Hare, R.D. (2006). *Snakes in suits: When psychopaths go to work.* New York, NY: Regan.

Babiak, P., Neumann, C.S., & Hare, R.D. (2010). Corporate psychopathy: Talking the walk. *Behavioral Sciences and the Law*, *28*, 174–193.

Baskin-Sommers, A.R., Brazil, I.A., Ryan, J., Kohlenberg, N.J., Neumann, C.S., & Newman, J.P. (2015a). Mapping the association of global functioning onto diverse measures of psychopathic traits. *Personality Disorders: Theory, Research and Treatment*, *6*, 336–346.

Baskin-Sommers, A.R., Curtin, J.J., & Newman, J.P. (2011). Specifying the attentional selection that moderates the fearlessness of psychopathic offenders. *Psychological Science, 22*, 226–234. doi: 10.1177/0956797610396227.

Baskin-Sommers, A.R., Curtin, J.J., & Newman, J.P. (2015b). Altering the cognitive-affective dysfunctions of psychopathic and externalizing offender subtypes with cognitive remediation. *Clinical Psychological Science, 3*, 45–57.

Bechara, A., Tranel, D., Damasio, H., & Damasio, A.R. (1996). Failure to respond autonomically to anticipated future outcomes following damage to prefrontal cortex. *Cerebral Cortex, 6*(2), 215–225.

Benning, S.D., Patrick, C.J., & Iacono, W.G. (2005). Psychopathy, startle blink modulation and electrodermal reactivity in twin men. *Psychophysiology, 42*, 753–762. doi: 10.1111/j.1469-8986.2005.00353.x.

Benning, S.D., Venables, N.C., & Hall, J.R. (2018). Successful psychopathy. In C.J. Patrick (Ed.), *Handbook of psychopathy* (2nd ed.) (pp. 585–608). New York, NY: Guilford Press.

Bernhardt, B.C., & Singer, T. (2012). The neural basis of empathy. *Annual Review of Neuroscience, 35*, 1–23.

Birbaumer, N., Veit, R., Lotze, M., Erb, M., Hermann, C., Grodd, W., & Flor, H. (2005). Deficient fear conditioning in psychopathy: A functional magnetic resonance imaging study. *Archives of General Psychiatry, 62*, 799–805.

Blair R. J. (1995). A cognitive developmental approach to mortality: Investigating the psychopath. *Cognition, 57*, 1–29.

Blair, R.J.R. (2005). Responding to the emotions of others: Dissociating forms of empathy through the study of typical and psychiatric populations. *Consciousness and Cognition, 14*, 698–718.

Blair, R.J.R. (2008a). Fine cuts of empathy and the amygdala: Dissociable deficits in psychopathy and autism. *Quarterly Journal of Experimental Psychology, 61*, 157–170.

Blair, R.J.R. (2008b). The amygdala and ventromedial prefrontal cortex: Functional contributions and dysfunction in psychopathy. *Philosophical Transactions: Biological Sciences, 363*(1503), 2557.

Blair, R.J.R. (2017). Emotion-based learning systems and the development of morality. *Cognition, 167*, 38–45.

Blair, R.J.R. (2018). Traits of empathy and anger: Implications for psychopathy and other disorders associated with aggression. *Philosophical Transactions of the Royal Society B: Biological Sciences, 373*(1744), 1.

Blair, R.J.R., Meffert, H., Hwang, S., & White, S.F. (2018). Psychopathy and brain function: Insights from neuroimaging research. In C.J. Patrick (Ed.), *Handbook of psychopathy* (2nd ed) (pp. 401–421). New York, NY: Guilford Press.

Book, A., Methot, T., Gauthier, N., Hosker-Field, A., Forth, A., Quinsey, V., & Molnar, D. (2015). The mask of sanity revisited: Psychopathic traits and affective mimicry. *Evolutionary Psychological Science, 1*(2), 91–102. doi: 10.1007/s40806-015-0012-x.

Book, A.S., Quinsey, V.L., & Langford, D. (2007). Psychopathy and perception of affect and vulnerability. *Criminal Justice and Behavior, 34*, 531–544.

Cleckley, H. (1976). *The mask of sanity: An attempt to clarify some issues about the so-called psychopathic personality.* St. Louis, MO: C.V. Mosby.

Cooke, D.J., Michie, C., Hart, S.D., & Clark, D.A. (2004). Reconstructing psychopathy: Clarifying the significance of antisocial and socially deviant behavior in the diagnosis of psychopathic personality disorder. *Journal of Personality Disorders, 18*, 337–356.

Dawel, A., O'Kearney, R., McKone, E., & Palermo, R. (2012). Not just fear and sadness: Meta- analytic evidence of pervasive emotion recognition deficits for facial and vocal expressions in psychopathy. *Neuroscience and Biobehavioral Reviews, 36*, 2288–2304.

Decety, J. (2015). The neural pathways, development and functions of empathy. *Current Opinion in Behavioral Sciences, 3*, 1–6.

Decety, J., Chen, C., Harenski, C., & Kiehl, K.A. (2013). An fMRI study of affective perspective taking in individuals with psychopathy: Imagining another in pain does not evoke empathy. *Frontiers in Human Neuroscience, 7*, 489. doi: 10.3389/fnhum.2013.00489.

Decety, J., & Cowell, J.M. (2017). Interpersonal harm aversion as a necessary foundation for morality: A developmental neuroscience perspective. *Development and Psychopathology, 30*, 153–164.

Decety, J., & Howard, L.H. (2013). The role of affect in the neurodevelopment of morality. *Child Development Perspectives, 7*(1), 49–54.

Deeley, Q., Daly, E., Surguladze, S., Tunstall, N., Mezey, G., Beer, D., Ambikapathy, A., Robertson, D., & Murphy, D.G. (2006). Facial emotion processing in criminal psychopathy. Preliminary functional magnetic resonance imaging study. *British Journal of Psychiatry, 189*, 533–539.

Drayton, L.A., Santos, L.R., & Baskin-Sommers, A. (2018). Psychopaths fail to automatically take the perspective of others. *Proceedings of the National Academy of Sciences of the United States, 115*(13), 3302–3307. doi: /10.1073/pnas.1721903115.

Eres, R., Decety, J., Louis, W.R., & Molenberghs, P. (2015). Individual differences in local gray matter density are associated with differences in affective and cognitive empathy. *NeuroImage, 117*, 305–310.

Flor, H., Birbaumer, N., Hermann, C., Ziegler, S., & Patrick, C.J. (2002). Aversive Pavlovian conditioning in psychopaths: Peripheral and central correlates. *Psychophysiology, 39*, 505–518. doi: 10.1017.S0048577202394046.

Fowles, D.C. (2003). Electrodermal hyporeactivity in psychopathy: Does it reflect disinhibition, low anxiety, or both? In M.F. Lenzenweger & J.M. Hooley (Eds.), *Principles of experimental psychopathology: Essays in honor of Brendan A. Maher* (pp. 255–268). Washington, DC: American Psychological Association. doi: http://dx.doi.org/10.1037/10477-016.

Gao, Y., & Raine, A. (2010). Successful and unsuccessful psychopaths: A neurobiological model. *Behavioral Sciences & the Law, 28*, 194–210. doi: 10.1002/bsl.924.

Gao, Y., & Tang, S. (2013). Psychopathic personality and utilitarian moral judgment in college students. *Journal of Criminal Justice, 41*, 342–349.

Glenn, A.L., & Raine, A. (2009). Psychopathy and instrumental aggression: Evolutionary, neurobiological, and legal perspectives. *International Journal of Law and Psychiatry, 32*(4), 253–258. doi: 10.1016/j.ijlp.2009.04.002.

Glenn, A.L., & Raine, A. (2014). *Psychopathy: An introduction to biological findings and their implications*. New York, NY: New York University Press.

Hare, R., & Neumann, C. (2009). Psychopathy: Assessment and forensic implications. *Canadian Journal of Psychiatry, 54*, 791–802. doi: 10.1177/070674370905401202.

Hare, R.D. (1965). Psychopathy, fear arousal, and anticipated pain. *Psychological Reports, 16*, 499–502.

Hare, R.D. (1993). *Without conscience: The disturbing world of the psychopaths among us*. New York, NY: Guilford Press.

Hare, R.D. (1996). Psychopathy: A clinical construct whose time has come. *Criminal Justice and Behavior, 23*, 25–54.

Hare, R.D. (2001). Psychopaths and their nature: Some implications for understanding human predatory violence. In J. Sanmartin & A. Raine (Eds.), *Violence and psychopathy* (pp. 5–34). Dordrecht: Kluwer.

Hare, R.D. (2003). *The Hare Psychopathy Checklist-Revised*. Toronto: Multi-Health Systems.

Hare, R.D. (2006). Psychopathy: A clinical and forensic overview. *Psychiatric Clinics of North America, 29*(3), 709–724. doi: org/10.1016/j.psc.2006.04.007.

Hare, R.D., & Neumann, C.S. (2008). Psychopathy as a clinical and empirical construct. *Annual Review of Clinical Psychology, 4*, 217–246. doi: 10.1146/annurev.clinpsy.3.022806.091452.

Hare, R.D., Neumann, C.S., & Mokros, A. (2018). The PCL-R assessment of psychopathy: Development, properties, debates, and new directions. In C.J. Patrick (Ed.), *Handbook of psychopathy* (2nd ed.) (pp. 39–79). New York, NY: Guilford Press.

Henderson, D.K. (1947). *Psychopathic states* (2nd ed.). New York, NY: W.W. Norton.

Hervé, H. (2007). Psychopathy across the ages: A history of the Hare psychopath. In H. Hervé & J.C. Yuille (Eds.), *The psychopath: Theory, research, and practice* (pp. 31–55). Mahwah, NJ: Lawrence Erlbaum Associates.

Hiatt, K.D., Schmitt, W.A., & Newman, J.P. (2004). Stroop tasks reveal abnormal selective attention among psychopathic offenders. *Neuropsychology, 18*, 50–59.

Hosker-Field, A., Gauthier, N.Y., & Book, A.S. (2016). If not fear, then what? A preliminary examination of psychopathic traits and the fear enjoyment hypothesis. *Personality and Individual Differences*, *90*, 278–282. doi: 10.1016/j.paid.2015.11.016.

James, S., Kavanagh, P.S., Jonason, P.K., Chonody, J.M., & Scrutton, H.E. (2014). The Dark Triad, schadenfreude, and sensational interests: Dark personalities, dark emotions, and dark behaviors. *Personality and Individual Differences*, *68*, 211–216. doi: doi.org/10.1016/j.paid.2014.04.020.

Kiehl, K.A. (2006). A cognitive perspective on psychopathy: Evidence for paralimbic system dysfunction. *Psychiatry Research*, *142*, 107–128.

Kiehl, K.A., Hare, R.D., McDonald, J.A., & Brink, J. (1999). Semantic and affective processing in psychopaths: An event-related potential (ERP) study. *Psychophysiology*, *36*, 765–844.

Kiehl, K.A., Smith, A.S., Hare, R.D., Mendrek, A., Forster, B.B., Brink, J., & Liddle, P.F. (2001). Limbic abnormalities in affective processing by criminal psychopaths as revealed by functional magnetic resonance imaging. *Biological Psychiatry*, *50*, 677–684.

Koenigs, M. (2017). Archival report: Impulsive-antisocial dimension of psychopathy linked to enlargement and abnormal functional connectivity of the striatum. *Biological Psychiatry: Cognitive Neuroscience and Neuroimaging*, *2*, 149–157.

Kolb, B., & Whishaw, I.Q. (2003). *Fundamentals of human neuropsychology* (5th ed.). New York, NY: Worth.

Korponay, C., Pujara, M., Deming, P., Philippi, C., Decety, J., Kosson, D.S., Kiehl, K.A., & Koenigs, M. (2017). Impulsive-antisocial psychopathic traits linked to increased volume and functional connectivity within prefrontal cortex. *Social Cognitive & Affective Neuroscience*, *12*(7), 1169–1178.

Kosson, D.S., Lorenz, A.R., & Newman, J.P. (2006). Effects of comorbid psychopathy on criminal offending and emotion processing in male offenders with antisocial personality disorder. *Journal of Abnormal Psychology*, *115*(4), 798–806. doi: 10.1037/0021-843X.115.4.798.

Lantrip, C., Towns, S., Roth, R.M., & Giancola, P.R. (2016). Psychopathy traits are associated with self-report rating of executive functions in the everyday life of healthy adults. *Personality and Individual Differences*, *101*, 127–131. http://dx.doi.org/10.1016/j.paid.2016.05.051.

Larson, C.L., Baskin-Sommers, A.R., Stout, D.M., Balderston, N.L., Curtin, J.J., Schultz, D.H., …,… & Newman, J.P. (2013). The interplay of attention and emotion: Top-down attention modulates amygdala activation in psychopathy. *Cognitive, Affective & Behavioral Neuroscience*, *13*(4), 757. doi: 10.3758/s13415-013-0172-8.

Larsson, H., Andershed, H., & Lichtenstein, P. (2006). A genetic factor explains most of the variation in psychopathic personality. *Journal of Abnormal Psychology*, *115*, 221–230.

Levenston, G.K., Patrick, C.J., Bradley, M.M., & Lang, P.J. (2000). The psychopath as observer: Emotion and attention in picture processing. *Journal of Abnormal Psychology*, *109*(3), 373–385.

Lilienfeld, S.O. (2015). Presidential address: Should the Society for the Scientific Study of Psychopathy put itself out of business? Talk presented at the biannual meeting of the Society for the Scientific Study of Psychopathy, Chicago, IL.

Lilienfeld, S.O., Waldman, I.D., Landfield, K., Watts, A.L., Rubenzer, S., & Faschingbauer, T.R. (2012). Fearless dominance and the U.S. presidency: Implications of psychopathic personality traits for successful and unsuccessful political leadership. *Journal of Personality and Social Psychology, 103*(3), 489–505.

Lilienfeld, S.O., Watts, A., & Smith, S.F. (2015). Successful psychopathy: A scientific status report. *Current Directions in Psychological Science, 24,* 298–303. E4RERW2F4OI: 10.1177/0963721415580297.

Lilienfeld, S.O., Watts, A.L., Smith, S.F., & Latzman, R.D. (2018). Boldness: Conceptual and methodological issues. In C.J. Patrick (Ed.), *Handbook of psychopathy* (2nd ed.) (pp. 165–186). New York, NY: Guilford Press.

Lingnau, V., Fuchs, F., & Dehne-Niemann, T.E. (2017). The influence of psychopathic traits on the acceptance of white-collar crime: Do corporate psychopaths cook the books and misuse the news? *Journal of Business Economics, 87*(9), 1193–1227.

Lopez, R., Poy, R., Patrick, C.J., & Molto, J. (2013). Deficient fear conditioning and self-reported psychopathy: The role of fearless dominance. *Psychophysiology, 50,* 210–218. doi: 10.1111/j.1469-8986.2012.01493.x.

Lykken, D.T. (1957). A study of anxiety in the sociopathic personality. *Journal of Abnormal Social Psychology, 55,* 6–10.

Lykken, D.T. (1995). *The antisocial personalities.* Hillsdale, NJ: Lawrence Erlbaum Associates.

Marsh, A.A., Finger, E.C., Schechter, J.C., Jurkowitz, I.T.N., Reid, M.E., & Blair, R.J.R. (2011). Adolescents with psychopathic traits report reductions in physiological responses to fear. *Journal of Child Psychology and Psychiatry, 52,* 834–841. doi: 10.1111/j.1469-7610.2010.02353.x.

Mathieu, C., & Babiak, P. (2016). Corporate psychopathy and abusive supervision: Their influence on employees' job satisfaction and turnover intentions. *Personality and Individual Differences, 91,* 102–106.

Mathieu, C., Babiak, P., Jones, D.N., Neumann, C., & Hare, R.D. (2012). What are the effects of psychopathic traits in a supervisor on employees' psychological distress? *Journal of Organizational Culture, Communications and Conflict, 16*(2), 81.

Mathieu, C., Neumann, C.S., Hare, R.D., & Babiak, P. (2014). A dark side of leadership: Corporate psychopathy and its influence on employee well-being and job satisfaction. *Personality and Individual Differences, 59,* 83–88.

McCord, W., & McCord, J. (1964). *The psychopath: An essay on the criminal mind.* Princeton, NJ: Van Nostrand.

Morgan, A.B., & Lilienfeld, S.O. (2000). A meta-analytic review of the relation between antisocial behavior and neuropsychological measures of executive function. *Clinical Psychology Review, 20*, 113–136.

Patrick, C., Fowles, D., & Krueger, R. (2009). Triarchic conceptualization of psychopathy: Developmental origins of disinhibition, boldness, and meanness. *Development and Psychopathology, 21*(3), 913–938. doi: 10.1017/ S0954579409000492.

Patrick, C.J. (1994). Emotion and psychopathy: Startling new insights. *Psychophysiology, 31*, 319–330.

Patrick, C.J. (2018). Cognitive and emotional processing in psychopathy. In C.J. Patrick (Ed.), *Handbook of psychopathy* (2nd ed.) (pp. 422–455). New York, NY: Guilford Press.

Patrick, C.J., & Bernat, E. (2009). Neurobiology of psychopathy: A two-process theory. *Handbook of Neuroscience for the Behavioral Sciences, 2*, 1110–1131.

Patrick, C.J., Bradley, M.M., & Lang, P.J. (1993). Emotion in the criminal psychopath: Startle reflex modulation. *Journal of Abnormal Psychology, 102*, 82–92.

Patrick, C.J., Cuthbert, B.N., & Lang, P.J. (1994). Emotion in the criminal psychopath: Fear image processing. *Journal of Abnormal Psychology, 103*, 523–534. doi: 10.1037/0021-843X.103.3.523.

Polaschek, D.L.L., & Daly, T.E. (2013). Treatment and psychopathy in forensic settings. *Aggression and Violent Behavior, 18*(5), 592–603. http://dx.doi.org /10.1016/j.avb.2013.06.003.

Poythress, N.G., & Skeem, J.L. (2006). Disaggregating psychopathy: Where and how to look for subtypes. In C.J. Patrick (Ed.), *Handbook of psychopathy* (2nd ed.) (pp. 172–192). New York, NY: Guilford Press.

Rothemond, Y., Ziegler, S., Hermann, C., Gruesser, S.M., Foell, J., Patrick, C.J., & Flor, H. (2012). Fear conditioning in psychopaths: Event-related potentials and peripheral measures. *Biological Psychology, 90*, 50–59. doi: 10.1016/j. biopsycho.2012.02.011.

Sethi, A., McCrory, E., Puetz, V., Hoffman, F., Knodt., A.R., Radtke, S.R., ..., & Viding, E. (2018). Primary and secondary variants of psychopathy in a volunteer sample are associated with different neurocognitive mechanisms. *Biological Psychiatry: Cognitive Neuroscience and Neuroimaging, 3*, 1013–1021.

Sonne, J.W.H., & Gash, D.M. (2018). Psychopathy to altruism: Neurobiology of the selfish- selfless spectrum. *Frontiers in Psychology, 9*, 575. doi: 10.3389/ psyg.2018.00575.

Veit, R., Konicar, L., Klinzing, J., Barth, B., Yilmaz, O., & Birbaumer, N. (2013). Deficient fear conditioning in psychopathy as a function of interpersonal and affective disturbances. *Frontiers in Human Neuroscience, 7*, 1–12. doi: 10.3389/fnhum.2013.00706.

Waldman, I.D., Rhee, S.H., LoParo, D., & Park, Y. (2018). Genetic and environmental influences on psychopathy and antisocial behavior. In C.J. Patrick

(Ed.), *Handbook of psychopathy* (2nd ed.) (pp. 335–353). New York, NY: Guilford Press.

Wilson, K., Juodis, M., & Porter, S. (2011). Fear and loathing in psychopaths: A meta-analytic investigation of the facial affect recognition deficit. *Criminal Justice and Behavior, 38*, 659–668. doi: 10.1177/0093854811404120..

Woodworth, G.W., & Porter, S. (2002). In cold blood: Characteristics of criminal homicides as a function of psychopathy. *Journal of Abnormal Psychology, 3*, 436–445. doi: 10.1037//0021-843X.111.3.436.

Yang, Y., & Raine, A. (2018). The neuroanatomical bases of psychopathy: A review of brain imaging findings. In C.J. Patrick (Ed.), *Handbook of psychopathy* (2nd ed.) (pp. 380–400). New York, NY: Guilford Press.

Yang, Y., Raine, A., Colletti, P., Toga, A.W., & Narr, K.L. (2010). Morphological alterations in the prefrontal cortex and the amygdala in unsuccessful psychopaths. *Journal of Abnormal Psychology, 119*(3), 546–554. doi: org/10.1037/a0019611.

Yang, Y., Raine, A., Narr, K.L., Colletti, P., & Toga, A.W. (2009). Localization of deformations within the amygdala in individuals with psychopathy. *Archives of General Psychiatry, 66*(9), 986–994. doi: 10.1001/archgenpsychiatry.2009.110.

Zeier, J.D., Baskin-Sommers, A.R., Hiatt Racer, K.D., & Newman, J.P. (2012). Cognitive control deficits associated with antisocial personality disorder and psychopathy. *Personality Disorders: Theory, Research, And Treatment, 3*(3), 283–293. doi: 10.1037/a0023137.

Index

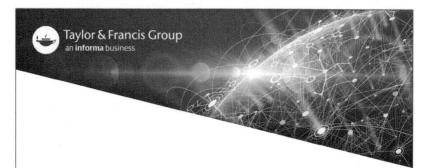